Supply Chain - Perspectives and Applications

Edited by Ágota Bányai

Published in London, United Kingdom

Supply Chain - Perspectives and Applications
http://dx.doi.org/10.5772/intechopen.107808
Edited by Ágota Bányai

Contributors
Jan Jansen, Benedikte Borgström, Leif-Magnus Jensen, Susanne Hertz, Shankar Subramanian Iyer, Ameeta Rawool, Antje P. Wittenberg, Daniel de Oliveira, Julie Hollis, Siim Nirgi, Håvard Gautneb, Rafael Navarro Domínguez, Martiya Sadeghi, Gorazd Žibret, Boris Malyuk, Tom Bide, Thomas Ernst E. Müller, Marisol Hernández, Luis Alfonso Bonilla Cruz, Lizbeth Cobián-Romero

First published in London, United Kingdom, 2024 by IntechOpen
IntechOpen is the global imprint of INTECHOPEN LIMITED, registered in England and Wales, registration number: 11086078, 5 Princes Gate Court, London, SW7 2QJ, United Kingdom

British Library Cataloguing-in-Publication Data
A catalogue record for this book is available from the British Library

Additional hard and PDF copies can be obtained from orders@intechopen.com

Supply Chain - Perspectives and Applications
Edited by Ágota Bányai
p. cm.
Print ISBN 978-1-83769-105-0
Online ISBN 978-1-83769-106-7
eBook (PDF) ISBN 978-1-83769-107-4

For EU product safety concerns:
IN TECH d.o.o., Prolaz Marije Krucifikse Kozulić 3, 51000 Rijeka, Croatia,
info@intechopen.com or visit our website at intechopen.com.

Meet the editor

Ágota Bányai was awarded an MSc in Mechanical Engineering from the University of Miskolc, Hungary, in 1993 and a Ph.D. in Engineering Sciences from the same institution in 1999. She is currently an associate professor at the Institute of Logistics, University of Miskolc, Hungary. She has more than 25 years of teaching and research experience in the design and control of logistic systems and supply chain management, with special emphasis on purchasing and distribution. She has worked in academia for nearly 25 years and has published more than 200 research papers, book chapters, and conference proceedings.

Contents

Preface

This book offers a selection of chapters on supply chain solutions, promoting new research results in the field. Authors from the Netherlands, Germany, Sweden, Mexico, United Arab Emirates, Portugal, the United Kingdom, Belgium, Estonia, Slovenia, Norway, and France have contributed work examples and case studies from their research in supply chain management.

The book covers six topics, determined by the theoretical and practical aspects of supply chain solutions.

Chapter 1, "Supply Chain Finance Perspectives", shows potential perspectives on supply chain finance The author discusses the basic model of supply chain finance, from supply chain management, logistics management, finance and control, enterprise resource planning (ERP) and information technology (IT) platforms, and supply chain finance instruments points of view. The author also proposes a novel conceptual model of supply chain finance.

Chapter 2, "Supply Chains for Hydrogen and Carbon Dioxide for Sustainable Production of Base Chemicals", extensively discusses the supply chain solutions for hydrogen and carbon dioxide. It describes various hydrogen production methods, including hydrogen production by steam methane reforming, partial oxidation, autothermal reforming, methane pyrolysis, water electrolysis, and more. The chapter also discusses a sustainable supply chain for carbon dioxide.

Chapter 3, "Improvement of Validated Manufacturing Processes with Fuzzy Logic", addresses an important and, by now, much-needed step in improving the efficiency of manufacturing processes focusing on the modeling of uncertainties in production and related logistics operations. The chapter proposes a novel fuzzy approach to improve the efficiency of manufacturing processes.

Chapter 4, "Europe's Raw Materials Supply Chain: Front-End Considerations", focuses on the raw materials supply chain front-end approach, including the political dimension of exploration and mining data in the raw material supply chain and the elements of a strong raw materials supply chain. The chapter delves into how exploration and extraction fit into the supply chain. The chapter also describes Europe's geological potential.

Chapter 5, "Road Haulier Competition: Implications for Supply Chain Integration", highlights how road hauliers are part of logistics service chains as well as the industrial supply chain and how the many links and relationships increase the magnitude and implications of hauliers' performances. The chapter also presents potential strategic moves for hauliers.

Chapter 6, "Resilient Supply Chain in United Arab Emirates", proposes a novel approach to the multi-level integrated process theory for the conceptual model. It focuses on the resilience of supply chains, providing valuable insights into strategies, practices, and factors that enhance resilience.

This book aims to help students as well as managers and researchers to understand and appreciate the concept, design, and implementation of different supply chain solutions and the different aspects of the design and operation of a supply chain.

The editors thank the chapter authors for their scientific contributions. The chapters were edited and published following a rigorous selection process. I also wish to thank and acknowledge the many individuals who helped us throughout the editorial process that made this book possible.

Ágota Bányai
University of Miskolc,
Institute of Logistics,
Miskolc, Hungary

Chapter 1

Supply Chain Finance Perspectives

Jan Jansen

Abstract

This chapter briefly introduces supply chain finance (SCF) and its four building blocks: supply chain management, finance, IT & ERP, and SCF instruments. After introducing the four building blocks, each block will be discussed in detail. Finally, state-of-the-art issues in supply chain management and finance will be discussed to bridge the gap to the real (international) business world of volatility, uncertainty, complexity, and ambiguity. To provide an answer to issues such as liquidity in the supply chain (deep tier financing), dealing with all sorts of risks in the supply chain (resilient supply chains), and being sustainable/circular in the supply chain and its finance.

Keywords: supply chain finance, finance, working capital, supply chain management, ERP, IT platform, sustainability, circularity, FinTech

1. Introduction

Supply chain finance (SCF) is a relatively new development in supply chain management [1], where the (financial) value flow of working capital (and related issues) in the supply chain is the main topic of study (see **Figure 1**).

Steeman [2] outlines SCF from a more general point of view with no links to such SCF instruments like reverse factoring and dynamic discounting as defined by the European Banking Association [3]:

> *Supply chain finance is defined as the use of financing and risk mitigation practices and techniques to optimize the management of the working capital and liquidity invested in supply chain processes and transactions. SCF is typically applied to open account trade and is triggered by supply chain events. Visibility of underlying trade flows by the finance provider(s) is a necessary component of such financing arrangements which can be enabled by a technology platform.*

So, the physical flow of goods and services is the supply chain finance event of the EBA definition, and the information flow is often managed in the supply chain by using an IT platform.

In this chapter, we will develop an overview of supply chain finance perspectives from the building blocks of supply chain finance such as were presented by Templar et al. [4] and Tate et al. [5]: supply chain management, corporate finance, business

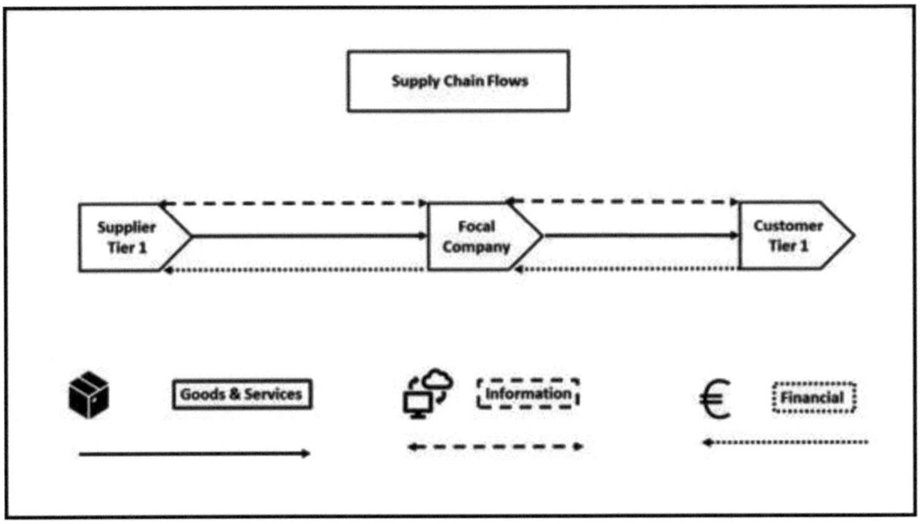

Figure 1.
Supply chain of the focal company (developed by the author).

processes (including Enterprise Resource Planning (ERP), and information technology (IT) platforms), and SCF instruments (including the role of banks).

Finally, the chapter ends with state-of-the-art developments in international business concerning supply chain finance such as volatility, uncertainty, complexity, and ambiguity (VUCA), sustainability, and FinTech.

2. Basics of supply chain finance

The essence of supply chain finance can be found in **Figure 1**, of course, is the plotted supply chain simple with only a tier 1 supplier and tier 1 client. Real-life supply chains are far more complex, and in some SCF research, we observe so-called deep-tier supply chain finance [6].

For reasons of convenience, we will stick to the supply chain in **Figure 1**. If we observe the focal company (as a dominant firm in the supply chain network [7]), there are three main activities:

I. Buying raw materials and/or components from tier 1 suppliers (including transport).

II. Processing raw materials and components into final products.

III. Selling final products to tier 1 clients (including transport).

The impact on the ledgers (income statement and/or balance sheet, see **Table 1**) of the three activities of the focal company are:

Ad I Buying raw materials & components will increase the inventories of raw materials and components (RM & C) (+) and increase the creditors or accounts payables (+), both on the balance sheet of the focal company.

#	Activity	Ledgers	Ledgers
I	Buying	Inventories RM & C+	Creditors +
II	Transformation	Inventories RM & C – Inventories FP+	
III	Selling	Inventories FP–COGS +	Debtors + Revenues +

Table 1.
Impact of business activities on ledgers (developed by the author).

Ad II Producing final products (or transforming raw materials and components) will decrease the inventories RM & C (−) and increase the inventories of final products (FP) (+), both on the balance sheet of the focal company.

Ad III Selling final products will result in two sub-transactions for the ledgers:

- Sending the final goods to the customers will decrease inventories FP (−) on the balance sheet and increase costs of goods sold or COGS (+) on the income statement.
- Sending the invoice to the customers will increase debtors or accounts receivables (+) on the balance sheet and increase revenues or sales (+) on the income statement.

The ledgers inventories (raw materials & components, work in progress (WIP), and final products), debtors, and creditors are part of the concept of net operating working capital (NOWC), the following formula [8, 9] is used:

$$NOWC = Inventories + Debtors - Creditors \tag{1}$$

In some financial literature, the word induced is used instead of operational Dorsman [10, 11] and Gieskens [12].

From this accounting analysis, we can deduce two important topics for the supply chain finance metrics of the net operating working capital (NOWC): Static value analysis of NOWC and dynamic analysis of NOWC.

In the static analysis of NOWC, we often use ratios (or relative numbers) to characterize a company for its static working capital position, the following formulas [8, 13] often used:

$$Inventory\ turnover = \frac{Cost\ of\ goods\ sold}{Inventories} \tag{2}$$

$$Receiveables\ turnover = \frac{Sales\ or\ Revenues}{Debtors\ or\ Accounts\ receiveable} \tag{3}$$

$$Payables\ turnover = \frac{Cost\ of\ goods\ sold}{Creditors\ or\ Accounts\ payable} \tag{4}$$

$$NOWC\ turnover = \frac{Sales\ or\ Revenues}{NOWC} \tag{5}$$

$$Current\ Ratio\ (CR) = \frac{Current\ Assets}{Current\ Liabilities} \tag{6}$$

$$Quick\ Ratio\ (QR) = \frac{Current\ Assets - Inventories}{Current\ Liabilities} \tag{7}$$

The NWOC turnover formula was developed in the analogy of Preve & Sarria-Allende [14] by the author. The inverse value of the NWOC turnover is the average number of days of net operating working capital in sales.

In the dynamic analysis of NOWC, we use the following ratios (or relative numbers) to characterize a company for its dynamic working capital position [8, 13] the following formulas are often used:

$$Days\ in\ Inventories\ (DIO) = \frac{Inventories}{Cost\ of\ goods\ sold} * 365\ days \tag{8}$$

$$Days\ of\ Sales\ Outstanding\ (DSO) = \frac{Debtors\ or\ Accounts\ receiveable}{Sales\ or\ Revenues} * 365\ days \tag{9}$$

$$Days\ of\ Purchases\ Outstanding\ (DPO) = \frac{Creditors\ or\ Accounts\ payable}{Cost\ of\ goods\ sold} * 365\ days \tag{10}$$

$$Cash\ to\ Cash\ Cycle\ (C2C) or\ Cash\ Conversion\ Cycle\ (CCC) = DIO + DSO - DPO \tag{11}$$

To provide you with some data from the following five companies (based on their annual reports): Unilever (fast-moving consumer goods) Heineken (beverages and beer), Philips (electronics), Volkswagen (automotive), and Ahold-Delhaize (supermarket chain).

We observe in **Table 2** that for some companies (Unilever, Heineken, and Ahold-Delhaize) the cash-to-cash cycle is negative and for some positive (Philips, and Volkswagen). The explanation is that for companies with a negative CCC; the DPO is higher than the sum of DIO + DSO. This implies that those companies pay their supplier quite late in 2021. The suppliers of Unilever had to 124 days on average for payment and Heineken the suppliers had to wait for 149 days to receive payment.

In the case of Philips, we observe a very high DIO (126 days in 2022), which might be due to some issues with storing special raw materials, and/or some issues in the market for electronic hospital equipment.

From **Table 2**, we can also conclude that we can observe differences in sectors of industries, as well as in the market power between suppliers (of tier 1, tier 2, tier 3, etc.) and focal companies. The distribution advantages of early payment of creditors/suppliers using supply chain finance programs (such as reverse factoring and dynamic discounting) are not always very clear. From a theoretical point of view, this so-called split-up issue is not solved [15]. Depending on the purchase market situation of the focal company, rules of thumb are used in negotiations of the financial and nonfinancial advantages [16].

The following example (see **Table 3**) might illustrate this split-up issue of advantages of a supply chain finance program issued by the focal company for tier 1 and tier s suppliers.

Assume we have a net operating working capital position for each company in US Dollars ($), each company has a different credit rating (that is why domestic interest rates differ), and each company has a different number of days invested in net operating working capital.

Company	SCF metric	2018	2019	2020	2021	Average
Unilever	DIO	40,9	35,1	38,4	39,1	38,4
	DSO	46,4	47,0	35,5	37,7	41,7
	DPO	137,6	124,6	121,6	124,0	126,9
	CCC	−50,3	−42,4	−47,7	−47,2	−46,9
Company	SCF metric	2018	2019	2020	2021	
Heineken	DIO	36,1	39,5	37,6	46,9	40,0
	DSO	50,9	52,8	43,1	50,3	49,3
	DPO	129,6	134,3	117,4	149,0	132,6
	CCC	−42,6	−42,0	−36,6	−51,9	−43,3
Company	SCF metric	2018	2019	2020	2021	
Philips	DIO	105,8	92,0	115,1	126,1	109,7
	DSO	81,3	85,3	87,6	80,6	83,7
	DPO	87,9	71,9	81,5	68,4	77,4
	CCC	99,2	105,5	121,2	138,2	116,0
Company	SCF metric	2018	2019	2020	2021	
Volkswagen	DIO	88,1	83,8	87,0	78,6	84,4
	DSO	27,7	25,9	26,6	22,6	25,7
	DPO	45,5	40,8	45,0	42,5	43,4
	CCC	70,3	69,0	68,6	58,8	66,7
Company	SCF metric	2018	2019	2020	2021	
AholdDelhaize	DIO	25,4	25,3	21,9	24,8	24,4
	DSO	10,2	10,5	9,6	9,9	10,1
	DPO	46,3	47,8	45,8	50,3	47,5
	CCC	−10,7	−12,0	−14,3	−15,6	−13,1
Company	SCF metric	2018	2019	2020	2021	
Average	DIO	59,3	55,2	60,0	63,1	59,4
	DSO	43,3	44,3	40,5	40,2	42,1
	DPO	89,4	83,9	82,2	86,8	85,6
	CCC	13,2	15,6	18,2	16,5	15,9

Table 2.
Supply chain finance metrics of some international companies (retrieved by the author).

The interest costs are calculated using the formula:

$$Interest\ costs\ NOWC = NOWC * Interest\ rate * \frac{Number\ of\ days}{365} \tag{12}$$

So, we observe the costs of domestic interest expenses for supplier tier 1 ($ 4.734,25), supplier tier 2 ($ 118.356,16), and focal company (73.972,60). So, in total $ 197.063,01.

	Tier 2 supplier	Tier 1 supplier	Focal company	Total
Credit rating	C	B	A	
NOWC position	$ 80.000,00	$ 4.000.000,00	$ 10.000.000,00	
Domestic interest rate	12%	9%	3%	
Number of days	180	120	90	
Days in a year	365	365	365	
Domestic interest expenses	$ 4.734,25	$ 118.356,16	$ 73.972,60	$ 197.063,01
SCF interest rate	3,00%	3,00%	3,00%	
Interest costs SCF program	$ 1.183,56	$ 39.452,05	$ 73.972,60	$ 114.608,22
Difference	$ 3.550,68	$ 78.904,11	$ -	$ 82.454,79

Table 3.
Costs of net operating working capital in the supply chain.

When the focal company introduces a supply chain finance program, the focal company will get a good interest rate (slightly above its domestic interest rate). Let us assume this interest rate will be 3,0%. So, now all three companies can borrow against this interest rate (via the focal company!).

This results in the following interest costs for the net operating working capital: Supplier tier 1 ($ 1.183,56), supplier tier 2 ($ 39.452,05), and focal company ($ 73.972,60). So, in total $ 114.608,22, an advantage of $ 82.454,79 (lower costs for the supplier tier 1 and supplier tier 2). The question that now arises is how to distribute this advantage in the supply chain. In **Table 4** some scenarios are provided, although it is from a theoretical point of view not backed up, just a rule of thumb (often passed on the power position in the supply chain).

Managing net operating working capital in the supply chain is one of the so-called "real" aspects of supply chain finance, in the following section of this chapter, we will add the role of IT and the role of financial institutions.

In the supply chain finance cube model [1] the capital costs of the volume (=amount) of net (operating) working capital are calculated like:

$$Capital\ costs = Volume\ (amount) * Duration\ (= time) * Capital\ cost\ rate\ (e.g. WACC) \tag{13}$$

The interest costs of net (Operating) working capital are one of the basic supply chain finance metrics because trade-offs can be made in the working capital policy in the supply chain of the focal company.

An example of how supply chain finance works in Asia can be found in the Trade and Supply Chain Finance Program of the Asian Development Bank [17].

3. Supply chain management

As was mentioned in the first section, the definition of supply chain finance is highly event-driven, so it is now time to understand the concept of supply chain management (**Figure 1**). Although supply chain finance has not only an operational

Split-up SCF advantage	Scenario I			Scenario II			Scenario III			Scenario IV	
Focal company	$	-	0%	$	27.484,93	33,3%	$	4.122,74	5%		
Tier 1 Supplier	$	3.550,68	4%	$	27.484,93	33,3%	$	2.473,64	3%		
Tier 2 Supplier	$	78.904,11	96%	$	27.484,93	33,3%	$	75.858,41	92%		
Total	$	82.454,79		$	82.454,79		$	82.454,79		$	-

Table 4.
Split-up scenarios of the supply chain finance program.

level but also tactical and strategic levels [18]. Logistics and supply chain management (SCM) are sometimes seen as different entities, but sometimes also seen as something similar. For this chapter, we follow two basic opinions about supply chain management, based on Stock and Lambert [19]:

> *The integration of key business processes from end user through original suppliers that provides products, services, and information that add value for customers and other stakeholders.*

and Harrison and Van Hoek [7]:

> *SCM encompasses the planning and controlling of all processes involved in procurement, conversion, transportation, and distribution across the supply chain. SCM includes coordination and collaboration between partners, which can be suppliers, intermediaries, third-party service providers, and customers. In essence, SCM integrates supply and demand management within and between companies in order to serve the needs of the end customer.*

Based on both definitions we have now some idea about supply chain management and logistics, the Association of Supply Chain Management [20, 21], confirms this academic concept from a professional point of view. Leeman [22] developed an overview of supply chain management following supply chain management as an academic topic:

Especially for supply chain finance the role of sourcing/procurement/purchasing is an important one from the perspective of the focal company and the (tier 1) supplier. Supply chain finance programs are discussed between the focal company and its suppliers in terms of payment terms (including early payments), the discussion is of course based on the market power between the focal company and its suppliers, as well as the position in the Kraljic's matrix of the purchase portfolio [23]. In Kraljic's matrix, we have four positions to characterize their procurement portfolio: leverage products, strategic or critical products, non-critical or routine products, and Bottleneck products. In Kraljic's matrix, the impact on the financial results (e.g., profit) is compared with the supplier risk. Depending on the position in the portfolio, it is clear if the focal company can easily swap suppliers or not (especially in the case of one supplier), and this also has an impact on the choice of a supply chain finance program.

4. Corporate finance

In corporate finance [8] the Economic Value Added (EVA®) is one of the cornerstones of the theory to explain the economic performance of a company. Economic Value Added is defined as:

$$EVA = NOPAT - WACC * Capital\ Employed \tag{14}$$

In which NOPAT stands for the net operating profit after taxes, WACC stands for weighted average costs of capital, and capital employed stands for the total assets minus the current liabilities (= Fixed Assets + Net Working Capital = Equity + Long term Debts).

The weighted average cost of capital (WACC) is defined as follows:

$$WACC = R_E * (1 - \lambda) + R_D * \lambda * (1 - \tau) \tag{15}$$

Lambda or λ stands for the debt to assets ratio, thus (1-λ) stands for the equity to assets ratio, per definition λ + (1-λ) = 1. The return to equity (R_E) is the expected value for the remuneration of shareholder's equity. The return on debt (R_D) is the remuneration for the use of debt by the combination, it is corrected for the tax deduction of interest cost (tax rate = τ = tau). R_{RF} is the so-called risk-free interest rate on premium state debt, for instance, the USA, Germany, the Netherlands, etc.

Finally, the capital assets pricing (CAPM) model is used for the determination of the return on equity (=R_E):

$$R_E = R_{RF} + \beta * (R_M - R_{RF}) \tag{16}$$

On page 417 of the 2022 Annual Report of Volkswagen [24] the value contribution (EVA) is + € 4.376 (million). In the 2022 annual report of Volkswagen AG, the WACC is 8.3%, NOPAT is in 2002 € 14.078 million and capital employed € 117.412 million, so EVA® for Volkswagen in 2022 is:

$$EVA = 14.078 - 0{,}083 * 117.412 = 14.078 - 9.702 = +€\ 4.376\ (million) \tag{17}$$

Economic Value Added or EVA® is a yardstick to measure the financial value of a company, also ratios such as return on investment (or Assets) or ROI [25] and return on capital employed or ROCE [26] are commonly used.

$$ROIorROA = \frac{NetProfitAfterTaxes}{TotalAssets} * 100\% \tag{18}$$

$$ROCE = \frac{OperatingProfit}{TotalAssets - CurrentLiabilities} * 100\% \tag{19}$$

Schoenmaker and Schramade developed in their books Principles of Sustainable Finance [27] and Corporate Finance for Long-term Value [28] a model for integrated value. Integrated values (IV) consist of financial value (FV), social value (SV), and environmental value (EV); or in a formula:

$$IV = FV + SV + EV \tag{20}$$

The three values have the following constraints: Accounting for transitions (FV), social foundations (SV), and planetary boundaries (EV). The value flows (VF) consists of a shadow price (SP) multiplied by a quantity (Q), so the value flow is:

$$VF = SP * Q \tag{21}$$

The shadow price [29] of a factor (e.g., quantity) expresses the increase in value (e.g., profit) if an additional unit of a factor is allocated. By using the discounted cash flow (DCF) model [8] the integrated value (IV) can be calculated as follows [28]:

$$IV = \sum_{n=0}^{N} \frac{VF_n}{(1+R)^n} \tag{22}$$

The symbol r stands for the cost of integrated capital (including a risk premium) and is an adjusted version of the WACC or weighted costs of capital [8], the weighted average of the return of integrated value (R) consists of the returns for financial value (R_{FV}), social value (R_{SV}), and environmental value (R_{EV}). The integrated return (R) can be approximately 1617% depending on data from case studies.

In corporate finance we can calculate days of sales outstanding with the supply chain finance metrics formula:

$$Days\ of\ Sales\ Outstanding\ (DSO) = \frac{Debtors\ or\ ARs}{Sales\ or\ Revenues} * 365\, days \tag{23}$$

In our example, we assume that sales are \$ 45.000.00 and the debtors are \$ 9.487.000, so the DSO is 77,0 days, using the formula above.

In **Table 5** an aging schedule [25] for debtors was downloaded from the company's data out of the Enterprise Resource Planning software (ERP). We can observe from the data in **Table 5** which customers (= debtors) are within the time limit of 90 days, and which are not. Based on the data in **Table 5** the average number of days can be calculated, using this calculation:

$$Average\ number\ of\ debtor's\ days = 0,31 * 15 = 0,30 * 45 + 0,25 * 75 + 0,14 * 120 = 53,9\, days \tag{24}$$

From the aging schedule, we have more insight into the structure of the aging portfolio of debtors, than using only the supply chain finance metric of days of sales outstanding (DSO).

Similar approaches to an aging schedule can be provided for creditors and/or inventories, using ABC or Pareto analysis [22].

One of the topics of corporate finance is working capital management [8, 25], net working capital (NWC) is often defined like:

$$NWC = Current\ Assets - Current\ Liabilities \tag{25}$$

	1–30 days	31–60 days	61–90 days	> = 91 days	Total
Average	15	45	75	120	
			Customer		
Neptunus NV	$ 70.000,00	$ 250.000,00	$ 60.000,00	$ -	$ 380.000,00
Poseidon BV	$ 400.000,00	$ 50.000,00	$ 150.000,00	$ 200.000,00	$ 800.000,00
Zeus AG	$ 80.000,00	$ 85.000,00	$ 20.000,00	$ -	$ 185.000,00
Apollo GmbH	$ 800.000,00	$ 300.000,00	$ 400.000,00	$ 100.000,00	$ 1.600.000,00
Hades SA	$ 250.000,00	$ 140.000,00	$ 80.000,00	$ 12.000,00	$ 482.000,00
Hestia SARL	$ 60.000,00	$ 280.000,00	$ 300.000,00	$ -	$ 640.000,00
Artemis Ltd	$ 500.000,00	$ 700.000,00	$ 300.000,00	$ 400.000,00	$ 1.900.000,00
Dionysos INC	$ 300.000,00	$ 200.000,00	$ 100.000,00	$ -	$ 600.000,00
Hermes LLC	$ 400.000,00	$ 800.000,00	$ 900.000,00	$ 600.000,00	$ 2.700.000,00
Panecea SLNE	$ 40.000,00	$ 80.000,00	$ 60.000,00	$ 20.000,00	$ 200.000,00
Total	$ 2.900.000,00	$ 2.885.000,00	$ 2.370.000,00	$ 1.332.000,00	$ 9.487.000,00
Total in percentages	31%	30%	25%	14%	100%

Table 5.
Aging schedule debtors (developed by the author).

Net working capital management manages the short-time value flows [14] in the company between the primary activities of buying (purchase), transformation or production, and sales (distribution), this approach in working capital management is also known as the net operating working capital (NOWC) [10–12]). The formula of this working capital variant is plotted here:

$$Net\ Operating\ Working\ Capital\ (NOWC) = Inventories + Debtors - Creditors) \quad (26)$$

Net operating working capital is also known as induced net working capital because it is linked (or induced) to the three primary activities in business:

- Input (buying of raw materials and components)
- Throughput (production or transformation of input into final products and/or services)
- Output (sales of finished products and/or services)

For managing net operating working capital, the following supply chain finance metrics are used:

- Static supply chain finance metrics
    - Value of net operating working capital (NOWC)
    - Current ratio (CR)
    - Quick ratio (QR)
    - NOWC turnover ratio
- Dynamic supply chain finance metrics
    - Days in inventories outstanding (DIO)
    - Days of sales outstanding (DSO)
    - Days of purchases outstanding (DPO)
    - Cash to cash cycle (C2C = DIO + DSO – DPO)

In some supply chain finance programs (such as reverse factoring and dynamic discounting), we see that there is a discount for early payment of the focal company to its suppliers. To calculate the effective interest for such a decision, the flowing example was developed (using simple interest rate calculation and compound interest rate calculation. Assume there is an invoice of $ 120.000,00 that the focal company has to pay to its suppliers, under the payment condition of 90 days. Early payment is possible within 10 days, the focal company is allowed to deduct 2% of the amount of the invoice. So, the discount amount is $ 2.400,00 to pay 80 days earlier (80 days = 90 days – 10 days), and the supplier will receive 98% of the original amount of the invoice.

The effective annual rate (EAR) based on simple interest (SI) is as follows:

$$EAR\ (SI) = 2\% * \frac{365}{80} = 9,1\% \tag{27}$$

The effective annual rate (EAR) based on compound interest (CI) is as follows:

$$EAR\ (CI) = \left[\left\{\left(1 + \frac{2}{100-2}\right)^{\frac{365}{80}}\right\} - 1\right] * 100\% = 9,7\% \tag{28}$$

This example illustrates the impact of small discounts in a supply chain finance program on an annual base for financing a company [13].

Suppose the payment term in the example is lowered to 60 days (ceteris paribus), the outcome of the effective rate will be 14,6% (simple interest) and 15,9% (compound interest). Similar calculations can be made when the discount rate is increased to 3% in the original example (ceteris paribus), the outcome of the effective rate will be 13,7% (simple interest), and 14,9% (compound interest).

5. Business process, ERP, and IT platforms

As supply chain finance is event-driven [3], we have to process the three events (buying, production, and selling) into the business processes of the focal company [30], as was plotted at the beginning of this chapter in **Figure 1**.

Input of resources (such as raw materials, components, labor force, and energy) will lead to transformation by production and finally end to the sales of final products (and services). This is a nutshell of the basics of operations management [30], in which topics like just in time (JIT), lean operations, material requirement planning (MRP), total quality management (TQM), and inventory management are integrated into one business system: enterprise resource planning (ERP). Enterprise resource planning (ERP) integrates business functions, such as planning, operations (execution), and control (including the accounting function) (**Figure 2**).

Nowadays enterprise resource systems from the different companies in a supply chain are connected via systems like electronic data interchange (EDI) and IT-cloud platforms [31]. An IT-cloud platform (Tradecloud [32]) is not only connecting financial events such as invoicing and payments in the supply chain, but also improving collaboration in the supply chain (by sharing forecasts by the focal company to tier-1 and tier-2 suppliers) and bringing back process time and processing costs of invoices in the supply chain of order to cash (O2C) [33] and purchase to pay (P2P).

The integrated overview of all business processes will be presented in **Figure 3** (a conceptual model of supply chain finance).

The latest development in this topic [34] is called Sales and Operational Planning (S&OP), so in this latest approach, there is a focus on coordination (in the ecosystem), planning (an integrated and dynamic structure), technology (as a transformation enabler), and collaboration (in an engaged planning culture). So, S&OP includes the focal company, their suppliers, and their customers to a more resilient approach in their supply chain to deal unstable environment (we will come on that later in the section about the VUCA world).

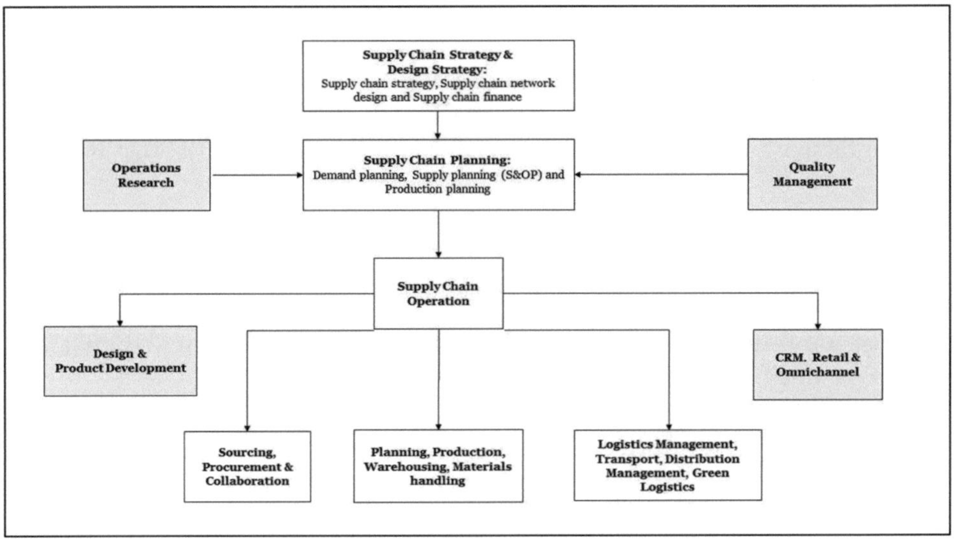

Figure 2.
Overview of supply chain management based on Leeman [22].

6. Supply chain finance instruments and banking

In **Table 6** an overview is provided for the most common supply chain finance instruments. The overview is composed by the author, and based on De Boer et al. [18], EBA [3], and Hollinger et al. [35].

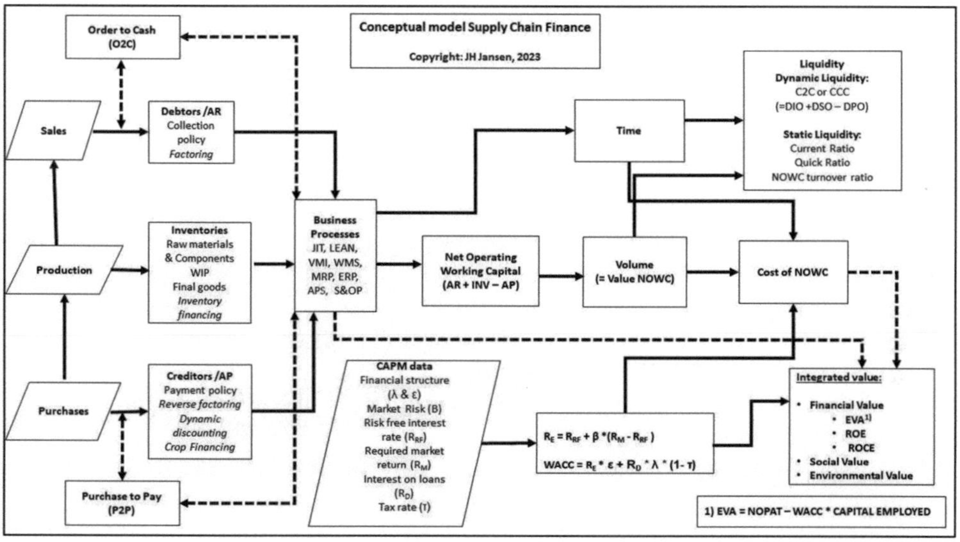

Figure 3.
Conceptual model of supply chain finance (developed by the author).

Management level	Supply chain finance instruments
Strategical	• Take ovar • Merge • Joint venture • Minority interest
Tactical	• Equipment financing • Pay on production • Supply risk sharing • Currency risk sharing • ERP • IT platform
Operational	• Working capital management • Dynamic discounting • Reverse factoring • Factoring • Inventory financing • Crop financing • Purchase order financing • Trade finance instruments • Letter of Credit (LC) • Bank guarantee • Documentary credit • Bank payment obligation (BPO)

Table 6.
Supply chain finance instruments (developed by the author).

We will select five supply chain finance instruments:

I. Minority interest

II. Equipment financing

III. Reverse factoring

IV. Dynamic discounting

V. Crop financing

The choice of these five instruments is based on the fact that they are most commonly used [36], in a more specialized report [3] more detailed information about most instruments can be retrieved.

Minority interest is used when a company like ASML [37]—that produces equipment for the chip industry—has investors (shareholders) that are important buyers such as chip producers. The reason that chip producers would like to have a stake in ASML is based on the fact to be sure of the future supply of equipment and reasons for co-development and innovation.

Equipment financing is often used in the supply chain, where the focal company is financing equipment (such as harvesters, tractors, and trucks) to help (agricultural) suppliers to finance this kind of capital expenditure (often in combination with a bank loan)). The main reason for a focal = company to use this type of tactical instrument is to be sure of future services and/or delivery of products from the suppliers.

Reverse factoring is one of the traditional supply chain finance instruments and is often combined with a financial institution (e.g., a bank) as an intermediary. The following five steps (see **Figure 4**) are normally in a reverse factoring program: The buyer places the order (step 1), the order is processed by the supplier and delivered to the buyer/focal company (step 2), the supplier sends the invoice to the buyer (step 3) with a payment term of 90 days (and with 1% discounts with payment within 5 days), the supplier receives payment within 5 days from the bank with a discount of 1%, finally (step 5) the buyer pays the full amount (100%) to the bank within 90 days (payment term). The effective annual rate (EAR based on compound interest) is 4.8% in this case.

Dynamic discounting is a method where suppliers receive early payment from the focal company. The discount rate is based on a schedule provided by the focal company. The supplier can select a date and corresponding discount rate and receive the amount of the invoice minus the selected discount rate. **Table 7** is an example provided by a dynamic discounting system; we observe that the discount rate is a function of time (day paid earlier).

Finally, crop financing is a supply chain finance tool used in (international) agricultural business [35], we observe in practice that besides the producers (often small farmers) a focal company (often a large multinational) and a financier (e.g., bank), during the growth season the farmers need liquidity. The liquidity is provided with a pre-payment via often a bank loan or a promissory note (IOU) issued by the framer, where the collateral is the future harvest of the crops. The World Bank Group (for instance IFC, International Finance Corporation) developed a lot of customized solutions for agricultural finance [38].

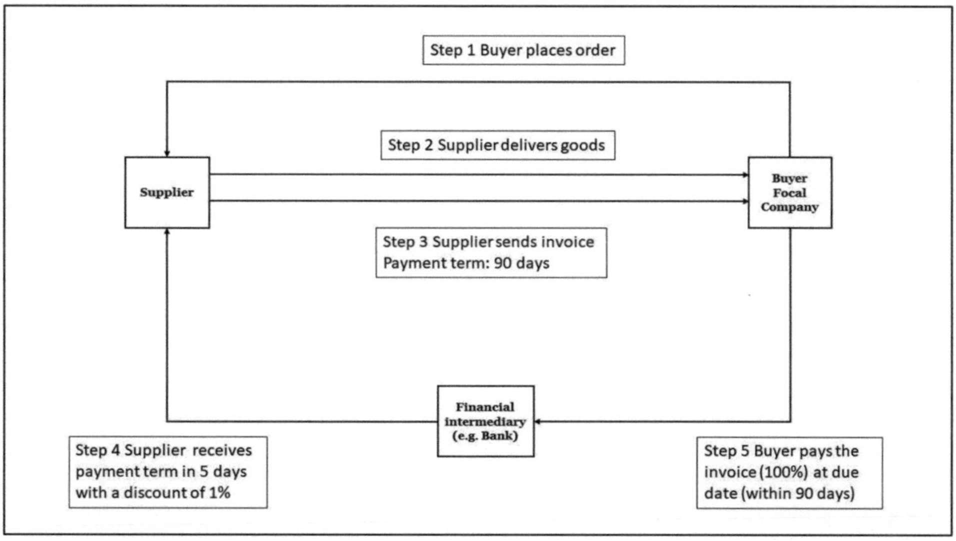

Figure 4.
Reverse factoring in five steps (developed by the author).

Discount rate	Days paid earlier
2,0%	20
1,9%	19
1,8%	18
1,7%	17
1,6%	16
1,5%	15
Etc.	Etc.
0%	0

Table 7.
Example of dynamic discounting (developed by the author).

7. State-of-the-art discussion: VUCA world, FinTech, and sustainability

Volatility, uncertainty, complexity, and ambiguity (VUCA) are four characteristics of the world we live in Ref. [39]. We observe more risks in the three supply chain flows, because of wars, scarcity of fossil fuels, large accidents (like recently in the Suez Channel), volatility of currencies, etc. Supply chain finance is often involved, because of financing (larger) inventories for a longer period, financing suppliers (especially so-called deep-tier finance), dealing with increased risks, etc.

An example of the leading principles (green, resilient, and inclusive) of a supply chain finance program can be found in the Trade and Supply Chain Finance Program of the Asian Development Bank [17].

Sustainability in supply chain finance has at least two dimensions:

I. Sustainability in finance.

II. Sustainability in supply chains.

Sustainability in finance was already discussed in paragraph 4 about corporate finance based on the publications of Schoenmaker and Schramade, introducing their integrated value model (in which financial value, social value, and ecological value were integrated). Similar approaches can be found in Gleeson-White [40] and Raworth [41] introducing besides financial value, other sorts of values based on externalities (e.g., social value and ecological value). Externalities are positive and/or negative influences on consumers and/or producers that are not reflected in the market price [42]. All those developments of integrated value are materialized in integrated annual reports for businesses [43].

Another trend in finance is to include externalities in the cost price of the product or service, this concept of true costing [44]. So, the true cost price of the product includes the costs of goods sold (such as procurement costs and direct labor costs), the costs of social externalities (such as extra labor costs for a fair wage), and environmental externalities (additional costs of preventing pollution or any cost to recover harm to the environment). This has a huge impact on the traditional way of calculating revenues and cost, and the traditional way [45], of calculating profit and economic value according to EVA® [8].

Sustainability in the supply chain can be demonstrated by the "butterfly" model of the Ellen MacArthur Foundation [46] by using the following loops:

- Maintenance
- Reuse/Redistribute
- Refurbish/Redistribute
- Recycle

The goals of the loops are to lower the use of virgin material, have lifetime extension, and minimize waste of production (and consuming products). A similar approach [47] can be read in **Figure 5**, where the restoration cycles and the regeneration cycles are plotted.

The restoration cycle consists of the following sub-cycles:

- Share, maintain, and prolong
- Reuse and redistribute
- Refurbish and remanufacture
- Recycle

The regeneration cycle consists of the following sub-cycles:

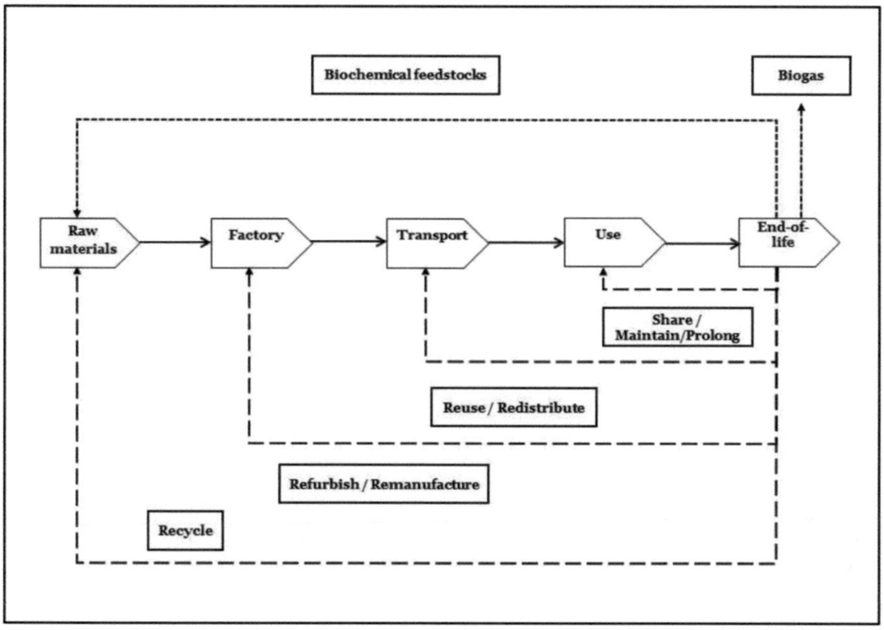

Figure 5.
Sustainable logistics [47].

- Biogas
- Biochemical feedstocks

In both cycles, it is the general goal to reduce pollution and lower extraction of virgin raw materials [46], in **Figure 5** this is made more specific for logistics and supply chain management [47].

The consequence of such new logistics models is that they have an impact on the product or service that will be offered. For instance, you need equipment or trucks as a company, in traditional business you buy such an investment from your supplier. In new business models [48], you can think about all sorts of leasing (operational or financial lease) or make a contract for the use of equipment or a truck as a service (in the case of the truck: Mobility as a Service or MaaS, or with a computer with software: SaaS). This has an impact on sales and inventories (supplier) and fixed capital and costs (buyer), as well as on the financial needs of suppliers and buyers.

In the logistics trend radar 6.0 of DHL [49] about 40 trends are playing an important role in the logistics industry, some of them a link to sustainable supply chain finance, such as:

- Circularity
- Environmental stewardship
- Sharing economy
- Blockchains

- Cloud & Application Programming Interfaces (APIs)
- Next generation wireless
- Physical Internet
- Digital marketplaces
- Supply chain diversification
- ...

DeSmet [50] introduces the supply chain triangle of service, cost, and cash, in his model he develops the relationship between service and revenue, capital employed (e.g., net operating working capital), and cost into one formula: ROCE (Return On Capital Employed).

$$ROCE = \frac{Revnues - Cost}{Capital\ Employed\ (= Fixed\ Assets + Net\ Working\ Capital)} * 100\% \quad (29)$$

DeSmet's model was adapted by two practitioners [51] into a pentagon:

So, five forces play a role in the value metrics of supply chain management: services (and sales), costs, capital employed, risk and resilience [52], and sustainability from a more integrated value perspective [28].

Another new development is the combination of IT-cloud technology and the role of financiers, called FinTech [53]. The advantages of the role of FinTech companies are more efficient and effective, introducing new technology systems such as distributed ledger technology (e.g., Blockchain) and introducing new business models.

8. Conceptual model of supply chain finance

A conceptual model is defined as a *conceptual model consists of units with attributes (concepts, theoretical constructs) and relations between those attributes and concepts based on theoretical constructs';* and has the following functions [54]:

1. What theoretical concepts (existing body of knowledge) are used in this research?
2. Helpful in structuring the problem.
3. Linking to a system, according to system theory (cause and effect relationships)

A similar approach to the definition can be found in Verschuren & Doorewaard [55] in which assumed causal relationships (based on existing theories) between the core concepts of research are plotted, as shown in **Figure 3**.

Of course, in a conceptual model, the eclectic approach will be used, eclectic means you combine different (parts) of theories for the conceptual model [54].

The goal of the conceptual model of supply chain finance (see **Figure 6**) is to understand the main financial (and non-financial) flows, based on real events (such as

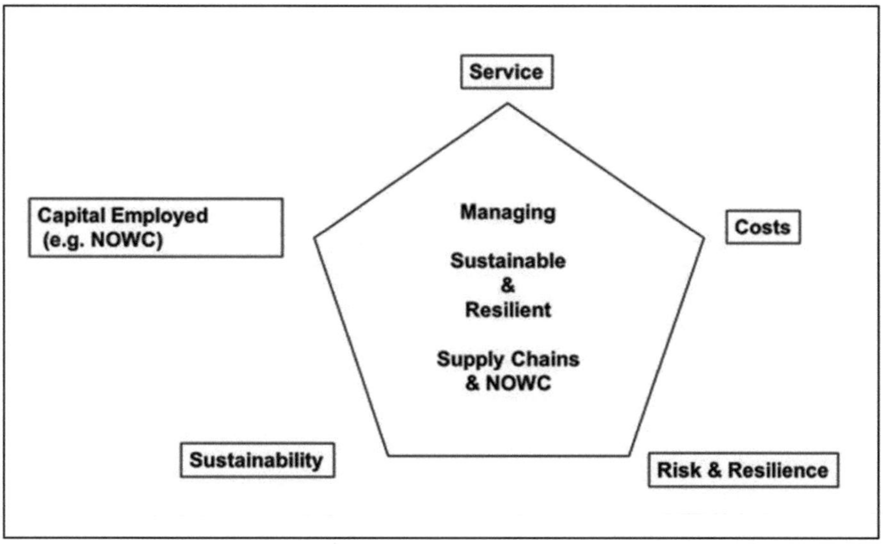

Figure 6.
Five forces in logistics/supply chain management.

buying, producing, and selling) in the supply chain, and their impact on business flows in the focal company, and at the end the impact on: static and dynamic liquidity (of the net operating working capital), and the integrated value performance (financial value or profit, social value, and environmental value).

The model has one important limitation, the impact of sustainability (see **Figure 6**) on the supply chain is not plotted in **Figure 3**, otherwise, the model would have been more complex (than it already is).

The conceptual model of supply chain finance is constructed based on an input-transformation-output model [30], so we start reading **Figure 3** from the left to the right. We observe the following parts in the conceptual model:

8.1 Supply chain events (Inputs A)

An important input is the twisted supply chain (see also **Figure 1**) on the left-hand side, starting with purchases, production, and sales. This is also the start of the Purchase to Pay (P2P) and the Order to Cash (O2C) processes. The supply chain events are:

- Buying of raw materials and components from suppliers, which results in the purchase-to-pay (P2P) process.

- Transformation respectively production from raw materials and components to work in progress (WIP) and finalized into products and services.

- Selling (Including distribution) of final products and services to the customers.

Each sub-process has an impact on creditors/account payables, inventories and debtors/account receivables.

8.2 Business processes (throughput/transformation)

From the supply chain events (Step I) we arrive at the box of business processes, in which all sorts of data are processed by the focal company. Data of incoming invoices (from suppliers), outgoing invoices (to customers), and production (from inventories) will have an impact on the different business systems of the focal company. We will use the enterprise resource planning (ERP) system as the overall business system that includes functionalities such as accounting (ledgers), warehouse management system (WMS), and materials resource planning (MRP). Often the structure/design of this business application is according to principles [30] such as lean management, just-in-time (JIT), and sales & operational planning (S&OP).

This has an impact on the supply chain finance metrics (see also step IV) according to the cube model [1], the value of net operating working capital (NOWC), duration or time, and the interest rate (e.g., WACC) play a role in the connecting three boxes in this section of the conceptual model.

8.3 Financial data (inputs B)

Another important input is the Capital Asset Pricing Model (CAPM) data of the focal company and from the macroeconomic environment. The data of the capital asset pricing model are exogenous data, which implies the focal company cannot influence them. Part of the data is strategically chosen by the strategic management of the company (Chief Executive Officer and/or Chief Financial Officer) and is data for the operations in the focal company. The financial structure of the focal company (materialized in the ε or equity ratio and λ or debt ratio) is an example of such a strategic choice by the executive management.

The market risk of the company (β) is a yardstick for the risk of the focal company compared to the stock market, it informs us how volatile the share of the focal company is (compared to the stock market).

The risk-free interest rate (R_{RF}), the required market return (R_M), as well as the interest rate on loans (R_D) are dictated by the financial market. So, the focal company does not influence those factors.

Finally, the government determines the corporate tax rate (τ).

All these inputs result in the CAPM basic formula of the return on equity:

$$R_E = R_{RF} + \beta * (R_M - R_{RF}) \tag{30}$$

This will continue in the weighted average costs of the capital formula:

$$WACC = R_E * \varepsilon + R_D * \lambda * (1 - \tau) \tag{31}$$

The WACC formula will be used to calculate EVA® in the next step (Step IV)

8.4 Supply chain finance outcomes or SCF metrics (outputs)

In the final step of the supply chain finance conceptual model, we have left two final boxes (one on the right-hand top and one on the right-hand bottom). One box is about static and dynamic liquidity. In the supply chain finance dynamics plays an important role (Cash to Cash cycle), in which the three components of net operating working capital are expressed in time: DIO, DSO and DPO.

The static ratio such as Quik Ratio (QR), Current Ratio (CR), and the NOWC turnover ratio are not so much used in supply chain finance ratios, although they might be quite relevant for the CFO of the focal company to evaluate the financial needs of the company in the short term of the business [8].

From the business processes (Step 2) and the CAPM data (Step 3) the costs of net operating capital can be calculated, using the cube model [1].

The final box (right-hand bottom) is about the integrated value model [28]. The financial value is calculated based on the traditional finance theory [8] with metrics such as EVA®, ROE, and ROCE. All financial metrics represent the Anglo-Saxon paradigm of the slogan "Cash is King."

The social value measures the added value of nonfinancial stakeholders such as suppliers, workers, and customers. That are not materialled in the financial value. Social value is typically an externality [42]. There are studies (True [56]) about the social costs of for instance a cotton t-shirt (estimated at around € 13), often based on a few types of cheap labor. Also, multinational enterprises try to estimate social value (often based on non-financial metrics [57].

The environmental value measures the impacts on the planet (the well-known triple bottom line: people, planet, and profits). The impact on the environment can be measured during the extraction from nature (such as extraction of oil and metals), during the production (deforestation, dehydration, pollution of water, air, and soil) and the economic life of products (waste of materials like glass, paper, batteries, etc.).

A big issue is also her to find a financial and/or a nonfinancial metric to measure the environmental impact. In a case study of the Impact Institute, we observe an estimation of environmental costs of cotton t-shirts of about € 5 (True [56]). In the Annual Report 2022 of Philips, we observe a serious attempt to quantify environmental impact often in a nonfinancial way in the ESG statements [57].

In the logistics industry, we observe huge attention to downsizing the impact of pollution of different transport modalities (sea, air, and road).

Recently historical foundations, current research, and future developments were published by Caniato et al. [36]. In one of the current eight studies, there was some attention to a framework; and one of the future developments is about real-time information and the use of blockchain (distributed ledger technology). A case study in which this was implemented by a focal company (Heering-Holland) in a supply chain using an IT platform (Tradecloud-One) was quite recently published by Jansen et al. [31].

9. Conclusion

The author developed in this chapter a few perspectives on supply chain finance. The basic model of supply chain finance was discussed, based on supply chain management/logistics management, finance and control, ERP & IT platforms, and supply chain finance instruments (including FinTechs).

This basic model of supply chain fiancé is very financially driven (Cash is King), while nowadays financial models are based on the integrated value concept. In the integrated value concept, financial value, social value, and environmental value are combined into one model.

Finally, the world is turbulent and supply chains have to deal with risk and volatility to be resilient in such a VUCA world. This will also have an impact on the traditional way supply chain finance looks at their instruments and business models.

Acknowledgements

The author thanks the Supply Chain Finance Community, the Research Group of Supply Chain Finance at Windesheim University of Applied Sciences, and the Research Group of Logistics and Alliances of HAN University of Applied Sciences.

Conflict of interest

The author declares no conflict of interest.

Notes/thanks/other declarations

None.

Author details

Jan Jansen
Emeritus HAN University of Applied Sciences, Research Group Logistics and Alliances, Arnhem, Netherlands

*Address all correspondence to: jansen.janh@gmail.com

References

[1] Pfohl H-C, Gomm M. Supply chain finance: Optimising financial flows in supply chains. Logistics Research. 2009: 149-161

[2] Steeman M. The Power of Supply Chain Finance. Zwolle: Windesheim University of Applied Sciences; 2014

[3] EBA. Standard Definitions for Techniques of Supply Chain Finance. Paris: European Banking Association (EBA); 2016

[4] Templar S, Hofmann E, Findlay C. Financing the End-to-End Supply Chain. London: Kogan Page; 2016

[5] Tate W, Bals L, Ellram L. Supply Chain Finance. London: Kogan Page; 2019

[6] Mascarenhas S, Sanstad B, Bhalla AS, Ramirez Ortiz CM. Deep-Tier Supply Chain Finance. ADB Briefs; 2022. p. 129

[7] Harrison A, Van Hoek R. Logistics Management & Strategy - Competing Through the Supply Chain. Harlow: Pearson Education Limited; 2011

[8] Brealy RA, Myers SC, Allen F. Principles of Corporate Finance. New York (USA): McGrawHill; 2020

[9] Zhao L, Huchzermeier A. Supply Chain Finance - Integrating Operations and Finance in Global Supply Chains. Cham (CH): Springer International Publishing AG; 2018

[10] Dorsman A. Vlottend Financieel Management - Analyse en Planning. Amsterdam: Elsevier; 2002a

[11] Dorsman AB. Vlottend Financieel Management. Amsterdam (NL): Elsevier; 2002b

[12] Gieskens JH. Strategic Working Capital Management. Amstelveen: Alex van Groningen; 2014

[13] Hillier D, Clacher I, Ross S, Westerfield R, Jordan B. Fundamentals of Corporate Finance. Maidenhead: McGraw-Hill Higher Education; 2011

[14] Preve L, Sarria-Allende V. Working Capital Management. Oxford: Oxford University Press; 2010

[15] Dekkers R, De Boer R, Gelsomino L, De Goeij C, Steeman M, Zhou Q, et al. Evaluating theoretical conceptualisations for supply chain and finance integration: A Scottish focus group. International Journal of Production Economics. 2020; **220**

[16] Malaket A. Financing Trade and International Supply Chains. Farnham: Gower; 2014

[17] ADB. Trade and Supply Chain Finance Program (TSCFP). Asian Development Bank. 2023. Available from: https://www.adb.org/what-we-do/trade-supply-chain-finance-program/main

[18] De Boer R, Van Bergen M, Steeman M. Supply Chain Finance, its Practical Relevance and Strategic Value. Zwolle: Supply Chain Finance Community; 2015

[19] Stock J, Lambert D. Strategic Logistics Management. New York: McGraw-Hill Higher Education; 2001

[20] ASCM. What is logistics? Retrieved from Association for Supply Chain Management (ASCM). 2023a. Available from: https://www.ascm.org/scm/logistics/

[21] ASCM. Supply Chain Management. Association Foir Supply Chain Management (ASCM). 2023b. Available from: https://www.ascm.org/scm/

[22] Leeman J. Supply Chain Management. Amsterdam: Pearson; 2018

[23] Van Weele A. Inkoop in Strategisch Perspectief. Alphen an den Rijn: Samson; 1997

[24] Volkswagen. Annual Report 2022. Wolfsburg: Volkswagen AG; 2023

[25] Van Horne J, Wachowicz J. Fundamentals of Financial Management. New Jersey: Prentince Hall; 2001

[26] Atrill P. Financial Management for Decision Makers. Harlow: Pearson Education; 2009

[27] Schoenmaker D, Schramade W. Principles of Sustainable Finance. Oxford: Oxford University Press; 2019

[28] Schoenmaker D, Schramade W. Corporate Finance for Long-Term Value. Cham: Springer; 2023

[29] Koutsoyiannis A. Modrern Microeconomics. London: Macmillan Press; 1976

[30] Slack N, Brandon-Jones A, Johnston R. Operations management. Harlow: Pearson Education; 2016

[31] Jansen J, Kaledinova E, Wolters A. The use of cloud technology for sustainable performance of international supply chains: A case study. Transportation Research Procedia. 2022:224-231

[32] Tradecloud One. Business Case for Supply Chain Collaboration. 2023. Available from https://www.tradecloud1.com/en/business-case-supply-chain-collaboration-benefits/

[33] De Goeij C, Van Weelden R, Breijer M, Jansen J, Holman R. Inefficiencies in order to cash processes in the logistics industry empirical evidence from the Netherlands. In: Weijers S, Bart V, editors. Vervoerslogsitiekewerkdagen 2022. Zelzate: University Press; 2022. pp. 217-230

[34] Jonsson P, Kaipia R, Barratt M. The future of S&OP: Dynamic complexity, ecosystems and reslience. International Journal of Physical Distribution & Logistics Management. 2021:553-565

[35] Hollinger F, Gross A. Crop Receipts - A New Financing Instrument for Africa. Washington: IFC; 2019

[36] Caniato F, Henke M, Zsidisin G. Supply chain finance: Historical foundations, current research, future developments. Journal of Purchasing and Supply Management. 2019:99-104

[37] ASML. Annual Report 2022. Veldhoven: ASML; 2023

[38] The World Bank. Agricultural Finance & Agricultural Insurance. The World Bank. 2023. Available from: https://www.worldbank.org/en/topic/financialsector/brief/agriculture-finance

[39] Bennis W, Nanus B. Leaders: The Strategies for Taking Charge. New York: Harper & Row; 1985

[40] Gleeson-White J. Six Capitals. Crows Nest: Allen & Unwin; 2014

[41] Raworth K. Doughnut Economics. London: RHB Books; 2017

[42] Perloff J. Microeconomics with Calculus. Harlow: Pearson Education; 2014

[43] IIRC. International <IR> Framework. Integrated Reporting Council (IIRC): Deleware; 2021

[44] Maxwell S. The Price Is Wrong. Danvers: Wiley; 2008

[45] Horngren C, Datar S, Rajan M. Cost Accounting. Harlow: Pearson Education; 2012

[46] Webster K. The Circular Economy a Wealth of Flows. Cowes: Ellen MacArthur Foundation; 2017

[47] Grant D, Trautrims A, Wong C. Sustainable Logistcs and Supply Chain Management. London: Kogan Page; 2017

[48] Jonker J. Nieuwe Business Modellen. Amsterdam: Academic Service; 2015

[49] Dohrmann K, Toy J, Pitcher E, Selders J, Grauf T. The Logistics Trend Radar 6.0. DHL. 2023. Available from: https://www.dhl.com/global-en/home/insights-and-innovation/insights/logistics-trend-radar.html

[50] DeSmet B. Supply Chain and Financial Metrics. London: Kogan Page; 2017

[51] Ebel T & Mohrschladt R. Mastering Uncertainty by Preparing for the Unxepected. Camelot Consulting Group. 2022. Available from: https://blog.camelot-group.com/2022/08/mastering-uncertainty-in-supply-chains-by-preparing-for-the-unexpected/

[52] Waters D. Supply Chain Risk Management - Vulnerability and Reslienece in Logistics. London: Kogan Page; 2011

[53] Le W. Fintech: Digital transformation in finance. In: 7th International Conference on Economic Management and Green Development. London: MDPI; 2023. pp. 22-27

[54] Jonker J, Bennink B. Conceptual models. In: Jonker J, Bennink B, editors. The Essence of Research Methodology. Berlin: Springer; 2010. pp. 43-63

[55] Verschuren P, Doorewaard H. Designing a Research Project. Den Haag: Eleven International Publishing; 2010

[56] Price T. Reducing the True Cost of Cotton T-Shirts. Brussels: Greens/EFA Group; 2012

[57] Philips. Annual Report 2022. Amsterdam: Philips; 2023

Chapter 2

Supply Chains for Hydrogen and Carbon Dioxide for Sustainable Production of Base Chemicals

Thomas E. Müller

Abstract

In pursuit of global climate goals, the emergence of a hydrogen economy is a promising avenue, emphasizing the environmentally friendly production and versatile applications of hydrogen as an energy carrier, raw material, and cornerstone for energy-intensive sectors such as power, transportation, and especially the chemical industry. This evolution requires profound changes in the supply chain, ranging from the establishment of a robust hydrogen infrastructure to the realization of efficient transportation, distribution, and storage mechanisms. Amidst a plethora of potential hydrogen supply modalities, determining the path to a carbon-neutral hydrogen economy presents complex challenges. This chapter explores these transition complexities in the context of sustainable technology development. It also critically assesses the symbiosis between this transition and emerging carbon supply chains, particularly those aiming for closed carbon cycles, and presents a holistic vision for future sustainable frameworks in the chemical sector.

Keywords: hydrogen, supply chain, renewable energy potential, energy transport, feedstock, chemical industry, carbon sources, sustainability

1. Introduction

With its vast array of products and intricate processes, the chemical industry is one of the influential sectors of the global economy. At the heart is a progressively branching, yet mostly linear, supply chain originating from fossil resources (**Figure 1**) that ensures the seamless flow of raw materials, intermediates, and finished products across continents and markets. This supply chain, honed over decades, is the silent engine that powers our modern world, from the materials to the chemicals and fuels we use in our daily lives. In this chapter, we will analyze today's chemical supply chain to understand its intricacies, challenges, and the innovations [1] that are driving their evolution in a rapidly changing global landscape.

As our collective awareness of the fragility of the planet grows, the concept of sustainability has evolved from a niche concern to a global imperative. For industry, including the chemical sector, the call for sustainability is not only a moral obligation, but also an economic and strategic necessity. Traditional paradigms that emphasized

IntechOpen

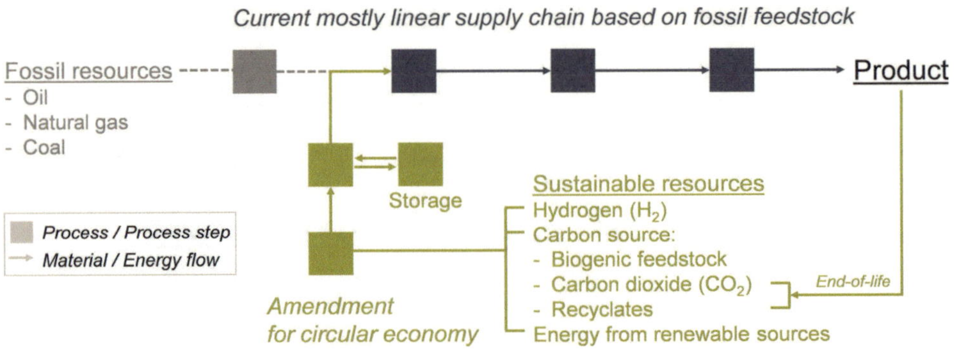

Figure 1.
Schematic representation of the linear fossil-based supply chain and the amendments needed to make the supply chain sustainable.

efficiency and output are now converging with environmental protection, resource conservation, and social responsibility. The pressing challenges of climate change, resource depletion, and environmental degradation underscore the need for sustainable transformation in chemical supply chains [2]. This chapter explores emerging sustainable amendments to the supply chain (**Figure 1**) and how these changes are reshaping the very fabric of chemical production, distribution, and consumption.

In the midst of this transformative shift, the world is eyeing the contours of a sustainable hydrogen economy as an indispensable part of a clean energy supply. Hydrogen stands out not only as an energy vector, but as a keystone for the sustainable evolution of the chemical industry. At the same time, the push toward closed carbon cycles [3] promises a breakthrough solution to some of the world's greatest environmental challenges. By capturing and reusing carbon dioxide (CO_2), we can forge supply chains that significantly reduce carbon footprints [4] and ensure a circular economy (**Figure 1**). As we navigate the complex realm of possibilities, it is critical to merge these two paradigms—building an infrastructure that promotes hydrogen while optimizing the sustainable use of carbon. The goal of this chapter is to demonstrate the synergies between a sustainable hydrogen economy and a closed-loop carbon supply chain, with the aim of outlining a blueprint for sustainable production in the chemical industry.

1.1 Sustainable hydrogen economy

One promising strategy to meet global climate objectives is transitioning to the so-called "hydrogen economy" [5]. This concept is based on producing hydrogen in a climate-friendly manner and then using it as an energy source, raw material, and feedstock in energy-intensive sectors such as power generation, transportation, and the chemical industry [6, 7]. In 2020, global hydrogen production was about 120 million tons per annum (t/a) [8]. Hydrogen is used for oil refining and as important feedstock in the chemical industry (39 million t/a), for methanol production and the production of platform and high-value chemicals (14 million t/a) as well as ammonia synthesis (32 million t/a) [9]. Hydrogen plays roles in steel production by the direct reduced iron process (5 million t/a) and in the generation of electricity and heat (30 million t/a) [8]. By 2050, once a hydrogen economy takes shape, the worldwide demand of hydrogen could rise to about 530 million t/a [10]. Transitioning to this hydrogen economy requires fundamental changes in the supply chain including establishing new technologies for hydrogen production and a suitable hydrogen infrastructure. This comprises creating new transport, distribution, and storage systems. Given the diverse methods available for hydrogen supply, determining the best way to provide hydrogen sustainably in the future hydrogen economy needs to be carefully analyzed.

2. Sustainable supply chains for hydrogen

An overview of various hydrogen production technologies, distinguishing between those derived from fossil fuels and those derived from renewable resources, is given in **Table 1**. The technologies are classified according to the primary feedstock. A notable advance in reducing the process-related CO_2 emissions of conventional hydrogen production is the incorporation of Carbon Capture Utilization and Storage (CCUS) technologies. While relying on the same fossil resources and production process, these methods focus on capturing a significant part of the arising CO_2. After capture, this CO_2 can either be reused (termed as "Carbon Capture and Utilization" or CCU) or stored (known as "Carbon Capture and Storage" or CCS) [11].

Hydrogen production technologies vary significantly in their development stage, the raw materials or feedstocks they employ (e.g., natural gas, oil, coal, biomass, water), the utilities they require, and their associated Greenhouse Gas (GHG) emissions. To facilitate differentiation, common color-based terms are used to categorize these technologies. For example, the colors "gray," "blue," "turquoise," and "green" often refer to conventional low-CO_2, CO_2-free, and carbon-free production pathways, respectively (**Figure 2**) [12, 13]. Several other color descriptors, such as "yellow," "purple," "pink," "brown," and "black," have been introduced to classify hydrogen production technologies [14].

Hydrogen produced from fossil resources is commonly termed "gray" or conventional hydrogen. The most common technology for producing hydrogen is through steam reforming of natural gas. This is often combined with two other fossil-based technologies that are widely used on an industrial scale, autothermal reforming, and partial oxidation [13]. The carbon dioxide resulting from these processes is emitted into the atmosphere, contributing to GHG emissions and, consequently, to global warming [15, 16].

"Blue" hydrogen, often referred to as low-CO_2 hydrogen, uses the same process technologies as "gray" hydrogen [12]. The key difference is how the off-gases from

Technologies based on fossil resources				Technologies based on sustainable resources	
	Natural gas	**Oil**	**Coal**	**Biomass**	**Water**
Steam reforming	X			Dark fermentation	Electrolysis
Autothermal reforming	X	X		Photofermentation	Thermolysis
Partial oxidation	X	X		Bio-photolysis	Photolysis
Pyrolysis	X	X		X	
Gasification		X	X	X	

Table 1.
Hydrogen production technologies categorized according to the primary feedstock.

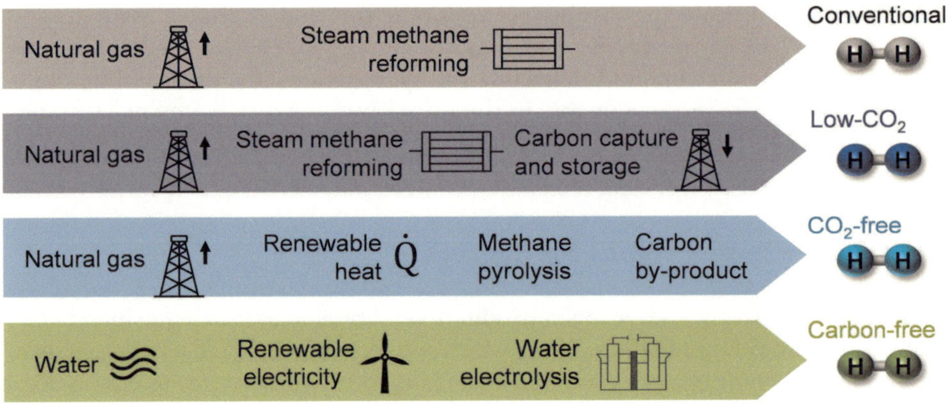

Figure 2.
Hydrogen production pathways and frequently associated colors, adapted from Ref. [12].

hydrogen production are managed. Before these gases are released into the atmosphere, they are treated to capture most of the resultant CO_2. This captured CO_2 is then stored in geological formations. For a process to earn the "low-CO_2" label, it is essential to ensure that the CO_2 is stored safely. Over time, the CO_2 gradually reacts with the surrounding rock. It is worth noting that there is no universally accepted definition specifying the minimum percentage of CO_2 that must be captured and stored to qualify for this classification [13].

"Turquoise" hydrogen is produced through methane pyrolysis (MP) [12], a process that cleaves methane into gaseous hydrogen and solid carbon. Notably, this process results in no direct CO_2 emissions, earning it the "CO_2-free" label. Similar to the captured CO_2 in "blue" hydrogen production [12], the solid carbon byproduct from MP requires long-term storage to keep it out of the atmospheric carbon cycle [3]. It is also important to note that for the process to be truly CO_2-free, the heat required for the process must be generated without the burning of fossil fuels and the associated release of CO_2 into the atmosphere [15, 17].

"Green" hydrogen is classified as such when its production is based entirely on renewable resources [12]. One notable method of producing "green" hydrogen is water electrolysis powered by electricity derived from renewable primary energy sources. This process does not involve any carbon-based feedstocks. Furthermore, neither the upstream value chain of electricity generation nor the operation of the electrolysis system produces CO_2 emissions, except for those associated with the construction and eventual disposal of the necessary plants and infrastructure. As a result, water electrolysis is often labeled as "carbon-free" [15, 17]. However, similar to the classification of "blue" hydrogen, the label for "green" hydrogen can be ambiguous [12]. There may be instances where the electricity used in the electrolysis cells is supplied by a mix that includes fossil-based primary energy sources [13]. Such a mix might be needed to maintain a high utilization of the electrolysis cells, given the intrinsically fluctuating availability of renewable primary energy sources [18].

Technologies that are poised for large-scale hydrogen production in the near to midterm future are characterized by their reliance on feedstocks with the established, extensive distribution networks and a high Technology Readiness Level (TRL).

2.1 Hydrogen production by steam methane reforming

Today, hydrogen production relies primarily on fossil hydrocarbons as the primary feedstock. The annual production of 70 million t/a of hydrogen is based mostly on the reforming and gasification of natural gas (76%) and coal (23%) [9]. The leading processes are steam reforming, partial oxidation, and autothermal reforming. The remainder of global hydrogen production is attributed to electrolysis, with chlor-alkali electrolysis being the predominant process [9].

Steam reforming [19] is a process that typically uses natural gas as a hydrocarbon feedstock. Methane (CH_4) is the major constituent of natural gas with a molar fraction of 75 to 99% [20]. Therefore, steam reforming is mostly termed Steam Methane Reforming (SMR). However, natural gas also contains varying quantities of higher alkanes. Additionally, it comprises inert gases such as nitrogen and helium, and acidic "sour" gases, predominantly carbon dioxide and hydrogen sulfide [20]. It is worth noting that hydrogen sulfide, when present in hydrogen, can be harmful for downstream processes. This is because sulfur compounds can poison catalysts by chemisorbing to the metal centers that form the active sites of the catalysts [21]. Therefore, it is critical to remove hydrogen sulfide from the hydrocarbon feed [22]. This removal is typically accomplished by hydrotreating or by reaction with activated zinc oxide [15].

The main process steps in SMR are depicted in **Figure 3**. Initially, methane undergoes catalytic cleavage, forming carbon monoxide (CO) and hydrogen (H_2). This reaction takes place in the presence of steam (H_2O) at temperatures ranging from 700 to 900°C [24] and pressures between 3 and 35 bar [6, 25]. Commonly used heterogeneous catalysts for this process include nickel sponges [15], as well as metal-supported catalysts like nickel/aluminum oxide (Ni/Al_2O_3) [26, 27] or ruthenium/zirconium dioxide (Ru/ZrO_2) [28].

Reacting hydrocarbons with water (as shown in Eqs. (1) and (2)) is highly endothermic that requires substantial external heat supply [19]. The necessary reaction temperatures depend on the hydrocarbon feedstock and typically fall within the 700 to 900°C range [24]. Specifically, for methane, hydrogen formation commences at temperatures above 750°C [24, 25]. The required heat is usually supplied through superheated steam, external reactor heating, or both. Natural gas and off-gases from hydrogen purification are frequently used as fuels for this purpose [6]. In addition, the

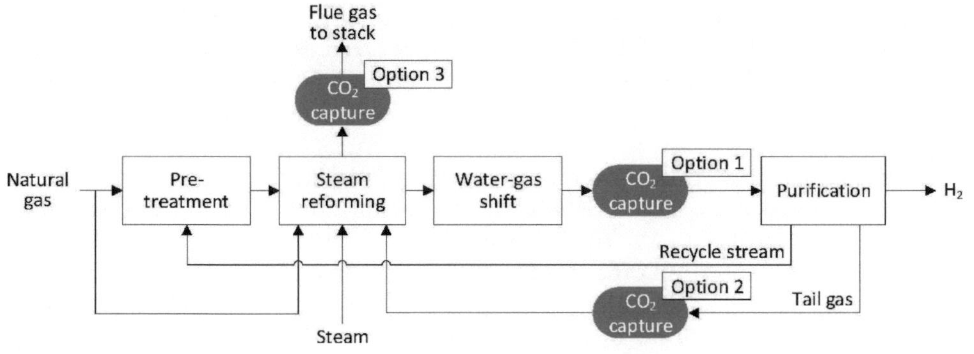

Figure 3.
Main process steps in hydrogen production by steam methane reforming and options for carbon capture, adapted from Ref. [23].

subsequent step in the SMR process chain, the exothermic Water-Gas-Shift (WGS) reaction (as detailed in Eq. (3)), can be harnessed to contribute to heat integration [19].

$$C_nH_m + n\ H_2O \rightarrow n\ CO + \left(n + \frac{m}{2}\right) H_2 \tag{1}$$

$$CH_4 + H_2O \rightleftharpoons CO + 3\ H_2\ \Delta H^0_R = +206.3\ kJ/mol \tag{2}$$

$$CO + H_2O \rightleftharpoons CO_2 + H_2\ \Delta H^0_R = -41.2\ kJ/mol \tag{3}$$

After the reforming step, the resulting hydrogen stream contains more than 10 vol.% CO [28]. The WGS reaction addresses this aspect by converting CO and water to CO_2 and H_2, enhancing the hydrogen yield (Eq. (3)). There are two distinct WGS methods, characterized by their operating temperature ranges and catalyst types:

- *High-temperature shift WGS:* This operates at temperatures between 310 and 500° C and at pressures between 25 and 35 bar. The catalysts used are iron/chromium (Fe/Cr) [29, 30] or cobalt/molybdenum (Co/Mo) [28].

- *Low-temperature shift WGS:* This operates at temperatures between 190 and 280° C. The catalysts used are copper oxide/zinc oxide (CuO/ZnO) [29] or brass-type catalysts [28].

Typically, a two-stage reactor is used combining these WGS conversion steps. After the dual-step WGS conversion, the carbon monoxide content in the product stream is reduced to about 1% [28]. Carbon dioxide is removed by physical absorption in gas scrubbers. If the hydrogen is destined for ammonia production, residual traces of carbon oxides are methanized, since methane does inhibit ammonia formation. For the generation of high-purity hydrogen, further purification is augmented by methods such as freezing, selective catalytic oxidation, Pressure Swing Adsorption (PSA), hydride storage, and membrane diffusion [6, 15, 25].

Steam Methane Reforming's (SMR's) performance is influenced by several factors. According to the Le Chatelier principle, higher temperatures and lower pressures enhance the process [25]. Introducing excess steam avoids coke formation, which is represented by the steam-to-carbon ratio. Typically, this ratio ranges between 2 [19] and 5 [24, 25]. For a balance between hydrogen yield, efficiency, and compact plant dimensions, a ratio between 2.5 [31] and 3.5 [19] is often deemed optimal. Current developments in SMR focus on elevating energy efficiency, particularly in steam preheating. This aims to reduce fuel consumption and increase the reformer's outlet temperature [32].

Steam Methane Reforming is a mature, well-established technology with a TRL of 9 [25, 27]. Some of the largest SMR plants have capacities of up to 120,000 Nm^3/h of hydrogen, primarily to serve the downstream production of ammonia (NH_3) [33]. When evaluating the overall process efficiency based on a Higher Heating Value (HHV), SMR operates at about 65 to 70% [34, 35]. Any excess heat—for instance, steam [36] from cooling of the flue gas or from intermediate product stream cooling—can be repurposed. The steam can either be used to supply adjacent industrial facilities or to produce electricity in steam turbines. The theoretical efficiency limit of SMR stands between 88.9 and 90.7% on a HHV basis [36]. A significant drawback of SMR is its notable process-related CO_2 emissions. With annual emissions currently at 530 million t/a, SMR contributes considerably to exacerbating climate change [9].

2.2 Hydrogen production by partial oxidation

Partial oxidation is currently the second most prevalent method for hydrogen production [9]. While SMR mostly utilizes natural gas, partial oxidation primarily processes higher hydrocarbons [22, 25]. A major advantage of partial oxidation is its flexibility with regard to feedstock quality [37]. In fact, a wide range of carbonaceous materials, ranging from heavy oil and coal to biomass and waste, can serve as potential feedstocks for partial oxidation [38]. The chemical equations of the partial oxidation of hydrocarbons and, specifically, of methane are given in Eqs. (4) and (5), respectively.

$$C_nH_m + \frac{n}{2}\ O_2 \rightarrow n\ CO + \frac{m}{2}\ H_2 \tag{4}$$

$$CH_4 + \frac{1}{2}\ O_2 \rightleftharpoons CO + 2\ H_2\ \Delta H_R^0 = -35.6\ \text{kJ/mol} \tag{5}$$

Partial oxidation can operate without the need for a catalyst, depending on the chosen feedstock [25]. This non-catalytic approach, also known as thermal partial oxidation, is especially advantageous, when processing sulfur-rich feedstocks such as crude oil or coal [37]. Compared to SMR, the thermal partial oxidation process is carried out at higher temperatures ranging from 1200 to 1500°C [38] and elevated pressures between 20 and 100 bar [6, 25].

To enhance the hydrogen yield and facilitate the use of reduced process temperatures in the range of 800–900°C [15, 19, 38], a catalyst can be introduced. Both, noble metals (such as Pt, Rh, Ir, Pd) and non-noble metals (like Ni, Co), are commonly used as heterogeneous catalysts for partial oxidation [38]. For catalytic partial oxidation to be effective, the sulfur content of the feed must, however, be below 50 ppm to prevent catalyst poisoning [38]. If the feed has higher sulfur contents, the non-catalytic partial oxidation is preferable. Otherwise, similar to SMR, there is a prerequisite to desulfurize the feedstock [38].

After any necessary pre-treatment, the hydrocarbon feedstock undergoes partial oxidation. This is achieved by adding less than the stoichiometrically required amount of an oxidant [38]. While air, oxygen, and oxygen-enriched air can be used [38], pure oxygen is the preferred choice. Using pure oxygen avoids the reaction of nitrogen and hydrogen, leading to a cleaner, more concentrated product stream [25].

As in SMR, hydrogen and carbon monoxide are the main products. Moreover, the use of sulfur-containing feedstocks results in the formation of hydrogen sulfide and a small amount of carbonyl sulfide as by-products [25]. The raw product gas may also contain particles such as soot. To remove these unwanted contaminants, the hydrogen stream must be cleaned, for example, by a gas scrubber [28, 39]. For feedstocks with relatively high sulfur contents above 3–4 wt.%, elemental sulfur can be recovered as a marketable byproduct [40].

The subsequent process steps resemble those of the SMR process [25]. The WGS reaction (Eq. (3)) is carried out to further increase the hydrogen yield, followed by the final purification of the product stream.

The concept of partial oxidation surpasses that of SMR in terms of a more compact process design and higher reaction rates [41]. In addition, no external heat is required as sufficient energy is recovered from the exothermic oxidation reaction [41, 42]. A disadvantage of partial oxidation is the need for pure oxygen as oxidant. Oxygen is usually provided by a cryogenic air separation unit [15], which is typically the most expensive part of the plant [25, 43]. In the future, however, sample amounts of pure oxygen may be available from water electrolysis plants, as this technology becomes widely available.

2.3 Hydrogen production by autothermal reforming

Autothermal reforming [44] is a process that combines steam reforming and non-catalytic partial oxidation in a single reactor to take advantage of both technologies [22, 37, 38, 43]. The reactor is configured in two successive sections: In the first section, called the combustion zone, the partial oxidation takes place. The heated gas is then passed to a fixed bed catalytic section where the reforming reactions take place [45]. After syngas production, as in SMR and partial oxidation, the WGS reaction is performed to further increase the hydrogen yield [22, 46].

Gaseous and liquid hydrocarbon feedstocks can be processed. At a process temperature of 850°C, a crude product gas with about 60 to 65% hydrogen is obtained [28]. As with the individual processes, it is advantageous to operate the autothermal reforming process with an excess of steam, high process temperatures, and pure oxygen as the oxidant. These measures prevent the formation of solid carbon particles such as coke in the reactor [6, 28, 39]. Assuming methane as feedstock, the net enthalpy is $\Delta H_R^0 = +170$ kJ/mol. Noteworthy, the process can be operated as an exothermic, endothermic, and thermoneutral type depending on the selected ratio of hydrocarbon feedstock, oxygen, and steam supply [45].

By integrating the excess heat of exothermic partial oxidation (Eqs. (4) and (5)) for endothermic steam reforming (Eq. (1)), the combined autothermal reforming process results in higher thermal efficiencies than the individual processes [47]. Furthermore, autothermal reforming shows higher feedstock flexibility [45] and entails a lower risk of coking than SMR [31]. Autothermal reforming is considered to be suited for relatively small production plants [28, 39] and producing syngas with a low hydrogen/carbon monoxide (H_2/CO) ratio [38, 48].

2.4 Hydrogen production by methane pyrolysis

In MP, methane (CH_4) is cleaved into gaseous hydrogen (H_2) and elemental carbon (C) [49, 50], as given by Eq. (6).

$$CH_4 \rightleftharpoons C + 2\,H_2 \quad \Delta H_R^0 = +74.9 \text{ kJ/mol} \tag{6}$$

In the MP process, methane is primarily sourced from natural gas, a fossil hydrocarbon feedstock. As shown in **Figure 4**, the main process steps in MP include the actual cleavage of methane into gaseous hydrogen and solid carbon, the removal of the solid carbon from the product stream, and the purification of the hydrogen produced [44]. MP requires greater amounts of methane for hydrogen production, given that the molar ratio of H_2 product to CH_4 feedstock is 2:1, compared to 4:1 for SMR. A notable advantage of MP over SMR is its reduced environmental impact [12]: MP does

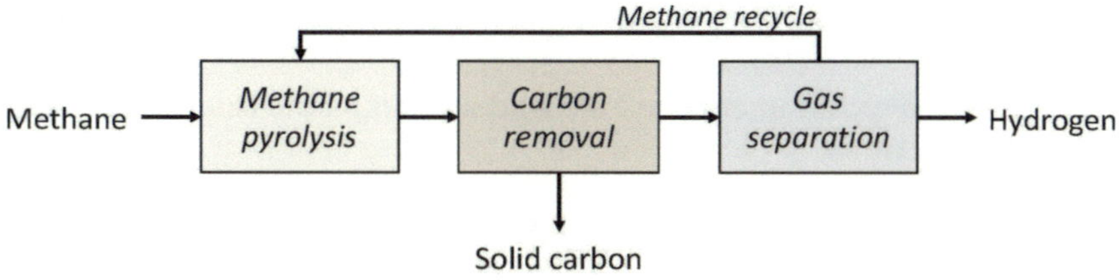

Figure 4.
Main process steps of hydrogen production by methane pyrolysis.

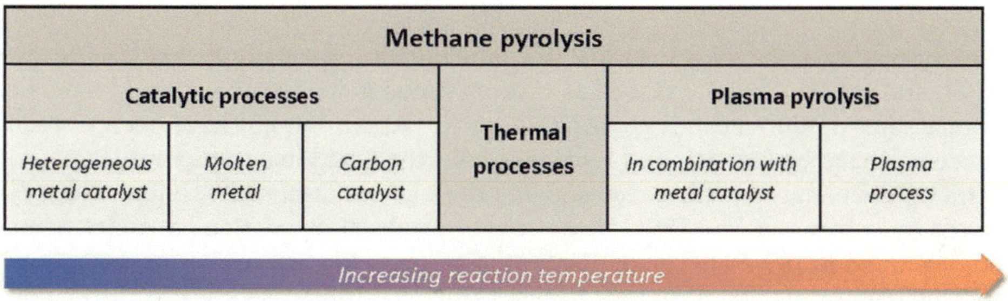

Figure 5.
Classification of methane pyrolysis concepts adapted from Ref. [53].

not result in direct CO_2 emissions. Therefore, hydrogen produced by MP is frequently labeled as "turquoise" or CO_2-free hydrogen [12, 13]. Because of this environmental advantage, MP is regarded as a potential bridging technology for more climate-friendly hydrogen production [51].

As methane is chemically very stable and MP an endothermal reaction, high temperatures are necessary to trigger the chemical conversion [52]. MP technologies are classified according to the characteristic temperature range, into catalytic, non-catalytic thermal, and plasma-based processes (**Figure 5**). By using a suitable catalyst, the methane conversion can be achieved at temperatures as low as 500°C [54]. It should be noted that the reaction rate increases with temperature [50, 55]. In contrast, the thermal, non-catalytic conversion of methane necessitates temperatures of at least 700°C [54]. Plasma technologies are particularly suitable for achieving the high temperatures required for thermal MP. To achieve practical space-time yields in industrial applications, anticipated temperatures are above 800°C for catalytic processes, 1000°C for non-catalytic processes, and up to 2000°C for plasma-based processes [53, 56, 57]. Significant research is currently underway to determine the optimal choice of catalyst for MP, to understand the kinetics of the reaction, and to elucidate the underlying reaction mechanism. This research is aimed at developing a robust and scalable process concept [58].

Numerous reactor concepts have been proposed for MP. These include plasma [59–61], packed bed [62], (circulating) fluidized bed [63–65], monolithic [66, 67], liquid bubble column [49, 68–72], and moving bed reactors [53]. Most of these concepts, however, are still in the early stages of development, predominantly explored at the laboratory scale (TRL 3–4) [53]. Scaling up MP for commercial hydrogen production presents several challenges [53] that must be overcome:

1. Meeting the significant heat demand to achieve practical space-time yields.

2. Managing the deposition of coke and solid carbon on the catalyst surface and within the reactor.

3. Use of natural gas, as opposed to pure methane, as a feedstock. This requires understanding the effects of a more complex gas composition on both process performance and product gas purity.

4. Effective processing and finding commercial applications for the resulting solid carbon that is obtained as a byproduct.

Catalysts play a pivotal role in MP. Various metals, especially nickel [73–75], iron [76, 77], and cobalt [78, 79], as well as carbonaceous materials [63, 80–83] have been investigated as potential catalysts. Molten media [70–72, 84, 85] have been tested to enhance methane conversion and hydrogen selectivity at lower temperatures.

Among the metals tested, nickel showed the highest catalytic activities [86, 87], followed by cobalt and iron [88]. Nickel-based catalysts, in particular, suffer from rapid deactivation [89–91]. The deposition of coke on the active sites of the catalysts and in the reactor results in catalyst deactivation [92], decreased heat transfer [93], and reactor plugging [55, 94]. This progressively slows the chemical conversion and leads to a decline in the hydrogen yield. As a result, the catalyst must be periodically regenerated [58]. Suitable methods for removing the accumulated carbon are oxidation of the carbon and gasification with steam. However, both methods lead to the unwanted formation of CO or CO_2 and are contrary to the purpose of producing high-purity hydrogen [55, 69, 85]. In addition, the carbon byproduct may contain catalyst residues [58]. Nickel-based catalysts are relatively costly [95]. Cobalt-based catalysts have lower activity than Ni-based catalysts [79, 96], and their use raises toxicity concerns [74, 97]. In contrast, iron-based catalysts often show greater resistance to carbon accumulation [98, 99], and result in lower costs [95] and fewer environmental concerns [100, 101]. However, iron-based catalysts are less active and provide incomplete methane conversion at moderate temperatures [96].

Carbonaceous materials, such as activated carbon [102], carbon black [103], or graphite [104], combine many desirable properties for use as catalysts in MP, including resistance to high temperatures [52, 105], low cost [81], non-toxicity [58], and tolerance to sulfur compounds [82]. In addition, there is no need to regenerate the carbon catalyst [81], thus avoiding the unwanted formation of CO_2. However, the carbon catalysts require high reaction temperatures to provide reasonable hydrogen yields [106].

Certain metals (Ti, Pb, Sn) [49, 50, 68, 69], metal alloys (Ni-Bi, Cu-Bi) [72, 84], and salts (KBr, NaBr, NaCl, NaF, $MnCl_2$, KCl) [70, 71] have been proposed to catalyze the thermal cleavage of methane in the form of molten media [85]. In a bubble column reactor methane is introduced at the bottom of the melt, forming bubbles that rise to the surface. Methane cleavage occurs at the interface between the gas bubbles and the molten medium. The rapid physical motion of the gas-liquid mixture results in constant recirculation of gas bubbles and prevents the accumulation of carbon at the interphase [107]. Molten tin has been found to be a suitable medium, allowing operating temperatures up to 1200°C [69, 94]. Laboratory-scale tests of this technology have shown that hydrogen can be produced for many hours without reactor plugging [50, 69].

The bubbles are buoyant according to Archimedes' principle and rise to the surface of the melt. Since two moles of gaseous hydrogen are formed for each mole of methane, the amount of gas contained in the bubbles increases, resulting in an increasing buoyancy. As a result, the bubbles rise progressively faster until they burst open at the top of the melt. Gaseous hydrogen and residual methane escape upward often entraining some of the solid carbon that separates from the molten medium [85, 94]. Carbon floating on the surface of the melt can be removed and collected [69]. Carbon particles entrained in the gas stream are removed by a filtration system. Hydrogen is then separated from the product gas stream by PSA or by the use of metallic membranes [51, 94, 108]. Unconverted methane is recycled to the reactor.

Industrial applications of MP currently would be based on the use of natural gas. At a later stage, methane from biogas plants may also be used as a feedstock [44]. Few studies have addressed the influence of trace components in the feed gas on critical process parameters such as selectivity, product quality, and conversion [53, 58]. Nickel- and iron-based catalysts are progressively deactivated by contact with hydrogen sulfide [82]. Small amounts of higher alkanes may reduce the deactivation of carbon catalysts [80, 109]. Consequently, feed conditioning may be required. Natural gas components other than CH_4 can trigger the formation of undesirable byproducts such as (un-)saturated hydrocarbons and (poly-)cyclic aromatic compounds [57, 110, 111].

On a mass basis, MP yields a hydrogen-to-carbon ratio of 1:3, which means that only 25% of the product mass is attributable to the primary target product hydrogen [53]. Consequently, the utilization of the carbon byproduct will be critical to the economic feasibility and environmental performance of the process. Highly dispersed amorpous carbon with small particle sizes is currently marketed as carbon black [112]. Carbon black is primarily used as a reinforcing filler in tires and other rubber products, and as a black pigment in plastics, paints, coatings, and printing inks [94, 113]. Minor applications include the manufacture of dry cells and electrodes, and the enhancement of antistatic and conductive properties of polymers and resins [114]. Each application requires a different grade of carbon black with narrow specifications for physical and chemical properties [115].

Depending on the process and the feedstock, furnace black, gas black, channel black, lamp black, acetylene black, and thermal black are distinguished [112]. The internally heated furnace black process, based on petroleum and coal tar oil feedstocks, is most widely used today due to a wide range of accessible carbon black grades and economic viability [116]. The thermal black process provides carbon blacks specialized for high filler mechanical rubber goods. Mainly for economic reasons, industrial plants for example, by the company Monolith Materials have been decommissioned and production has been focused on carbon black [116].

A disadvantage of MP is that it produces two economically valuable products at the same time [53, 59, 117]. The existing carbon black market is of insufficient size considering the sheer scale of a potential future hydrogen production by MP [118–120]. Global annual carbon black consumption is projected to exceed 15 million t/a [113] in 2025. In comparison, meeting the current annual demand for pure H_2 of approximately 70 million t/a [9] by MP would result in approximately 210 million t/a of carbon [44], exceeding the estimated market demand for carbon black by a factor of 14.

The mismatch between supply and demand is even greater when considering the expected increase in hydrogen demand in the future. It is unlikely that the full range of carbon black grades can be produced by MP alone. Finally, increased material use of the carbon, for example, as a filler in polymeric materials, would result in renewed CO_2 emissions at a later stage of the life cycle. To achieve truly CO_2-free hydrogen production from MP, the carbon must be permanently removed from the atmosphere [44]. While storage does not add value, the use of carbon fillers in concrete and for other construction purposes could meet the criteria for long-term removal of the carbon from the atmosphere. Carbon-reinforced cement could also contribute to material savings and reduced energy demand [121–123].

2.5 Hydrogen production by water electrolysis

Water electrolysis [44] is the electrochemical cleavage of water (H_2O) into hydrogen (H_2) and oxygen (O_2), Eq. (7). Unlike other hydrogen production technologies, water electrolysis does not rely on fossil resources. As a result, hydrogen from water electrolysis is often referred to as "green" or carbon-free hydrogen [13]. Nevertheless, there may be significant climate change impacts from equipment manufacturing, infrastructure development, and the underlying water and electricity supply chains [44].

$$H_2O \rightleftharpoons H_2 + ½\, O_2 \;\; \Delta H_R^0 = +285.9\ \text{kJ/mol} \tag{7}$$

Water electrolysis [44] is based on an electrolysis cell, which consists of two electrodes that are spatially and electrically separated from one another by a an ion-conducting electrolyte [124]. Electricity is supplied in the form of a direct current to create a difference in electrical potential between the electrodes [124]. When a sufficiently high electric potential is applied, an endothermic ($\Delta H_R > 0$), non-spontaneous ($\Delta G_R > 0$) redox reaction is initiated [126]. At one of the electrodes, water is electrochemically converted to either O_2 and positively charged ions (cations) by oxidation, or H_2 and negatively charged ions (anions) by reduction [124]. The ions then migrate through the electrolyte to the other electrode, attracted by its opposite charge [127]. At the second electrode, the second part of the redox reaction takes place, forming either H_2 by reduction at the cathode, or O_2 by oxidation at the anode [128].

The thermodynamics of water cleavage is described by Eq. (8) in combination with Eq. (9) [129]. The minimal voltage (U_{min}) for a water electrolysis cell to operate can be derived by considering the electrons transferred per mol of water ($n = 2$) and the Faraday constant ($\text{F} = 96485$ C/mol) [129, 130].

$$\Delta H_R = \Delta G_R + \Delta S_R \times T \tag{8}$$

$$\Delta G_R = U_{\text{min}} \times n \times \text{F} \tag{9}$$

At a standard temperature of 25°C and pressure of 1 bar, the thermodynamic changes associated with water cleavage are as follows: $\Delta G_R^0 = 237.21\ kJmol^{-1}$, $\Delta S_R^0 = 0.1631\ kJ\ (mol\ K)^{-1}$, and $\Delta H_R^0 = 285.84\ kJ\ mol^{-1}$ [131]. When the entire process heat is supplied externally, the minimum cell voltage for water splitting, called the "reversible" cell voltage, is 1.23 V [126, 129, 130]. In many cases, both the electrical energy and the thermal energy are supplied electrically, resulting in a thermo neutral cell voltage of 1.48 V [126, 129, 130]. It is important to note that the actual cell voltage (U_{cell}) in practice is higher due to the cell overpotential, which results from activation losses at the electrodes, mass transport limitations, and ohmic resistances [130]. As described by Eq. (10), these factors contribute to a reduced efficiency (η_U) of the electrolysis cell, defined as the ratio of the minimal to the actual cell voltage [129].

$$\eta_U = \frac{U_{\min}}{U_{\text{cell}}} \tag{10}$$

The efficiency of electrolyzers is given by the ratio of the energy content of the hydrogen produced to the electricity consumed (E_{el}) [132]. Taking into account the energy demand of the entire process chain, the metrics used for calculating the efficiency is based on the Lower Heating Value (LHV, 3.00 kWh/Nm^3), as given in Eq. (11), or on the HHV value (3.54 kWh/Nm^3) of hydrogen, as shown in Eq. (12) [129]. The choice depends on the aggregate state of the supplied water, specifically whether the water is in a liquid or vapor state. When liquid water is introduced into the electrolyzer, the HHV value is used for calculations. However, when steam is supplied, the LHV value is selected because the energy for water evaporation has been accounted for before the water enters the electrolyzer. In addition, the choice between HHV and LHV depends on the intended use of the produced hydrogen: chemical applications prefer HHV, while energy-related applications favor LHV. Consideration is also given to whether the oxygen byproduct will be further used [132].

$$\eta_{\text{LHV}} = \frac{\text{LHV}}{E_{\text{el}}} \tag{11}$$

$$\eta_{\text{HHV}} = \frac{\text{HHV}}{E_{\text{el}}} \tag{12}$$

2.6 Water electrolysis technologies

The primary technologies for hydrogen production by water electrolysis [44] are Alkaline Electrolysis (AEL) [133], Polymer Electrolyte Membrane electrolysis (PEM) [134], and high-temperature electrolysis with Solid Oxide Electrolysis Cells (SOECs) [135]. These technologies differ in their stage of development, choice of electrolyte and charge carrier, operating conditions, and suitability for dynamic operation, especially when powered by intermittent renewable energy sources [124]. Commercial systems are available for both AEL and PEM, with AEL being the most advanced and dominant commercial technology [136]. Its leading position largely arises from the knowledge and experience acquired from chlor-alkali electrolysis, the main technology used for the production of chlorine and caustic soda [137]. In contrast, SOEC is still under development and has yet to gain a foothold in the industry [138–140]. Each electrolysis technology has its own set of advantages and disadvantages. The following is a brief overview of the three main technologies.

2.6.1 Alkaline water electrolysis

In AEL, a diaphragm that is permeable to OH^- ions separates the electrodes (**Figure 6**). Conventional AEL systems employ an alkaline solution, typically 20–40 wt.% aqueous potassium hydroxide, as the electrolyte [141, 142]. In the newer, advanced AEL concept, the electrodes are separated only by a gas-tight barrier, eliminating any spatial gap. This innovative "zero-gap" technology [143] achieves superior efficiencies compared to conventional AEL systems.

In the AEL process, deionized water is supplied in liquid form to the cathode. When an electric potential is applied to the electrodes, this water is cleaved into hydrogen gas and OH^- ions (Eq. (13)). The OH^- ions migrate through the electrolyte,

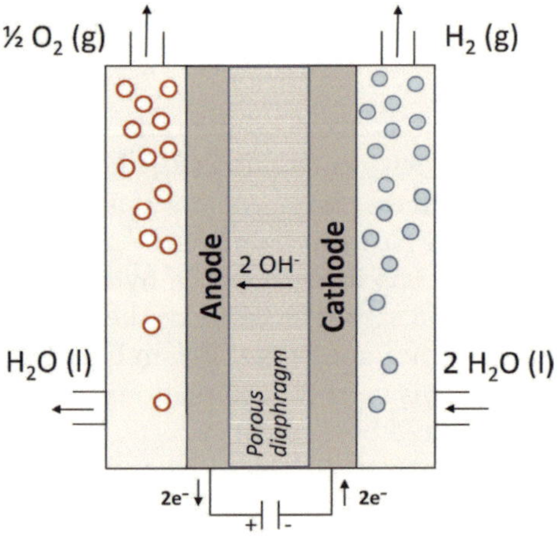

Figure 6.
Schematic representation of an alkaline water electrolysis cell for producing hydrogen adapted from Ref. [12].

pass through the diaphragm, and reach the anode, where they are converted to form water and oxygen (Eq. (14)).

$$\text{Cathode reaction } 2\,H_2O + 2\,e^- \rightleftharpoons H_2 + 2\,OH^- \quad (13)$$

$$\text{Anode reaction } 2\,OH^- \rightleftharpoons ½\,O_2 + H_2O + 2\,e^- \quad (14)$$

Alkaline electrolyzers typically operate at temperatures between 40 and 90°C, and pressures between 10 and 30 bar [130, 132]. Their current densities range from 0.13 [32] to 0.5 A/cm^2 [128], with cell voltages ranging from 1.80 [32, 132, 144] to 2.4 V [132, 144]. This results in stack efficiencies of 62 to 82% in modern commercial systems [144, 145].

Alkaline electrolysis is the most mature water electrolysis technology [132, 141, 144, 146], having reached the industrial scale (TRL 9) for several decades [126, 133]. Notably, the world's largest AEL plant, with a capacity of 156 MW, is situated at the Aswan Reservoir in Egypt. This plant, operating at ambient pressure, can produce up to 33,000 Nm^3/h of hydrogen per hour [132]. This maturity offers notable benefits. AEL electrolyzers tend to have lower capital costs [126, 136, 141, 144, 147] and are well suited for large-scale applications [126, 141, 144]. Their durability exceeds that of other water electrolysis technologies [126, 136, 141, 144]. The use of non-precious catalysts makes AEL even more attractive [144]. However, AEL also has its drawbacks. Conventional AEL systems are limited in terms of current densities [130, 136, 144, 146, 147] and operating pressures [144]. Consequently, the dimensions of AEL electrolyzers are significantly larger than those of PEM electrolyzers of equivalent capacity [133]. Their partial load range is limited [130, 132, 136, 141, 144, 146], and there is a risk of gas crossover at low loads [144]. This not only compromises the purity of the hydrogen gas produced but may also raises safety concerns.

2.6.2 Polymer electrolyte membrane water electrolysis

The main components of a PEM cell are shown in **Figure 7**. A typical PEM cell comprises a solid polymer electrolyte sandwiched between two electrodes, an anode and a cathode, both coated with noble metal catalysts. Adjacent to these electrodes are two porous transport layers, flanked by two bipolar plates [134, 148].

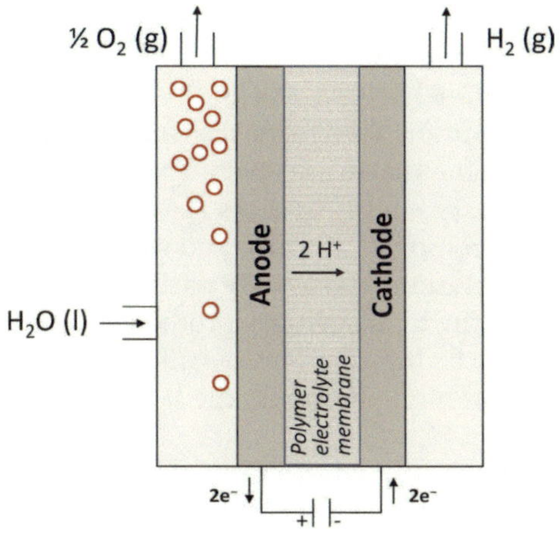

Figure 7.
Schematic representation of a polymer electrolyte membrane water electrolysis cell for producing hydrogen adapted from Ref. [12].

The electrolyte in a PEM cell is a proton-conducting membrane made of porous polymer materials, often either Nafion™ [134] or fumapem™ [144]. This membrane, which has a thickness varying between 60 [148] and 200 μm [130], promotes the flow of current and facilitates transport of water and gas.

Electrodes, with a thickness of about 10 μm [148], are coated directly onto the membrane, a design aimed at minimizing ohmic resistances [130]. These electrodes are decorated with noble metal catalysts: typically, iridium for the anode and platinum for the cathode [144, 149]. The need for rare and costly materials, including platinum, iridium, and titanium, is a challenge. Their use is necessary, given the resilience to high potentials at the anode and the corrosive acidic environment due to the proton-conducting ionomer [150]. Current research aims to achieve higher current densities, reduce catalyst loading, and minimize the use of rare materials [148].

Surrounding the membrane and electrodes is porous transport layers, measuring approximately 280 μm thick [151]. The transport layer for the cathode is made of carbon paper, while that for the anode is made of sintered titanium foam or felt. Firmly attached to these transport layers are bipolar plates, typically made of titanium [130, 152]. These plates have engraved flow channels that facilitate the transport of water and hydrogen gas [132], and ensure a uniform current distribution over the entire surface [152]. For industrial-scale capacities, multiple electrolysis cells are commonly linked in series to form a single electrolyzer stack, a practice seen across all electrolysis processes [134].

In PEM, deionized water is supplied in liquid form to the anode side [153, 154], where the application of an electric potential initiates the oxidation of water to O_2 and protons (Eq. (15)). The byproduct oxygen leaves the system in gaseous form. The protons travel through the membrane to the cathode, where they combine with electrons to form hydrogen (Eq. (16)), which is also removed in gaseous form [134].

$$\text{Anode reaction } H_2O \rightleftharpoons 2\,H^+ + \tfrac{1}{2}\,O_2 + 2\,e^- \tag{15}$$

$$\text{Cathode reaction } 2\,H^+ + 2\,e^- \rightleftharpoons H_2 \tag{16}$$

Typical operating conditions for PEM cells are temperatures of 20 [130, 132] to 150°C [32] and pressures of up to 200 bar [134]. To date, electrolyzers with pressures greater than 30 bar have only been tested on a small scale [126]. At current densities of up to 4.0 A/cm^2 [32] and cell voltages of 1.4 [32] to 2.2 V [132, 144], the energy efficiency of PEM stacks is 67–82% [132, 144].

Polymer Electrolyte Membrane electrolysis is well suited for dynamic operation, seamlessly aligning with the fluctuating availability of electricity generated from intermittent renewable primary energy sources [146, 155]. In this context, PEM has several coveted traits: short response, startup, and shutdown times; low degradation; energy-efficient standby operation; and a wide partial load range, all without compromising the purity of the hydrogen gas produced [130, 132, 136, 144, 147]. Other merits of PEM include its high current densities, compact system design, and the ability to operate safely at high pressures, the latter eliminating the need for post-compression [130, 136, 144, 147].

While PEM systems offer several advantages, they are not without drawbacks. One concern is their dependence on critical, scarce, and expensive materials, a necessity due to their corrosive acidic environment [144]. Their lifetime is compromised by high degradation rates [126, 136, 142]. Financially, they have higher investment costs compared to AEL systems [126, 136, 142, 144]. However, it is important to highlight that there is significant potential for cost reduction through economy of scale [136].

Polymer Electrolyte Membrane electrolysis development began in the 1960s [156]. Although PEM is not as frequently used as AEL [132], PEM electrolyzers are now commercially available (TRL 9) [146]. In 2020, the world's largest hydrogen production plant using PEM technology commenced commercial operation in Québec, Canada [157]. Powered by four 5 MW electrolyzers, the plant has a total capacity of 20 MW and produces about 3000 t/a of H_2 annually. Notably, both the hydrogen [147] and oxygen [158] produced are of high purity and are used directly without any further purification.

2.6.3 Solid oxide water electrolysis

In SOEC [44], the anode and cathode are separated by an electrolyte composed of oxygen-conducting solid oxides or ceramics, such as yttrium-stabilized zirconia (**Figure 8**) [144]. This gas-tight electrolyte becomes permeable to O^{2-} ions at high temperatures [138].

Unlike the other electrolysis technologies, SOEC uses superheated steam instead of liquid water, which is supplied to the cathode. When an electric potential is applied to the electrodes, the water is cleaved into hydrogen and O^{2-} ions (Eq. (17)). The hydrogen produced is then removed from the system. Meanwhile, the O^{2-} ions migrate through the solid oxide electrolyte membrane to the anode, where they are oxidized to oxygen (Eq. (18)) [126, 132].

$$\text{Cathode reaction } H_2O + 2\,e^- \rightleftharpoons H_2 + O^{2-} \tag{17}$$

$$\text{Anode reaction } 2\,O^{2-} \rightleftharpoons \tfrac{1}{2}\,O_2 + 2\,e^- \tag{18}$$

In SOEC stacks, operating temperatures range from 600°C [126, 159] to 1000°C [32, 130, 132, 143], markedly higher than those applied in other electrolyzer types [160–163]. Unlike other processes that use liquid water, SOEC uses steam, a feature that contributes to high efficiencies that can exceed 80% [32]. In terms of performance, the system typically operates at current densities range between 0.3 [32, 138, 141] and 2.0 A/cm^2 [138, 141], resulting in cell voltages of 0.7–1.5 V [138].

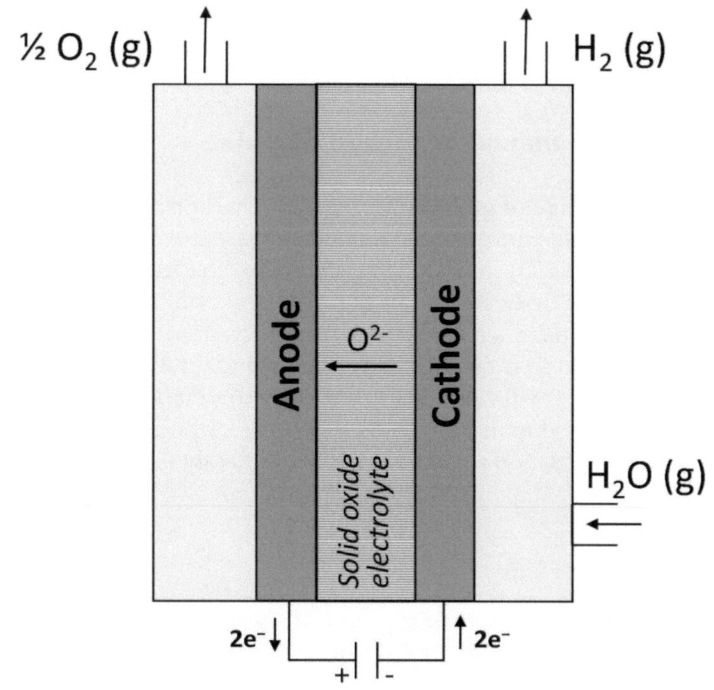

Figure 8.
Schematic comparison of a solid oxide electrolysis cell for generating hydrogen adapted from Ref. [12].

Solid oxide electrolysis cell is at an early development stage and has yet to be adopted by the industry [138–140]. Extensive research is needed to make the transition to industrial application, particularly in developing cost-effective, durable, and heat-resistant ceramic materials [126, 132, 136], achieving higher current densities [136], and reducing investment costs [136, 146].

Solid oxide electrolysis cell is emerging as a technology with significant potential for the future [144]. One of its major advantages is the use of steam instead of liquid water, which results in significantly lower operating potentials [132, 135, 136, 146]. This choice affects two thermodynamic properties. First, as the process temperature increases, the thermal component of the reaction enthalpy ΔH_R^0 (as seen in Eq. (8)) also increases. Conversely, the energy required for electrochemical water cleavage, represented by ΔG_R^0 (see Eq. (9)), decreases substantially. This improved efficiency stems from the fact that the use of steam eliminates the energy otherwise required for the phase change during electrolysis [132]. Interestingly, under certain conditions, where steam is supplied at extremely high temperatures, the efficiency can theoretically surpass 100% [144]. Overall thermal efficiency can also benefit from the use of waste heat sources, such as otherwise unused excess heat from nearby industrial facilities [126, 132, 146].

Another advantage of SOEC is its flexibility: Many solid oxide cells can function as either electrolytic cells or fuel cells [126], meaning that they can also use hydrogen as a fuel to generate electricity. This duality allows plant operators to store surplus energy for times when demand exceeds supply [18]. With its ability to buffer fluctuations in power supply and the resulting increase in plant operating hours, SOEC is attractive when combined with renewable power generation technologies [135]. However, in order to respond quickly to load changes, the cell must maintain a consistently high temperature due to its long cold start time. Therefore, a continuous and readily available source of (excess) heat is critical.

3. Sustainable supply chains for carbon dioxide

In the evolving narrative of global sustainability, carbon dioxide (CO_2) plays a central role, not only as an environmental concern, but also as a valuable resource. As industries move to utilize CO_2 in various applications, the focus is now on creating sustainable supply chains dedicated to its management and utilization. These supply chains must holistically address the capture, transportation, storage, and end-use of CO_2, ensuring that each step is optimized for environmental and economic viability. As we enter this arena, we will take a deep dive into understanding the intricacies and imperatives of building and maintaining a sustainable carbon supply chain, setting the stage for a future where carbon management is seamlessly integrated into our industrial fabric.

3.1 Carbon capture

Three technologies are used primarily for CO_2 capture: pre-combustion, oxyfuel combustion, and post-combustion [164, 165]:

- *Pre-combustion:* In this upstream process, the carbon in the fuel is converted to CO_2 prior to combustion. The CO_2 is then captured using techniques such as physicochemical absorption in aqueous amine scrubbing solutions, or physical absorption with solvents such as polyethylene glycol dimethyl ether (Selexol™) and cold methanol (Rectisol™) [166, 167].

- *Oxyfuel combustion:* This industrial-scale combustion method uses pure oxygen for combustion. This results in a CO_2-enriched flue gas stream, facilitating CO_2 sequestration.

- *Post-combustion:* Here, CO_2 is captured from the post-combustion flue gas stream in a downstream process. Technologies used for CO_2 capture include absorption by Monoethanolamine (MEA), adsorption on solid sorbents, cryogenic separation, and pressure swing adsorption [165, 168].

In the context of SMR, pre-combustion CO_2 capture from the shifted syngas by chemical absorption with aqueous Methyldiethanolamine (MDEA) is recognized as the standard practice [44]. This preference is largely due to the high partial pressure of CO_2 in the syngas stream (16 vol.% CO_2 at 25 bar) at this stage of the process [169]. Capturing CO_2 from the tail gas has often been viewed as less economically viable due to the lower CO_2 partial pressure (51 vol.% at 2 bar) [169], but remains an area of research [23]. For the post-combustion stages, CO_2 capture from the flue gas stream, which contains 21 vol.% CO_2 at 1 bar [169], is primarily accomplished by chemical absorption, typically using MEA scrubbing [170–172].

In the CO_2 absorption process, the gas stream is contacted with a solvent, commonly aqueous MEA or MDEA, in an absorption column [44]. This step effectively extracts CO_2 from the gas stream. Once saturated with CO_2, the solvent is regenerated by heating it in a stripper unit, releasing the CO_2 for subsequent use. A continuous solvent make-up stream is required to compensate for evaporation losses and degradation [171].

The efficiency of CO_2 capture varies, ranging from 53 to 95%. While it is technically possible to capture a larger fraction of the CO_2, this requires greater energy consumption [170–173]. Integrating carbon capture technologies into SMR plants results in a 5–14% reduction in their efficiency [168]. Often, the site where CO_2 is captured is spatially separated from the site where the CO_2 is used (CCU) or stored (CCS). Therefore, CCUS strategies involve require not only CO_2 capture, but also the transportation of CO_2—whether by pipeline, ship, or other means—to its intended destination. This often requires significant investment to develop the appropriate transportation infrastructure [173].

3.2 Carbon dioxide transport

To achieve a transport density that is both technically manageable and economically feasible, carbon dioxide (CO_2) may need to be compressed, liquefied, or solidified. Some key properties of CO_2 include its condensation at 57.28 bar at ambient temperature (20°C) [174], a critical point at 31.04°C and 73.83 bar [174], and its freezing point at −78.46°C at standard pressure (1 bar) [174]. CO_2 can be transported in various forms, including as a compressed gas, in liquid or supercritical state or even in its solid form [175, 176].

- *Compressed state:* Pipelines, due to their energy and economic efficiency, are commonly preferred for transporting large quantities of CO_2 over long distances [175, 177]. Maintaining a high density of CO_2 is critical for economical transport, which in turn minimizes the energy required for compression along the transport route [177, 178].

- *Liquid and supercritical state:* CO_2 can be easily liquefied, although this requires a significant energy input of 0.11 kWh/kg CO_2 [179]. Supercritical CO_2, which combines the density of a liquid with the low viscosity of a gas [180], is especially suitable for transportation [176, 178]. To ensure that CO_2 remains in this supercritical state [181, 182], pipelines typically operate at temperatures between 13 and 44°C and pressures between 85 and 150 bar [183–185].

- *Solid state (dry ice):* CO_2 can be converted to "dry ice," its solid form. This option requires substantial energy to cool the CO_2 to temperatures below −78.0°C [174]. Because dry ice sublimes continuously, even in well-insulated containers, it is typically produced on demand.

Ultimately, the optimal method of transporting CO_2 depends on factors such as distance, quantity, and the infrastructure available.

3.3 Carbon dioxide storage

Physical storage of CO_2 in salt caverns is suitable for temporary storage of large quantities [168]. For longer-term storage, especially in the context of CCS, CO_2 must be injected into suitable geological formations [11]. These include aquifers, depleted oil and gas reservoirs, and coal seams [186]. Typically, CO_2 is compressed and injected under supercritical conditions into these geological formations [170]. One notable monitoring project took place in the Williston Basin, a geological formation in Canada and the US. As part of the International Energy Agency Greenhouse Gas (IEAGHG) research program from 2000 to 2012, this study found no evidence of CO_2 leakage from the geologic storage site [187]. Estimates of annual leakage rates vary, ranging from 0.00001 to 1%, based primarily on the permeability of the rock formation [165]. Over time in the geological reservoirs, CO_2 undergoes chemical transformation with the adjacent rock formations [188, 189]. Silicates, for example, in the reservoir slowly react with CO_2 to form carbonates and silica, as exemplified by Eq. (19).

$$(\mathrm{Mg, Mn, Fe})_2[\mathrm{SiO_4}] + 2\ \mathrm{CO_2} \rightarrow 2\ (\mathrm{Mg, Mn, Fe})[\mathrm{CO_3}] + \mathrm{SiO_2} \tag{19}$$

To meet the Paris Agreement's goal of limiting global warming to 1.5°C [190], the amount of CO_2 that must be sequestered through CCS varies across different scenarios [191]. On a global scale, projections for annual CO_2 capture in the twenty-first century range widely, from none at all to over 1200 Gt/a per year [191]. Within Europe, the expected capture could reach up to 300 million t/a annually by 2050 [191].

The estimated global storage capacity for CO_2 spans from 3900 to 55,000 Gt of CO_2 [191, 192]. However, it should be noted that potential hazards associated with storage could lead to social or regulatory restrictions. After accounting for such constraints, Europe's CO_2 storage capacity is estimated at 134 Gt of CO_2 [193], which would last for about 400 years based on current emission rates [11].

The first CCS plant was commissioned in the US in 1972 as part of an Enhanced Oil Recovery (EOR) project [194]. EOR involves the injection of gaseous CO_2 into mature oil reservoirs. The dissolution of CO_2 in the oil reduces the oil's viscosity and interfacial tension, causing it to swell and restore the declining oil production rates [194]. Turning to Europe, the Sleipner oil field in Norway is home to the first permanent, dedicated CO_2 storage facility and has been in operation since 1996 [11]. Globally, there are now 26 commercial CCS facilities in operation, with a combined annual CO_2 capture of 40 million t/a [194]. Of these, six facilities are designed for dedicated geological storage, while the other 20 facilities use the CO_2 for EOR or Enhanced Gas Recovery (EGR) as a revenue-generating mechanism [194]. In addition, 34 pilot and demonstration facilities are either operational or in the development phase [194]. Given the maturity of the technologies involved throughout the value chain, the SMR-CCS approach is considered to be verified at an industrial scale, achieving a TRL of 8-9 [11].

3.4 Physical utilization of carbon dioxide

There are many possibilities for the industrial use of CO_2. In general, CO_2 can either be used directly in its physical form or it can be chemically converted into value-added products. Direct utilization technologies take advantage of the unique physicochemical properties of CO_2. At ambient conditions, CO_2 is an inert, non-flammable, and non-toxic gas.

Several applications make use of gaseous CO_2. For instance, it is used in fire extinguishers [174, 195] and acts as an economical shielding gas in arc welding [195, 196]. It also plays a role in food preservation [2, 174].

Carbon dioxide (CO_2) is readily soluble in a variety of liquids, including water. When dissolved in water, CO_2 forms carbonic acid. This reaction is harnessed by the beverage industry to produce carbonated beverages, such as soda and sparkling water [174]. The formation of carbonic acid plays a role in adjusting the pH of aqueous solutions applications in several industries [180], including the production of hydrogen peroxide by the reaction of hydrogen and oxygen [197, 198], bleaching in the textile and paper industries [199], and the treatment of alkaline wastewaters [200].

An intriguing characteristic of CO_2 near the critical point is its responsiveness to small changes in temperature and pressure. These small changes significantly alter the properties of CO_2, including its density, viscosity, miscibility and solubilizing power, and polarity. As a result, CO_2 is advantageous for tweaking the properties of switchable solvents, surfactants, and other materials. This adaptability promotes energy-efficient separation processes [201].

Its supercritical point at 31.1°C and 73.8 bar allows CO_2 to become supercritical under mild conditions [174]. Supercritical CO_2 is widely used across industries, acting as a reaction medium for catalysis [202], extractant in coffee decaffeination [203], and aiding the textile industry in dyeing and impregnating [204] fibers and polymers [205]. Its role also extends to other industrial processes, including dispersion polymerization [206, 207], fractionation, and powder polymer formation [208, 209]. One of its outstanding properties is its low heat of vaporization, which makes it an easily recoverable solvent, and suggests its potential as a substitute for other more harmful solvents [210]. In the context of sustainability, supercritical CO_2 stands out as an environmentally friendly substitute for more harmful and hazardous refrigerants, especially in refrigeration cycles [211].

In its solid form, CO_2 is known and marketed as dry ice, available in compressed blocks or pellets. Notably, below its triple point of −56.57°C and 5.18 bar [174], CO_2 sublimates, transitioning directly from its solid to its gaseous state without becoming a liquid. This property makes dry ice an attractive, residue-free, non-toxic, and lightweight refrigerant, commonly used in applications such as food preservation [195].

It is important to underscore that the physical applications of CO_2 do not result in its permanent removal from the atmospheric carbon cycle [3]. Instead, the captured CO_2 is emitted back into the atmosphere shortly after its use. As a result, its role in mitigating climate change is marginal [212].

3.5 Chemical utilization of hydrogen and carbon dioxide

Chemical utilization of CO_2 [213] provides a pathway [195] to transform the captured CO_2 into value-added products [2, 214], either integrating them into anthropogenic carbon cycles [3] or permanently removing the carbon [215]. Due to CO_2 being the most oxidized form with carbon in oxidation state +IV, it possesses a low-energy level making it thermodynamically stable [3]. This means CO_2 does easily engage in chemical conversions at low temperatures, given its inherent stability [216]. To promote chemical reactions involving CO_2 one of the following strategies is generally employed [2, 213, 217]:

1. Using energy-rich co-reactants such as hydrogen and epoxides.

2. Applying external energy sources, whether electrical, thermal, radiant, or other forms.

3. Adjusting variables like reaction temperatures, concentrations, and pressures to sway the chemical equilibrium, based on the Le Chatelier principle.

4. Aiming for low-energy target products.

Using an appropriate catalyst for CO_2 conversion can introduce alternative reaction pathways with a lower activation energy, accelerating the reaction rate and improving selectivities [218]. Reactions for converting CO_2 comprise redox reactions and carbonylation and carboxylation reactions [213]. This chapter will not delve further into the latter as they do not involve the use of hydrogen.

Catalytic hydrogenation, which employs hydrogen (H_2) as the reducing agent, is the predominant method for providing the energy required for CO_2 reduction [219]. CO_2 hydrogenation gives access to value-added products [124], with methane [220], methanol [221], formic acid [222], carbon monoxide [223], and syngas [224] being the primary focus of current research. These products are promising because they serve as important platform chemicals. Currently, their large-scale production in the chemical industry is energy intensive and results in significant GHG emissions. Their climate-friendly production (see, e.g., [225]) could significantly mitigate global warming [41, 226].

The integration of these novel chemical processes into the chemical industry could occur seamlessly at an early stage of the value chains without requiring significant changes to the existing downstream production chains. Hence, CO_2 hydrogenation holds the promise not only to utilize vast quantities of CO_2 as a renewable carbon source, but also to position H_2 as a key feedstock for manufacturing high-demand platform chemicals. This could further amplify the already significant demand for H_2 in the (petro)chemical sector. Nevertheless, for these hydrogenation-based CO_2 utilization techniques to reach their full environmental potential, an environmentally sound supply of both CO_2 and H_2 is essential [226, 227].

Chemical CO_2 utilization technologies represent a promising avenue, not only for utilizing CO_2 captured from flue gases that would otherwise be released to the atmosphere, but also as a means to transition away from fossil carbon-based, energy-intensive feedstocks [2, 228]. As such, CCU technologies have the potential to reduce the industry's impact on fossil resource depletion and global warming [212, 216].

However, it is important to recognize that the CO_2 used in these methods will eventually be released once the product's lifetime concludes. While this temporary carbon storage does not avoid the resulting climate change impacts, delaying its release may still bear environmental benefits [229]. Notably, contemporary assessment methods do not account for such temporary CO_2 storage [230], and there is ongoing discussion about accounting for it [213]. One possible solution is to assess time-corrected global warming potentials [230, 231]. Current guidelines suggest reporting the amount and duration of stored carbon independently [232, 233]. Ultimately, anthropogenic carbon cycles [3] need to be established (**Figure 9**).

Evaluating the environmental impact of CCU technologies presents unique challenges. One primary concern is the inherently temporary nature of CO_2 storage. Incorporating CCU technologies into existing production chains often leads to multifunctional systems producing multiple valuable products. While methods exist to account for these coproducts in life cycle assessments, meticulous attention is essential when setting the system boundaries and the functional unit [44]. This becomes especially pertinent in studies comparing alternative technologies for a singular product. The multitude of potential uses for captured CO_2 complicates the selection of a specific product or a technology. Emphasis should be on those technologies that promise longer storage durations of captured CO_2, aiming for its permanent removal from the atmospheric carbon cycle [3].

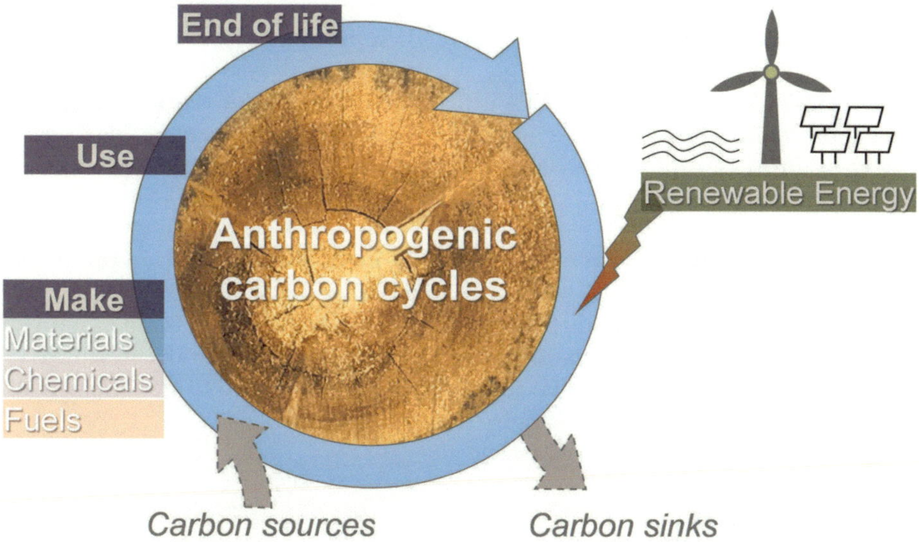

Figure 9.
Anthropogenic carbon cycles, adapted from Ref. [3].

4. Conclusions

In summary, we have navigated the intricate landscape of CO_2 utilization in its varied forms—gaseous, supercritical, and solid. We have explored its diverse applications spanning several industries and the potential of CO_2 as an indispensable element in the modern industrial ecosystem. Direct utilization, while beneficial in specific contexts, merely offers a transitory solution to the broader challenges of atmospheric CO_2 accumulation. In contrast, the chemical utilization of CO_2, despite its challenges, presents a more sustainable and promising avenue. These processes, while thermodynamically demanding, require specific reactants and often confront complexities in life cycle assessments, especially when integrated into current production chains. The widespread adoption and scaling of CO_2 utilization technologies will undoubtedly have profound implications for global supply chains. As these technologies become more integrated into industries, several shifts can be foreseen:

- *Focus on sustainability:* With a heightened emphasis on CO_2 utilization, supply chains will evolve to become more sustainable, significantly reducing the carbon footprint associated with manufacturing and distribution.

- *Demand for new reactants:* An increased demand for co-reactants, most notably hydrogen, will stimulate the growth of related industries, consequently reshaping supply chain dynamics.

- *Hydrogen supply chain:* As CO_2 hydrogenation processes become more prevalent, the importance of a robust and sustainable hydrogen supply chain becomes paramount. This implies sourcing hydrogen from green methods, efficient storage, and transportation solutions, and ensuring that the hydrogen infrastructure is equipped to handle the increased demand.

- *Integration:* Incorporating CCU technologies into existing supply chains will pose require thorough integration, especially when processes yield multiple products.

- *Temporary CO_2 storage:* While CO_2 utilization offers a brief reprieve, it does extend a valuable timeframe in our battle against climate change. The integration of these processes into supply chains for carbon-based industrial feedstock is a pivotal consideration.

In the future, supply chains will need to be more resilient and adaptive. As CO_2 utilization technologies advance, industries must brace for a shift toward environmentally conscious and sustainable production methods. The path is laden with challenges, but with collective efforts, technological breakthroughs, and a steadfast commitment to sustainability, global supply chains stand poised to lead the way in our fight against climate change.

Acknowledgements

This contribution was made possible by funding of the state of North Rhine-Westphalia, grant number IRR-2018-1, RWE Power AG, and the Faculty of Mechanical Engineering of Ruhr-Universität Bochum as part of the endowed chair CSC. Also, the financial support of the Bundesministerium für Bildung und Forschung (BMBF) for the project "Production of Ethene from Recycling Streams and Renewable Carbon Sources as a Sustainable and Economic Route to Basic Building Materials for the Chemical Industry" (Syngas2Ethene, grant number 01LJ2107A) is acknowledged. TEM would like to thank Prof. M. Dröscher for the lively scientific discussions on the subjects of raw material and energy supply to the chemical industry.

Conflict of interest

The authors declare no conflict of interest.

Acronyms and abbreviations

AEL	alkaline electrolysis
CCS	carbon capture and storage
CCU	carbon capture and utilization
CCUS	carbon capture utilization and storage
EGR	enhanced gas recovery
EOR	enhanced oil recovery
GHG	greenhouse gas
HHV	higher heating value
MP	methane pyrolysis
MDEA	methyldiethanolamine
MEA	monoethanolamine
LCA	life-cycle-assessment
LHV	lower heating value
PEM	polymer electrolyte membrane electrolysis

PSA	pressure swing adsorption
SOEC	solid oxide electrolysis cells
SMR	steam methane reforming
TRL	technology readiness level
WGS	water-gas-shift

Author details

Thomas E. Müller
Ruhr-Universität Bochum, Bochum, Germany

*Address all correspondence to: thomas-ernst.mueller@ruhr-uni-bochum.de

References

[1] Mechnig SP. Strengthening progress at the grassroots. 2023 [[Accessed: December 29, 2023], Global Corporate Website]. Available from: https://www.covestro.com/blog/strengthening-progress-at-the-grassroots?trk=article-ssr-frontend-pulse_x-social-details_comments-action_comment-text

[2] Peters M, Köhler B, Kuckshinrichs W, Leitner W, Markewitz P, Müller TE. Chemical technologies for exploiting and recycling carbon dioxide into the value chain. ChemSusChem. 2011;**4**(9):1216

[3] Tomkins P, Müller TE. Evaluating the carbon inventory, carbon fluxes and carbon cycles for a long-term sustainable world. Green Chemistry. 2019;**21**(15):3994

[4] Centi G, Perathoner S. CO_2-based energy vectors for the storage of solar energy. Greenhouse Gases: Science and Technology. 2011;**1**(1):21

[5] Blanc P, Zafar M, Martino FD, Fargere A, Carton J, Kolodziejczyk B. New hydrogen economy-hope or hype? In: Innovation Insights Brief. London, UK: World Energy Council; 2019

[6] Ausfelder F, Bazzanella A. In: Solten D, Emonts B, editors. Hydrogen in the Chemical Industry, Hydrogen Science and Engineering: Materials, Processes, Systems and Technology. Weinheim: Wiley-VCH Verlag GmbH & Co. KGaA; 2016. pp. 19-39

[7] Gielen D, Taibi E, Miranda R. Hydrogen: A Renewable Energy Perspective. Abu Dhabi, United Arab Emirates: International Renewable Energy Agency; 2019. Available from: www.irena.org/publications

[8] Abergel T, Armijo J, Bains P, Bennett S, Berghout N, Bibra EM, et al. Global Hydrogen Review 2021. Dubai: International Energy Agency; 2021. Available from: www.iea.org

[9] Birol F. The Future of Hydrogen - Seizing today's opportunities: Report prepared by the IEA for the G20, 2019, Japan

[10] Bouckaert S, Pales AF, McGlade C, Remme U, Wanner B, Varro L, et al. Net Zero by 2050: A Roadmap for the Global Energy Sector. Paris, France: International Energy Agency; 2021. p. 224

[11] Madrid Forum CCUS Taskforce. The Potential for CCS and CCU in Europe. London, UK: IOGP; 2019. pp. 1-47

[12] Hermesmann M, Müller TE. Green, Turquoise, Blue, or Grey? Environmentally friendly Hydrogen Production in Transforming Energy Systems. Progress in Energy and Combustion Science. 2022;**90**:100996

[13] Newborough M, Cooley G. Developments in the global hydrogen market: The spectrum of hydrogen colours. Fuel Cells Bulletin. 2020;**2020**:16

[14] Wilkinson A, Hughes N, Preece J, VanHoof J, Peterseim J, Hatop O, et al. Hydrogen on the horizon: ready, almost set, go? In: Working Paper National Hydrogen Strategies. London, UK: World Energy Council; 2021

[15] Zohuri B. Cryogenics and Liquid Hydrogen Storage. In: Zohuri B, editor. Hydrogen Energy: Challenges and Solutions for a Cleaner Future. Cham: Springer International Publishing; 2019. pp. 121-139

[16] Stolten D, Emonts B. Hydrogen Science and Engineering: Materials,

Processes, Systems, and Technology. Vol. 1. Weinheim, Germany: John Wiley & Sons; 2016

[17] Die Nationale Wasserstoffstrategie. Berlin, Germany: Bundesministerium für Wirtschaft und Energie (BMWi); 2020. Available from: https://www.bmwk.de/Redaktion/DE/Publikationen/Energie/die-nationale-wasserstoffstrategie.html

[18] Tsiklios C, Schneider S, Hermesmann M, Müller TE. Efficiency and optimal load capacity of E-Fuel-Based energy storage systems. Advances in Applied Energy. 2023;**10**:100140

[19] Ersöz A. Investigation of hydrocarbon reforming processes for micro-cogeneration systems. International Journal of Hydrogen Energy. 2008;**33**(23):7084

[20] Hammer G, Lübcke T, Kettner R, Pillarella MR, Recknagel H, Commichau A, et al. Natural Gas, in Ullmann's Encyclopedia of Industrial Chemistry. Hoboken, New Jersey: Wiley Online Library; 2006

[21] Bartholomew CH. Mechanisms of nickel catalyst poisoning. In: Delmon B, Froment GF, editors. Studies in Surface Science and Catalysis. Amsterdam: Elsevier; 1987. pp. 81-104

[22] Nikolaidis P, Poullikkas A. A comparative overview of hydrogen production processes. Renewable and Sustainable Energy Reviews. 2017;**67**:597

[23] Collidi G. Reference data and supporting literature reviews for SMR based hydrogen production with CCS. In: IEAGHG Technical Review. Cheltenham, UK: International Energy Agency (IEA); 2017

[24] Carapellucci R, Giordano L. Steam, dry and autothermal methane reforming for hydrogen production: A thermodynamic equilibrium analysis. Journal of Power Sources. 2020;**469**:228391

[25] Steinberg M, Cheng HC. Modern and prospective technologies for hydrogen production from fossil fuels. International Journal of Hydrogen Energy. 1989;**14**(11):797

[26] Yoo J, Bang Y, Han SJ, Park S, Song JH, Song IK. Hydrogen production by tri-reforming of methane over nickel–alumina aerogel catalyst. Journal of Molecular Catalysis A: Chemical. 2015;**410**:74

[27] Liu C-J, Ye J, Jiang J, Pan Y. Progresses in the preparation of coke resistant Ni-based catalyst for steam and CO_2 reforming of methane. ChemCatChem. 2011;**3**(3):529

[28] Kurzweil P. Brennstoffzellentechnik: Grundlagen, Materialien, Anwendungen, Gaserzeugung. Heidelberg, Germany: Springer-Verlag; 2016

[29] LeValley TL, Richard AR, Fan M. The progress in water gas shift and steam reforming hydrogen production technologies – A review. International Journal of Hydrogen Energy. 2014;**39**(30):16983

[30] Kung MC, Kung HH. The surface cation densities of iron oxide-chromium oxide solid solutions. Surface Science. 1981;**104**(1):253

[31] Hamelinck CN, Faaij APC. Future prospects for production of methanol and hydrogen from biomass. Journal of Power Sources. 2002;**111**(1):1

[32] Maack M. Generation of the energy carrier hydrogen in context with

electricity buffering generation through fuel cells. Icelandic New Energy. 2008:47

[33] Hamacher T. Wasserstoff als strategischer Sekundärträger. In: Töpler J, editor. Wasserstoff und Brennstoffzelle. Berlin, Heidelberg: Springer; 2017. pp. 1-23

[34] Godula-Jopek A, Jehle W, Wellnitz J. Hydrogen Storage Technologies, New Materials, Transport and Infrastructure. Weinheim: Wiley-VCH; 2012

[35] Spath PL, Mann MK. Life Cycle Assessment of Hydrogen Production via Natural Gas Steam Reforming. Golden, CO: National Renewable Energy Lab. (NREL); 2000

[36] Peng XD. Analysis of the Thermal Efficiency Limit of the Steam Methane Reforming Process. Industrial & Engineering Chemistry Research. 2012; **51**(50):16385

[37] Dybkjaer I. Tubular reforming and autothermal reforming of natural gas — An overview of available processes. Fuel Processing Technology. 1995;**42**(2):85

[38] Albonetti S, Perathoner S, Quadrelli EA. Horizons in Sustainable Industrial Chemistry and Catalysis. Oxford, Cambridge, MA: Elsevier; 2019

[39] Stiller C, Weikl MC. Industrielle Produktion und Nutzung von konventionellem, CO_2-armem und grünem Wasserstoff. In: Töpler J, Lehmann J, editors. Wasserstoff und Brennstoffzelle: Technologien und Marktperspektiven. Berlin, Heidelberg: Springer; 2017. pp. 189-206

[40] Speight JG. The Refinery of the Future. Cambridge, MA: Gulf Professional Publishing; 2020

[41] Ausfelder F, Bazzanella A, VanBrackle H, Wilde R, Beckmann C, Mills R, et al. Technology Roadmap Energy and GHG Reductions in the Chemical Industry via Catalytic Processes. Wien: International Energy Agency (IEA); 2013

[42] Vita A, Pino L, Italiano C, Palella A. Steam reforming, partial oxidation, and autothermal reforming of ethanol for hydrogen production in conventional reactors. In: Basile A, Iulianelli A, Dalena F, Veziroğlu TN, editors. Ethanol. Amsterdam: Elsevier; 2019. pp. 159-191

[43] Rostrup-Nielsen JR. Syngas in perspective. Catalysis Today. 2002; **71**(3):243

[44] Hermesmann M. Environmental assessment of climate-friendly supply chains in a prospective hydrogen economy. [Ph. D. Thesis]. Bochum, Germany: Ruhr-Universität; 2023

[45] Hacker V, Mitsushima S. Fuel Cells and Hydrogen: From Fundamentals to Applied Research. Amsterdam, Kidlington, Cambridge, MA: Elsevier; 2018

[46] Lutz AE, Bradshaw RW, Bromberg L, Rabinovich A. Thermodynamic analysis of hydrogen production by partial oxidation reforming. International Journal of Hydrogen Energy. 2004;**29**(8):809

[47] Ebrahimi H, Behroozsarand A, Zamaniyan A. Arrangement of primary and secondary reformers for synthesis gas production. Chemical Engineering Research and Design. 2010;**88**(10):1342

[48] Luque R, Speight J. Gasification for Synthetic Fuel Production: Fundamentals, Processes and Applications. Amsterdam: Elsevier; 2014

[49] Plevan M, Geißler T, Abánades A, Mehravaran K, Rathnam RK, Rubbia C, et al. Thermal cracking of methane in a liquid metal bubble column reactor: Experiments and kinetic analysis. International Journal of Hydrogen Energy. 2015;**40**(25):8020

[50] Geißler T, Abánades A, Heinzel A, Mehravaran K, Müller G, Rathnam RK, et al. Hydrogen production via methane pyrolysis in a liquid metal bubble column reactor with a packed bed. Chemical Engineering Journal. 2016;**299**:192

[51] Weger L, Abánades A, Butler T. Methane cracking as a bridge technology to the hydrogen economy. International Journal of Hydrogen Energy. 2017;**42**(1):720

[52] Ashik UPM, Wan Daud WMA, Abbas HF. Production of greenhouse gas free hydrogen by thermocatalytic decomposition of methane – A review. Renewable and Sustainable Energy Reviews. 2015;**44**:221

[53] Schneider S, Bajohr S, Graf F, Kolb T. State of the art of hydrogen production via pyrolysis of natural gas. ChemBioEng Reviews. 2020;7(5):150

[54] Steinberg M. Fossil fuel decarbonization technology for mitigating global warming. International Journal of Hydrogen Energy. 1999;**24**(8):771

[55] Amin AM, Croiset E, Epling W. Review of methane catalytic cracking for hydrogen production. International Journal of Hydrogen Energy. 2011;**36**(4):2904

[56] Dagle RA, Dagle V, Bearden MD, Holladay JD, Krause TR, Ahmed S. An Overview of Natural Gas Conversion Technologies for Co-Production of Hydrogen and Value-Added Solid Carbon Products. Oak Ridge, TN: Pacific Northwest National Lab (PNNL); 2017. Available from: https://www.osti.gov/servlets/purl/1411934

[57] Guéret C, Daroux M, Billaud F. Methane pyrolysis: Thermodynamics. Chemical Engineering Science. 1997;**52**(5):815

[58] Sánchez-Bastardo N, Schlögl R, Ruland H. Methane pyrolysis for CO_2-free H_2 production: A green process to overcome renewable energies unsteadiness. Chemie Ingenieur Technik. 2020;**92**(10):1596

[59] Gautier M, Rohani V, Fulcheri L. Direct decarbonization of methane by thermal plasma for the production of hydrogen and high value-added carbon black. International Journal of Hydrogen Energy. 2017;**42**(47):28140

[60] Bakken JA, Jensen R, Monsen B, Raaness O, Wærnes AN. Thermal plasma process development in Norway. Pure and Applied Chemistry. 1998;**70**(6):1223

[61] Gaudernack B, Lynum S. Hydrogen from natural gas without release of CO_2 to the atmosphere. International Journal of Hydrogen Energy. 1998;**23**(12):1087

[62] Pudukudy M, Yaakob Z, Takriff MS. Methane decomposition over unsupported mesoporous nickel ferrites: Effect of reaction temperature on the catalytic activity and properties of the produced nanocarbon. RSC Advances. 2016;**6**(72):68081

[63] Lee KK, Han GY, Yoon KJ, Lee BK. Thermocatalytic hydrogen production from the methane in a fluidized bed with activated carbon catalyst. Catalysis Today. 2004;**93**(95):81

[64] Dunker AM, Kumar S, Mulawa PA. Production of hydrogen by thermal

decomposition of methane in a fluidized-bed reactor—Effects of catalyst, temperature, and residence time. International Journal of Hydrogen Energy. 2006;**31**(4):473

[65] Keipi T, Tolvanen H, Konttinen J. Economic analysis of hydrogen production by methane thermal decomposition: Comparison to competing technologies. Energy Conversion and Management. 2018;**159**: 264

[66] Gatica JM, Cifredo GA, Blanco G, Trasobares S, Vidal H. Unveiling the source of activity of carbon integral honeycomb monoliths in the catalytic methane decomposition reaction. Catalysis Today. 2015;**249**:86

[67] Gatica JM, Gómez DM, Harti S, Vidal H. Monolithic honeycomb design applied to carbon materials for catalytic methane decomposition. Applied Catalysis A: General. 2013;**458**:21

[68] Serban M, Lewis MA, Marshall CL, Doctor RD. Hydrogen production by direct contact pyrolysis of natural gas. Energy & Fuels. 2003;**17**(3):705

[69] Geißler T, Plevan M, Abánades A, Heinzel A, Mehravaran K, Rathnam RK, et al. Experimental investigation and thermo-chemical modeling of methane pyrolysis in a liquid metal bubble column reactor with a packed bed. International Journal of Hydrogen Energy. 2015;**40**(41):14134

[70] Kang D, Rahimi N, Gordon MJ, Metiu H, McFarland EW. Catalytic methane pyrolysis in molten MnCl2-KCl. Applied Catalysis B: Environmental. 2019;**254**:659

[71] Rahimi N, Kang D, Gelinas J, Menon A, Gordon MJ, Metiu H, et al. Solid carbon production and recovery from high temperature methane pyrolysis in bubble columns containing molten metals and molten salts. Carbon. 2019;**151**:181

[72] Palmer C, Tarazkar M, Kristoffersen HH, Gelinas J, Gordon MJ, McFarland EW, et al. Methane pyrolysis with a molten Cu–Bi alloy catalyst. ACS Catalysis. 2019;**9**(9):8337

[73] Pudukudy M, Yaakob Z, Jia Q, Sobri Takriff M. Catalytic decomposition of undiluted methane into hydrogen and carbon nanotubes over Pt promoted Ni/CeO_2 catalysts. New Journal of Chemistry. 2018;**42**(18):14843

[74] Bayat N, Rezaei M, Meshkani F. COx-free hydrogen and carbon nanofibers production by methane decomposition over nickel-alumina catalysts. Korean Journal of Chemical Engineering. 2016;**33**(2):490

[75] Bayat N, Rezaei M, Meshkani F. Hydrogen and carbon nanofibers synthesis by methane decomposition over Ni–Pd/Al_2O_3 catalyst. International Journal of Hydrogen Energy. 2016; **41**(12):5494

[76] Fakeeha AH, Ibrahim AA, Khan WU, Seshan K, Al Otaibi RL, Al-Fatesh AS. Hydrogen production via catalytic methane decomposition over alumina supported iron catalyst. Arabian Journal of Chemistry. 2018;**11**(3):405

[77] Avdeeva LB, Reshetenko TV, Ismagilov ZR, Likholobov VA. Iron-containing catalysts of methane decomposition: Accumulation of filamentous carbon. Applied Catalysis A: General. 2002;**228**(1):53

[78] Ayillath Kutteri D, Wang IW, Samanta A, Li L, Hu J. Methane decomposition to tip and base grown

carbon nanotubes and COx-free H_2 over mono- and bimetallic 3d transition metal catalysts. Catalysis Science & Technology. 2018;**8**(3):858

[79] Silva RRCM, Oliveira HA, Guarino ACPF, Toledo BB, Moura MBT, Oliveira BTM, et al. Effect of support on methane decomposition for hydrogen production over cobalt catalysts. International Journal of Hydrogen Energy. 2016;**41**(16):6763

[80] Pinilla JL, Suelves I, Lázaro MJ, Moliner R. Influence on hydrogen production of the minor components of natural gas during its decomposition using carbonaceous catalysts. Journal of Power Sources. 2009;**192**(1):100

[81] Zhang J, Li X, Chen H, Qi M, Zhang G, Hu H, et al. Hydrogen production by catalytic methane decomposition: Carbon materials as catalysts or catalyst supports. International Journal of Hydrogen Energy. 2017;**42**(31):19755

[82] Fidalgo B, Muradov N, Menéndez JA. Effect of H_2S on carbon-catalyzed methane decomposition and CO_2 reforming reactions. International Journal of Hydrogen Energy. 2012; **37**(19):14187

[83] Guil-Lopez R, Botas JA, Fierro JLG, Serrano DP. Comparison of metal and carbon catalysts for hydrogen production by methane decomposition. Applied Catalysis A: General. 2011;**396**(1):40

[84] Upham DC, Agarwal V, Khechfe A, Snodgrass ZR, Gordon MJ, Metiu H, et al. Catalytic molten metals for the direct conversion of methane to hydrogen and separable carbon. Science. 2017;**358**(6365):917

[85] Abánades A, Rubbia C, Salmieri D. Thermal cracking of methane into hydrogen for a CO_2-free utilization of natural gas. International Journal of Hydrogen Energy. 2013; **38**(20):8491

[86] Ermakova MA, Ermakov DY. Ni/SiO_2 and Fe/SiO_2 catalysts for production of hydrogen and filamentous carbon via methane decomposition. Catalysis Today. 2002;**77**(3):225

[87] Ouyang M, Boldrin P, Maher RC, Chen X, Liu X, Cohen LF, et al. A mechanistic study of the interactions between methane and nickel supported on doped ceria. Applied Catalysis B: Environmental. 2019;**248**:332

[88] Bayat N, Rezaei M, Meshkani F. Methane decomposition over Ni–Fe/Al_2O_3 catalysts for production of COx-free hydrogen and carbon nanofiber. International Journal of Hydrogen Energy. 2016;**41**(3):1574

[89] Rastegarpanah A, Rezaei M, Meshkani F, Zhang K, Zhao X, Pei W, et al. Influence of group VIB metals on activity of the Ni/MgO catalysts for methane decomposition. Applied Catalysis B: Environmental. 2019;**248**:515

[90] Bayat N, Meshkani F, Rezaei M. Thermocatalytic decomposition of methane to COx-free hydrogen and carbon over Ni–Fe–Cu/Al_2O_3 catalysts. International Journal of Hydrogen Energy. 2016;**41**(30):13039

[91] Al-Fatesh AS, Fakeeha AH, Ibrahim AA, Khan WU, Atia H, Eckelt R, et al. Decomposition of methane over alumina supported Fe and Ni–Fe bimetallic catalyst: Effect of preparation procedure and calcination temperature. Journal of Saudi Chemical Society. 2018; **22**(2):239

[92] Parkinson B, Tabatabaei M, Upham DC, Ballinger B, Greig C,

Smart S, et al. Hydrogen production using methane: Techno-economics of decarbonizing fuels and chemicals. International Journal of Hydrogen Energy. 2018;**43**(5):2540

[93] Abánades A, Ruiz E, Ferruelo EM, Hernández F, Cabanillas A, Martínez-Val JM, et al. Experimental analysis of direct thermal methane cracking. International Journal of Hydrogen Energy. 2011;**36**(20):12877

[94] Abánades A, Rathnam RK, Geißler T, Heinzel A, Mehravaran K, Müller G, et al. Development of methane decarbonisation based on liquid metal technology for CO_2-free production of hydrogen. International Journal of Hydrogen Energy. 2016;**41**(19):8159

[95] Zhou L, Enakonda LR, Li S, Gary D, Del-Gallo P, Mennemann C, et al. Iron ore catalysts for methane decomposition to make COx free hydrogen and carbon nano material. Journal of the Taiwan Institute of Chemical Engineers. 2018; **87**:54

[96] Pudukudy M, Yaakob Z. Methane decomposition over Ni, Co and Fe based monometallic catalysts supported on sol gel derived SiO_2 microflakes. Chemical Engineering Journal. 2015;**262**:1009

[97] Ermakova MA, Ermakov DY, Kuvshinov GG. Effective catalysts for direct cracking of methane to produce hydrogen and filamentous carbon: Part I. Nickel catalysts. Applied Catalysis A: General. 2000;**201**(1):61

[98] Al-Fatesh AS, Amin A, Ibrahim AA, Khan WU, Soliman MA, Al-Otaibi RL, et al. Effect of Ce and Co addition to Fe/Al_2O_3 for catalytic methane decomposition. Catalysts. 2016;**6**(40): 2-15

[99] Wang J, Jin L, Li Y, Hu H. Preparation of Fe-doped carbon catalyst for methane decomposition to hydrogen. Industrial & Engineering Chemistry Research. 2017;**56**(39):11021

[100] Zhou L, Enakonda LR, Saih Y, Loptain S, Gary D, Del-Gallo P, et al. Catalytic methane decomposition over $Fe\text{-}Al_2O_3$. ChemSusChem. 2016;**9**(11): 1243

[101] Cunha AF, Órfão JJM, Figueiredo JL. Methane decomposition on Fe–Cu Raney-type catalysts. Fuel Processing Technology. 2009;**90**(10): 1234

[102] Moliner R, Suelves I, Lázaro MJ, Moreno O. Thermocatalytic decomposition of methane over activated carbons: influence of textural properties and surface chemistry. International Journal of Hydrogen Energy. 2005;**30**(3):293

[103] Lee EK, Lee SY, Han GY, Lee BK, Lee T-J, Jun JH, et al. Catalytic decomposition of methane over carbon blacks for CO_2-free hydrogen production. Carbon. 2004;**42**(12):2641

[104] Takenaka S, Ogihara H, Yamanaka I, Otsuka K. Decomposition of methane over supported-Ni catalysts: Effects of the supports on the catalytic lifetime. Applied Catalysis A: General. 2001;**217**(1):101

[105] Zhang J, Li X, Xie W, Hao Q, Chen H, Ma X. K_2CO_3-promoted methane pyrolysis on nickel/coal-char hybrids. Journal of Analytical and Applied Pyrolysis. 2018;**136**:53

[106] Abánades A. Low carbon production of hydrogen by methane decarbonization. In: Fang Z, Smith RL, Qi X, editors. Production of Hydrogen from Renewable Resources. Dordrecht: Springer; 2015. pp. 149-177

[107] Schultz I, Agar DW. Decarbonisation of fossil energy via methane pyrolysis using two reactor concepts: Fluid wall flow reactor and molten metal capillary reactor. International Journal of Hydrogen Energy. 2015;**40**(35):11422

[108] Postels S, Abánades A, von der Assen N, Rathnam RK, Stückrad S, Bardow A. Life cycle assessment of hydrogen production by thermal cracking of methane based on liquid-metal technology. International Journal of Hydrogen Energy. 2016; **41**(48):23204

[109] Ogihara H, Tajima H, Kurokawa H. Pyrolysis of mixtures of methane and ethane: activation of methane with the aid of radicals generated from ethane. Reaction Chemistry & Engineering. 2020;**5**(1):145

[110] Albright LF, Crynes BL, Corcoran WH. Pyrolysis, Theory and Industrial Practice. New York: Academic Press; 1983

[111] Fau G, Gascoin N, Gillard P, Steelant J. Methane pyrolysis: Literature survey and comparisons of available data for use in numerical simulations. Journal of Analytical and Applied Pyrolysis. 2013;**104**:1

[112] Voll M, Kleinschmit O. Carbon, carbon black. In: Gerhartz W, editor. Ullmann's Encyclopedia of Industrial Chemistry. Weinheim, Germany: Wiley-VCH; 2011

[113] Adams R. Market Study: Carbon Black. Konstanz, Germany: Converting Technical Institute (CTI); 2018. p. 270

[114] Bode R. Pigmentruße für Kunststoffe. Hanau, Germany: Degussa, Geschäftsbereich Anorganische Chemieprodukte; 1983

[115] Standard Classification System for Carbon Blacks Used in Rubber Products. West Conshohocken, PA: ASTM International; 2021. ASTM D1765-19

[116] Hardman NJ. The new carbon black and its role in the United States manufacturing renaissance. Reinforced Plastics. 2017;**61**(3):145

[117] Keipi T, Tolvanen KES, Tolvanen H, Konttinen J. Thermo-catalytic decomposition of methane: The effect of reaction parameters on process design and the utilization possibilities of the produced carbon. Energy Conversion and Management. 2016;**126**:923

[118] Muradov NZ, Veziroğlu TN. "Green" path from fossil-based to hydrogen economy: An overview of carbon-neutral technologies. International Journal of Hydrogen Energy. 2008;**33**(23):6804

[119] Abánades A, Rubbia C, Salmieri D. Technological challenges for industrial development of hydrogen production based on methane cracking. Energy. 2012;**46**(1):359

[120] Keipi T, Hankalin V, Nummelin J, Raiko R. Techno-economic analysis of four concepts for thermal decomposition of methane: Reduction of CO_2 emissions in natural gas combustion. Energy Conversion and Management. 2016; **110**:1

[121] Afzal A, Kausar A, Siddiq M. A review on polymer/cement composite with carbon nanofiller and inorganic filler. Polymer-Plastics Technology and Engineering. 2016;**55**(12):1299

[122] Alatawna A, Birenboim M, Nadiv R, Buzaglo M, Peretz-Damari S, Peled A, et al. The effect of compatibility and dimensionality of carbon nanofillers on

cement composites. Construction and Building Materials. 2020;**232**:117-141

[123] Jeyashree TM, Ganapathy C. Experimental studies on concrete elements using waste carbon black as filler material. Asian Journal of Civil Engineering. 2017;**18**:21

[124] Hermesmann M, Grübel K, Scherotzki L, Müller TE. Promising pathways: The geographic and energetic potential of power-to-x technologies based on regeneratively obtained hydrogen. Renewable and Sustainable Energy Reviews. 2021;**138**:110644

[125] Sato N, Okamoto G, Bockris JOM. In: Bockris JOM, Conway BE, Yeager E, White RE, editors. Comprehensive treatise of electrochemistry. Vol. 4. New York: Plenum Press; 1981. p. 223

[126] Ursua A, Gandia LM, Sanchis P. Hydrogen Production From Water Electrolysis: Current Status and Future Trends. Proceedings of the IEEE. 2012; **100**(2):410

[127] Ehl RG, Ihde AJ. Faraday's electrochemical laws and the determination of equivalent weights. Journal of Chemical Education. 1954; **31**(5):226

[128] Godula-Jopek A. Hydrogen Production: By Electrolysis. John Wiley & Sons; 2015

[129] Millet P. Fundamentals of water electrolysis. In: Godula-Jopek A, editor. Hydrogen Production: Electrolysis. Weinheim: Wiley-VCH; 2015. pp. 33-62

[130] Carmo M, Stolten D. Energy storage using hydrogen produced from excess renewable electricity: Power to hydrogen. In: de Miranda PEV, editor. Science and Engineering of Hydrogen-Based Energy Technologies. Cambridge, Massachusetts: Academic Press; 2019. pp. 165-199

[131] Keenan JH, Keyes FG, Hill PG, Moore JG. Steam Tables: Thermodynamic Properties of Water Including Vapor, Liquid, and Solid Phases. Hoboken, NJ: Wiley; 1969

[132] Smolinka T, Günther M, Garche J. Stand und Entwicklungspotenzial der Wasserelektrolyse zur Herstellung von Wasserstoff aus regenerativen Energien, in NOW-Studie: Kurzfassung des Abschlussberichts. Freiburg im Breisgau: Fraunhofer ISE; 2011

[133] Guillet N, Millet P. Alkaline water electrolysis. In: Godula-Jopek A, editor. Hydrogen Production: Electrolysis. Weinheim: Wiley-VCH; 2015. pp. 117-166

[134] Millet P. PEM water electrolysis. In: Godula-Jopek A, editor. Hydrogen Production: Electrolysis. Weinheim: Wiley-VCH; 2015. pp. 63-116

[135] Laurencin J, Mougin J. High-Temperature Steam Electrolysis. In: Godula-Jopek A, editor. Hydrogen Production: Electrolysis. Weinheim: Wiley-VCH; 2015. pp. 191-272

[136] Smolinka T, Wiebe N, Sterchele P, Palzer A, Lehner F, Jansen M, et al. Industrialisation of Water Electrolysis in Germany: Opportunities and Challenges for Sustainable Hydrogen for Transport, Electricity and Heat. Berlin: NOW GmbH; 2018

[137] Saba SM, Müller M, Robinius M, Stolten D. The investment costs of electrolysis – A comparison of cost studies from the past 30 years. International Journal of Hydrogen Energy. 2018;**43**(3):1209

[138] Laguna-Bercero MA. Recent advances in high temperature

electrolysis using solid oxide fuel cells: A review. Journal of Power Sources. 2012; **203**:4

[139] Töpler J, Lehmann J. Wasserstoff und Brennstoffzelle. Berlin, Heidelberg: Springer; 2017

[140] Chen K, Jiang SP. Review—Materials degradation of solid oxide electrolysis cells. Journal of the Electrochemical Society. 2016;**163**(11): F3070

[141] Lehner M, Tichler R, Steinmüller H, Koppe M. Power-to-Gas: Technology and Business Models, in SpringerBriefs in Energy. Cham: Springer International Publishing; 2014

[142] Zeng K, Zhang D. Recent progress in alkaline water electrolysis for hydrogen production and applications. Progress in Energy and Combustion Science. 2010;**36**(3):307

[143] Phillips R, Dunnill CW. Zero gap alkaline electrolysis cell design for renewable energy storage as hydrogen gas. RSC Advances. 2016;**6**(102):100643

[144] Carmo M, Fritz DL, Mergel J, Stolten D. A comprehensive review on PEM water electrolysis. International Journal of Hydrogen Energy. 2013; **38**(12):4901

[145] Smoot LD, Baxter LL. Fossil fuel power stations - coal utilization. In: Meyers RA, editor. Encyclopedia of Physical Science and Technology. Amsterdam: Elsevier; 2003. pp. 121-144

[146] Bertuccioli L, Chan A, Hart D, Lehner F, Madden B, Standen E. Study on development of water electrolysis in the European Union. Lausanne: Fuel Cells and Hydrogen Joint Undertaking; 2014. p. 160

[147] Schmidt O, Gambhir A, Staffell I, Hawkes A, Nelson J, Few S. Future cost and performance of water electrolysis: An expert elicitation study. International Journal of Hydrogen Energy. 2017; **42**(52):30470

[148] Bareiß K, de la Rua C, Möckl M, Hamacher T. Life cycle assessment of hydrogen from proton exchange membrane water electrolysis in future energy systems. Applied Energy. 2019; **237**:862

[149] Grigoriev SA, Porembsky VI, Fateev VN. Pure hydrogen production by PEM electrolysis for hydrogen energy. International Journal of Hydrogen Energy. 2006;**31**(2):171

[150] Lædre S, Kongstein OE, Oedegaard A, Karoliussen H, Seland F. Materials for proton exchange membrane water electrolyzer bipolar plates. International Journal of Hydrogen Energy. 2017;**42**(5):2713

[151] Bernt M, Gasteiger HA. Influence of ionomer content in IrO_2/TiO_2 electrodes on PEM water electrolyzer performance. Journal of the Electrochemical Society. 2016;**163**(11):F3179

[152] Rozain C, Millet P. Electrochemical characterization of polymer electrolyte membrane water electrolysis cells. Electrochimica Acta. 2014;**131**:160

[153] Pitschak B, Mergel J, Müller M. Elektrolyse-Verfahren. In: Töpler J, Lehmann J, editors. Wasserstoff und Brennstoffzelle: Technologien und Marktperspektiven. Berlin, Heidelberg: Springer; 2017. pp. 207-227

[154] Sterner M, Bauer F, Crotogino F, Eckert F, Olshausen CV, Teichmann D, et al. . In: Sterner M, Stadler I, editors. Chemische Energiespeicher, in Energiespeicher - Bedarf, Technologien,

Integration. Berlin, Heidelberg: Springer; 2017

[155] Rakousky C, Reimer U, Wippermann K, Kuhri S, Carmo M, Lueke W, et al. Polymer electrolyte membrane water electrolysis: Restraining degradation in the presence of fluctuating power. Journal of Power Sources. 2017;**342**:38

[156] Russel JH, Nuttall LJ, Fickett AP. Hydrogen generation by solid-polymer electrolyte water electrolysis. American Chemical Society Division of Fuel Chemistry Preprints. 1973;**18**(3):24-40

[157] Air Liquide starts up Cummins 20 MW PEM electrolyser in Canada. Fuel Cells Bulletin. 2021;**2021**(2):12

[158] Albrecht FG, König DH, Baucks N, Dietrich R-U. A standardized methodology for the techno-economic evaluation of alternative fuels – A case study. Fuel. 2017;**194**:511

[159] Zahid M, Schefold J, Brisse A. High-temperature water electrolysis using planar solid oxide fuel cell technology: A review. In: Stolten D, editor. Hydrogen and Fuel Cells, Fundamentals, Technologies and Applications. Weinheim: Wiley-VCH; 2010. p. 227

[160] Lim A, Cho MK, Lee SY, Kim H-J, Yoo SJ, Sung Y-E, et al. A review of industrially developed components and operation conditions for anion exchange membrane water electrolysis. Journal of Electrochemical Science and Technology. 2017;**8**(4):265

[161] Cho MK, Lim A, Lee SY, Kim H-J, Yoo SJ, Sung Y-E, et al. A review on membranes and catalysts for anion exchange membrane water electrolysis single cells. Journal of Electrochemical Science and Technology. 2017;**8**(3):183

[162] Gandía LM, Oroz R, Ursúa A, Sanchis P, Diéguez PM. Renewable hydrogen production: Performance of an alkaline water electrolyzer working under emulated wind conditions. Energy & Fuels. 2007;**21**(3):1699

[163] Le Bideau D, Mandin P, Benbouzid M, Kim M, Sellier M. Review of necessary thermophysical properties and their sensivities with temperature and electrolyte mass fractions for alkaline water electrolysis multiphysics modelling. International Journal of Hydrogen Energy. 2019;**44**(10):4553

[164] Pellegrini LA, De Guido G, Moioli S. Design of the CO_2 removal section for PSA tail gas treatment in a hydrogen production plant. Frontiers in Energy Research. 2020;**8**(77):1-10

[165] Cuéllar-Franca RM, Azapagic A. Carbon capture, storage and utilisation technologies: A critical analysis and comparison of their life cycle environmental impacts. Journal of CO_2 Utilization. 2015;**9**:82

[166] Rackley SA. Absorption Capture Systems. Carbon Capture and Storage. Amsterdam: Elsevier; 2010. pp. 103-131

[167] Mokhatab S, Poe WA. Natural Gas Sweetening. Handbook of Natural Gas Transmission and Processing. Amsterdam: Elsevier; 2012. pp. 253-290

[168] Metz B, Davidson O, De Coninck HC, Loos M, Meyer L. IPCC Special Report on Carbon dioxide Capture and Storage. Cambridge: Cambridge University Press; 2005

[169] Santos S, Collodi G, Azzaro G, Ferrari N. Techno-economic Evaluation of SMR Based Standalone (Merchant) Hydrogen Plant with CCS. IEAGHG Technical Report. Paris: International Energy Agency (IEA); 2017

[170] Koornneef J, van Keulen T, Faaij A, Turkenburg W. Life cycle assessment of a pulverized coal power plant with post-combustion capture, transport and storage of CO_2. International Journal of Greenhouse Gas Control. 2008;**2**(4):448

[171] Singh B, Strømman AH, Hertwich EG. Comparative life cycle environmental assessment of CCS technologies. International Journal of Greenhouse Gas Control. 2011;**5**(4):911

[172] Dufour J, Serrano DP, Gálvez JL, González A, Soria E, Fierro JLG. Life cycle assessment of alternatives for hydrogen production from renewable and fossil sources. International Journal of Hydrogen Energy. 2012; **37**(2):1173

[173] Noussan M, Raimondi PP, Scita R, Hafner M. The role of green and blue hydrogen in the energy transition—A technological and geopolitical perspective. Sustainability. 2021;**13** (298):1-26

[174] Topham S, Bazzanella A, Schiebahn S, Luhr S, Zhao L, Otto A. Carbon dioxide. In: Ullmann's Encyclopedia of Industrial Chemistry. Weinheim, Germany: Wiley-VCH; 2011. pp. 1-43

[175] Wang H, Chen J, Li Q. A review of pipeline transportation technology of carbon dioxide. IOP Conference Series: Earth and Environmental Science. 2019; **310**(3):032033

[176] Knoope MMJ, Ramírez A, Faaij APC. A state-of-the-art review of techno-economic models predicting the costs of CO_2 pipeline transport. International Journal of Greenhouse Gas Control. 2013;**16**:241

[177] Kuckshinrichs W, Hake J-F. CO_2-Abscheidung, -Speicherung und -Nutzung: Technische, wirtschaftliche, umweltseitige und gesellschaftliche Perspektive. In: Advances in Systems Analysis 2. Vol. 144. Jülich: Forschungszentrum Jülich; 2013. p. 367

[178] Zhang ZX, Wang GX, Massarotto P, Rudolph V. Optimization of pipeline transport for CO_2 sequestration. Energy Conversion and Management. 2006; **47**(6):702

[179] Fischedick M, Esken A, Pastowski A, Schüwer D, Supersberger N, Nitsch J, et al. RECCS Strukturell-ökonomisch-ökologischer Vergleich Regenerativer Energietechnologien (RE) mit Carbon Capture and Storage (CCS). Wuppertal: Deutsches Zentrum für Luft-und Raumfahrt (DLR); 2006. p. 210

[180] Wells SL, DeSimone J. CO_2 technology platform: An important tool for environmental problem solving. Angewandte Chemie International Edition. 2001;**40**(3):518

[181] Han C, Zahid U, An J, Kim K, Kim C. CO_2 transport: Design considerations and project outlook. Current Opinion in Chemical Engineering. 2015;**10**:42

[182] Peletiri SP, Rahmanian N, Mujtaba IM. CO_2 pipeline design: A review. Energies. 2018;**11**(2185):1-25

[183] Kang K, Huh C, Kang S-G, Baek J-H, Noh HJ. Estimation of CO_2 pipeline transport cost in South Korea based on the scenarios. Energy Procedia. 2014; **63**:2475

[184] Witkowski A, Rusin A, Majkut M, Stolecka-Antczak K. The analysis of pipeline transportation process for CO_2 captured from reference coal-fired 900 MW power plant to sequestration

region. Chemical and Process Engineering. 2014;**35**(4):497-514

[185] Patchigolla K, Oakey JE. Design overview of high pressure dense phase CO_2 pipeline transport in flow mode. Energy Procedia. 2013;**37**:3123

[186] Kelemen P, Benson SM, Pilorgé H, Psarras P, Wilcox J. An overview of the status and challenges of CO_2 storage in minerals and geological formations. Frontiers in Climate. 2019;**1** (9):1-20

[187] Brown K, Whittaker S, Wilson M, Srisang W, Smithson H, Tontiwachwuthikul P. The history and development of the IEA GHG Weyburn-Midale CO_2 monitoring and storage project in Saskatchewan, Canada (the world largest CO_2 for EOR and CCS program). Petroleum. 2017;**3**(1):3

[188] McKelvy MJ, Bearat H, Chizmeshya AVG, Nunez R, Carpenter RW. Understanding Olivine CO_2 Mineral Sequestration Mechanisms at the Atomic Level: Optimizing Reaction Process Design. Tempe, AZ: Arizona State University (US); 2003. Available from: https://www.osti.gov/biblio/1411934

[189] Rochelle CA, Czernichowski-Lauriol I, Milodowski AE. The impact of chemical reactions on CO_2 storage in geological formations: A brief review. Geological Society, London, Special Publications. 2004;**233**(1):87

[190] Fabius L. Report of the Conference of the Parties on its twenty-first session, held in Paris from 30 November to 13 December 2015. In: Part two: Action taken by the Conference of the Parties at its twenty-first session, Paris: Framework Convention on Climate Change FCCC/CP/2015/10. 2016. pp. 1-42

[191] Masson-Delmotte V. Global Warming of 1.5°C : An IPCC Special Report on Impacts of Global Warming of 1.5°C above Pre-industrial Levels and Related Global Greenhouse Gas Emission Pathways, in the Contex of Strengthening the Global Response to the Thereat of Climate Change, Sustainable Development, and Efforts to Eradicate Poverty. Cambridge: Intergovernmental Panel on Climate Change; 2022

[192] Bradshaw J, Bachu S, Bonijoly D, Burruss R, Holloway S, Christensen NP, et al. CO_2 storage capacity estimation: Issues and development of standards. International Journal of Greenhouse Gas Control. 2007;**1**(1):62

[193] Terlouw W, Peters D, Tilburg JV, Schimmel M, Berg T, Cihlar J, et al. Gas for climate. The Optimal Role for Gas in a Net-zero Emissions Energy System. Brussels, Belgium: European Biogas Association; 2019

[194] Barry J, Global CCS Institute. Global Status of CCS Update to 3rd Clean Energy Ministerial. Australia: Global CSS Institute; 2012

[195] Mikkelsen M, Jørgensen M, Krebs FC. The teraton challenge, A review of fixation and transformation of carbon dioxide. Energy & Environmental Science. 2010;**3**(1):43

[196] Blunt J, Balchin NC. In: Blunt J, Balchin NC, editors. Arc Welding and Cutting, in Health and safety in welding and allied processes. Boca Raton, FLA: CRC Press; 2002. pp. 106-132

[197] Karmee SK, Greiner L, Kraynov A, Müller TE, Niemeijer B, Leitner W. Nanoparticle catalysed oxidation of sulfides to sulfones by in situ generated H_2O_2 in supercritical carbon dioxide/water biphasic medium. Chemical Communications. 2010;**46**(36):6705

[198] Karmee SK, Roosen C, Kohlmann C, Lütz S, Greiner L, Leitner W. Chemo-enzymatic cascade oxidation in supercritical carbon dioxide/water biphasic media. Green Chemistry. 2009;**11**(7):1052

[199] Leigraf C, Besser J, Kleemann S. CO_2 for pH-stabilisation in Specialty Paper Production through Using of Adalka Process. Wochenblatt für Papierfabrikation; 2002;**130**:772

[200] Choi SK, Ko KS, Chun HD, Kim JG. Utilization of Carbon Dioxide for Neutralization of Alkaline Wastewater. Greenhouse Gas Control Technologies - Sixth International Conference. 2003;**II**: 1871

[201] Jessop PG, Mercer SM, Heldebrant DJ. CO_2-triggered switchable solvents, surfactants, and other materials. Energy & Environmental Science. 2012;**5**(6):7240

[202] Leitner W. Supercritical Carbon Dioxide as a Green Reaction Medium for Catalysis. Accounts of Chemical Research. 2002;**35**(9):746

[203] Ramalakshmi K, Raghavan B. Caffeine in coffee: Its removal. why and how? Critical Reviews in Food Science and Nutrition. 1999;**39**(5):441

[204] Molla Tadesse A, Ada F, Jinping G, Guoqiang C, Vincent N. Impregnation of materials in supercritical CO_2 to impart various functionalities. In: Igor P, editor. Advanced Supercritical Fluids Technologies. London, UK, Rijeka: IntechOpen; 2019. p. Ch. 8

[205] Kikic I, Vecchione F. Supercritical impregnation of polymers. Current Opinion in Solid State and Materials Science. 2003;**7**(4):399

[206] DeSimone JM, Maury EE, Menceloglu YZ, McClain JB, Romack TJ, Combes JR. Dispersion polymerizations in supercritical carbon dioxide. Science. 1994;**265**(5170):356

[207] Jennings J, Beija M, Kennon JT, Willcock H, O'Reilly RK, Rimmer S, et al. Advantages of block copolymer synthesis by RAFT-controlled dispersion polymerization in supercritical carbon dioxide. Macromolecules. 2013;**46**(17): 6843

[208] Knez Ž, Markočič E, Leitgeb M, Primožič M, Knez Hrnčič M, Škerget M. Industrial applications of supercritical fluids: A review. Energy. 2014;**77**:235

[209] Ramsey E, Sun Q, Zhang Z, Zhang C, Gou W. Mini-review: Green sustainable processes using supercritical fluid carbon dioxide. Journal of Environmental Sciences. 2009;**21**(6):720

[210] Leitner W. Reactions in Supercritical Carbon Dioxide ($scCO_2$). In: Knochel P, editor. Modern Solvents in Organic Synthesis. Berlin, Heidelberg: Springer; 2003. pp. 107-132

[211] Pearson A. Carbon dioxide—New uses for an old refrigerant. International Journal of Refrigeration. 2005;**28**(8):1140

[212] von der Aßen NV. From Life-cycle Assessment Towards Life-cycle Design of Carbon dioxide Capture and Utilization. Aachen: RWTH Aachen University; 2015

[213] Artz J, Müller TE, Thenert K, Kleinekorte J, Meys R, Sternberg A, et al. Sustainable conversion of carbon dioxide: An integrated review of catalysis and life cycle assessment. Chemical Reviews. 2018;**118**(2):434

[214] Müller TE, Leitner W, Markewitz P, Kuckshinrichs W. Opportunities for utilizing and recycling CO_2. In: Kuckshinrichs W, Hake J-F,

editors. Carbon Capture, Storage and Use: Technical, Economic, Environmental and Societal Perspectives. Cham: Springer International Publishing; 2015. pp. 67-100

[215] Prado A, Mac Dowell N. The cost of permanent carbon dioxide removal. Joule. 2023;7(4):700

[216] Markewitz P, Kuckshinrichs W, Leitner W, Linssen J, Zapp P, Bongartz R, et al. Worldwide innovations in the development of carbon capture technologies and the utilization of CO_2. Energy & Environmental Science. 2012;**5**(6):7281

[217] Sakakura T, Choi J-C, Yasuda H. Transformation of carbon dioxide. Chemical Reviews. 2007;**107**(6):2365

[218] Centi G, Quadrelli EA, Perathoner S. Catalysis for CO_2 conversion: A key technology for rapid introduction of renewable energy in the value chain of chemical industries. Energy & Environmental Science. 2013;**6**(6):1711

[219] Wang W, Wang S, Ma X, Gong J. Recent advances in catalytic hydrogenation of carbon dioxide. Chemical Society Reviews. 2011;**40**(7): 3703

[220] Su X, Xu J, Liang B, Duan H, Hou B, Huang Y. Catalytic carbon dioxide hydrogenation to methane: A review of recent studies. Journal of Energy Chemistry. 2016;**25**(4):553

[221] Jiang X, Nie X, Guo X, Song C, Chen JG. Recent advances in carbon dioxide hydrogenation to methanol via heterogeneous catalysis. Chemical Reviews. 2020;**120**(15):7984

[222] Bulushev DA, Ross JRH. Heterogeneous catalysts for hydrogenation of CO_2 and bicarbonates to formic acid and formates. Catalysis Reviews. 2018;**60**(4):566

[223] Medrano-García JD, Ruiz-Femenia R, Caballero JA. Optimal carbon dioxide and hydrogen utilization in carbon monoxide production. Journal of CO_2 Utilization. 2019;**34**:215

[224] Dasireddy VDBC, Vengust D, Likozar B, Kovač J, Mrzel A. Production of syngas by CO_2 reduction through reverse water–gas shift (RWGS) over catalytically-active molybdenum-based carbide, nitride and composite nanowires. Renewable Energy. 2021;**176**:251

[225] Müller TE, Hannes J, Graef I, Hagen V. SynGas2Ethen - Production of Ethene from Recycle Streams and Renewable Carbon Sources as a Sustainable and Economic Way to Basic Materials of the Chemical Industry. Bonn: Federal Ministry of Education and Research; 2022. [Accessed: October 28, 2023]. Available from: https://www.fona.de/en/measures/funding-measures/KlimPro/SynGas2Ethen_en.php

[226] Bazzanella A, Ausfelder F. Low Carbon Energy and Feedstock for the European Chemical Industry. Frankfurt: DECHEMA e.V.; 2017. p. 168. Available from: www.dechema.de

[227] Quadrelli EA, Centi G, Duplan J-L, Perathoner S. Carbon dioxide recycling: Emerging large-scale technologies with industrial potential. ChemSusChem. 2011;**4-9**:1194

[228] Aresta M, editor. Carbon dioxide as Chemical Feedstock. Hoboken, New Jersey: John Wiley & Sons; 2010

[229] Bruhn T, Naims H, Olfe-Kräutlein B. Separating the debate on CO_2 utilisation from carbon capture and

storage. Environmental Science & Policy. 2016;**60**:38

[230] Brandão M, Levasseur A, Kirschbaum MUF, Weidema BP, Cowie AL, Jørgensen SV, et al. Key issues and options in accounting for carbon sequestration and temporary storage in life cycle assessment and carbon footprinting. The International Journal of Life Cycle Assessment. 2013;**18**(1):230

[231] Levasseur A, Lesage P, Margni M, Deschênes L, Samson R. Considering time in LCA: Dynamic LCA and its application to global warming impact assessments. Environmental Science & Technology. 2010;**44**(8):3169

[232] Ranganathan J, Corbier L, Bhatia P, Schmitz S, Oren PG. The Greenhouse Gas Protocol: A corporate accounting and reporting standard. In: World Resources Institute and World Business Council for Sustainable Development. Washington: World Business Council for Sustainable Development; 2004

[233] Sinden G. PAS 2050–Specification for the Assessment of the Life Cycle Greenhouse Gas Emissions of Goods and Services. London: British Standards Institution (BSI); 2008. pp. 1-54. PAS 2050:2008

Chapter 3

Improvement of Validated Manufacturing Processes with Fuzzy Logic

Marisol Hernández-Hernández, Luis Alfonso Bonilla Cruz and Lizbeth Cobián-Romero

Abstract

SMEs are essential entities for the economy of countries, so they need to implement strategies to maintain and achieve economic stability. Technology is a great support tool to achieve this. Still, entrepreneurs, generally acting empirically, need to determine which technology to select, how to do it, and its scope of implementation. Fuzzy logic is a technology adapted to human linguistic thinking, which served as a methodology in this case study to measure the degree of behavior given by the implementation of software and hardware in a company. The result of the research validated the benefits that the gradual implementation of the technology presented to the company in terms of utility, time, and quantity of production, which were related in degrees of uncertainty with variables that were labeled as "high," "medium," and "low." The established membership was validated through fuzzy graphs, showing the company's status, and adjusted with the appropriateness of the technology until profits were placed within the "high" range. Thus, fuzzy logic is a tool that helps measure variables in degrees of belonging, with words used by business people to make it more understandable. Furthermore, the data coding in fuzzy terms showed the prediction of the behavior of the variables adjusted with technological processes.

Keywords: manufacturing, fuzzy logic, methodology, process evaluation, SMEs

1. Introduction

Manufacturing processes in the manufacturing industry differ from other sectors by their materials, their machinery, and how they carry out operations. In general, a process can be defined as the change of properties of an object, ranging from geometry, hardness, state, and content in the form of information data [1]. In the manufacturing industry, this definition applies perfectly.

The manufacturing industry is a vital sector for the countries' economy and can be of different sizes: large, medium, and trim. In this context, small and medium-sized enterprises (SMEs) comprise a large percentage of all companies; Mexico has 4.9 million economic establishments, of which 98.8% are SMEs and generate 27 million jobs [2]. Other sources state that SMEs comprise 99.80% of the entire business fabric

IntechOpen

and generate 70% of employment. In addition, they contribute 50% of the Gross Domestic Product (GDP) [3], measure that expresses the monetary value of the production of goods and services demanded by a country or region during a given period.

In Latin America and the Caribbean, SMEs generate formal productive employment for 60% of workers, making up 99.5% of companies [4]. In the world, SMEs represent approximately 90% of companies, generating more than 50% of employment and 40% of GDP, according to the World Bank SME Finance [5]. In addition, the OECD determined that SMEs represent 60% of employment and between 50 and 60% of added value, which is why they are considered drivers of productivity in many regions [6].

In the background of the benefits of the companies, the PYMES are an essential part of a country's economy. However, not all of them can survive the daily problems generated by the mismanagement of their processes, the inexperience of business people, and the nonexistence or poor adaptation of technology to support their businesses, is what can lead to the reduction of their profits, and to reaffirm this assertion [7], affirm that SMEs do not have practical management skills and have limited education and training of their workforce, so this type of problem often means that their life potential does not increase.

As a proposed solution to the above, innovation has created many types of technologies that would help increase their profits. Still, unfortunately, entrepreneurs do not know how to implement them since, by tradition, SMEs are made up of people who have acted empirically in the administration since their ancestors started them in a rustic or experimental way and without theoretical foundation and consequently, they are unaware of the benefits that it could give them and although the effects of technology on organizations and productivity in companies have not been analyzed for several years [8], it is time to return to them, mainly to explore the benefits of emerging technologies.

Manufacturing is one of our environment's leading small and medium-sized companies. Only in Mexico in the fourth quarter of 2022, the population employed in these was 9.59 million, registering a gross domestic product of 5.51 billion pesos. If you look further back, in 2019, there were a total of 579,828 economic units in Manufacturing Industries, according to the website of the Government of Mexico [9]; this was the reason to focus this study on them and thus implement improvement strategies in their processes so that they continue to exist and progress.

For SMEs to achieve stability and growth, their problems are detected to generate new ideas to improve their manufacturing processes; this is taking into account that five-sixths of the world population, equivalent to 6 billion people, live in emerging countries and better products are required [10]; Therefore, it is necessary to improve the quality of processes and their products, to satisfy consumers and, consequently, improve the productive life of companies.

The productive processes have been studied for their improvement, implementing several techniques. Favela-Herrera et al. [11], created a lean manufacturing model as an alternative to increase productivity and develop manufacturing skills, where the results were observed mainly in the increase in operational performance that reduced production costs, but this was only in theory.

In other contexts, Chinese manufacturing companies have opted for technological innovation strategies in the manufacturing industry, strengthening official industry-university-research-customer cooperation and taking advantage of the Industry 4.0 era [12]. This idea should be used in other countries, starting with Universities, since they can be great allies of companies and become business advisors. Even so, while that happens, it is necessary to propose solutions to ensure that SMEs continue to generate economic benefits for countries.

Regarding the evolution of industries, in recent years, they have met various requirements that satisfy the market's growing demands, so they must constantly evolve, trying to have innovation, greater productivity, and lower losses. For this, industrial researchers have been attempting to implement technology in manufacturing, where innovation requirements must cover logistics and administration aspects that encompass the production, supply, and distribution of materials used for manufacturing [13, 14]. However, it is essential to add methods to measure the results of this implementation and thus know if these changes are positive for companies and to what extent, as well as demonstrate to other companies that they can replicate the methodology with the confidence they already have.

The productive processes of a company were automated, attending to the strategies generated from an analysis based on fuzzy cognitive maps, from which the "consequents" generated from problems used as "background" were taken. A "case study" was carried out to analyze the benefits of innovation, review the results, and adjust the changes that technology made in the company, considering that everything can improve more and more, but being able to predict the best behavior from the study of the company in such a way that the change benefits the employer and its employees.

The study was achieved by analyzing the evolutionary process of the company, for which it was necessary to continuously adjust the changes, which make companies more mature and competitive; Socconini Luis [15] suggests that the adjustments made to companies should be corrective, prevention, improvement and innovation actions and, with this idea, an investigation proposing fuzzy models as a methodology, this to measure the results, in variables that can be adjusted as required by the innovation process.

A study was made of a family business with 20 workers, making it a small business. In this type of company, the leaders fulfill multiple complex functions that include the control of the company, although they still need a vision of the perspective of long-term growth. Instead, they see it as self-employment [16]. However, this idea is correct because this job earns money to live; it differs from what is required for its growth.

In the study company, the leaders need a comprehensive vision of growth and less of how to include technology since they need to see the antecedents and consequences to make decisions about its implementation. So, based on already established strategies, technology was implemented in the company to meet the most urgent needs and thus measure the benefit in terms of three selected study variables: production, time, and profits, which are essential for the company's growth.

With these parameters, diffuse linguistic variables were established by low, medium, and high categories related to the study variables and modeled under the fuzzy logic scheme. Results were obtained that show the benefit that technology gave to the company, which at the end of the study was reflected in high terms in company profits, low in production and management time, and high in terms of quantities produced.

With this study, it was possible to appreciate that with the fuzzy methodology, the company's behavior can be measured in terms of human language and adjust variables with the implementation of technology and forecast results.

2. Background

Fuzzy logic is a theory given by Lofti Zadeh in 1965, which is based on sets that have degrees of membership in them and are encoded in unitary intervals; that is, they have a membership function whose values are compatible with those sets in degrees of membership from 0 to 1. [17], mentions that this theory differs from classical logic, in that the data are complex, that is, a data has membership in a set, "all or nothing."

Classical logic is based on sets where their inclusion is resolved in degrees of "true or false," 0 or 1, all or nothing; unlike fuzzy logic, where a piece of data is part of a set to a certain extent, to a greater degree (0), sometimes to a medium degree (0.5) or can increase or decrease its vagueness, it can even be empty.

Classical logic has solved many problems, but it is necessary to solve those in which the membership of the data in a set is uncertain or, more specifically, in which they may belong to that set to a greater or lesser extent. To categorize elements into small or large with complex data, it would be said drastically and according to an established criterion, what is less or significant; However, how much do they cost? Who are they compared to? How small or big are they?; For example, if the number of employees of a company is measured and it is established that to be a "microenterprise" it must have 10 employees and to be "small" it must have more than 10, then a company with 13 employees, how small or what? Is it so big?

Most of the logic of human reasoning is not the classical logic of two values or even of several values rather, it is a logic of fuzzy truths, of fuzzy conjunctions, of fuzzy rules of deduction [18]. Fuzzy information locates its elements in degrees of belonging to one set or another, which means that in linguistic terms, not everything is genuine and not everything is false; that is, with this fuzzy logic, if a company has 13 employees, then it belongs to a certain degree to the small ones, although it is also part of the microenterprises to a greater degree, this example is shown analogically in **Table 1**.

Fuzzy logic manages the vagueness of the sets according to their degree of membership; for example, people would be classified into wide and thin. The thin membership set is translated linguistically with If-Then-Else statements. This technique has also been applied in various contexts, both electronic and in other sectors belonging to the social or health sciences. There are three fuzzy inference classification systems (FIS), which are Mamdani FIS, TSK/Sugeno FIS, and Tsukamoto FIS, and they have variations.

Ebrahim Mamdani's algorithm, proposed in 1974, maintains the "IF-THEN" rules given by linguistic expressions. Hence, its rule is "IF X is A THEN Y is B. Mamdani systems are made up of IF-THEN rules of the form "IF X is in A THEN Y is in B," such as "IF THE PRESSURE is HIGH THEN THE VOLUME is LOW." In these rules, the IF part "X is in A" is called the antecedent of the rule, and the THEN "Y are in B" part is called the consequent of the rule [19].

Rout et al. [20] describe the fuzzy inference model presented by Takagi, Sugeno, and Kang, called Sugeno and abbreviated TSK; it is based on three components: the rule base, the database, and the reasoning mechanism and its rules consist of antecedents and consequents that are stated "If A is antecedent then B is consequent, with a function

			Microenterprises							
0.0	0.1	0.2	0.3	0.4	0.5	0.6	0.7	0.8	0.9	1.0
						Small companies				
Source: prepared by the authors.										

Table 1.
Example of the location of companies with fuzzy logic.

that defines the degree of membership of an object and its rule is represented with a polynomial of the form: If there are two inputs "x" and "y," the output polynomial will have the form z = px + qy + r and its rule is If x is A and B then z = f(x,y).

Suharjito and Yulyanto [21], describe the Tsukamoto FIS model presented in 1979; it is little known and therefore little used; it is a decision-making method with monotonic reasoning rules, that is, they are systems with a single rule of the form "Cause and Effect" or "Input-Output" implication in which the antecedent and consequence have to be correlated and uses the "centered average method." An example of this model can be written as follows:

- If X is small then Y is C1
- If X is medium then Y is C2
- If X is big then Y is C3

As proposed, and based on the IF-Then denominator, fuzzy logic is a way of getting closer to human language since it handles vagueness in terms of words; the numbers are denoted in linguistic variables. Fuzzy data of some entities, for example, **Table 2**, shows the complex, imprecise data and their linguistic variables of the temperature of the day.

Another way of using fuzzy logic is through fuzzy cognitive maps (FCM), represented in a cognitive digraph that describes the behavior of a physical system in terms of nodes and edges that connect them and where each node of the graph is a fuzzy set described by variables, objects or entities of a system [22].

The FCM are oriented graphs, where a set of nodes represents notations in symbolic form and causal relationships in the form of weighted connections and, for the most part, the nodes are objects described by states or conditions, and the connections are actions or transfers functions, that transform a state in one node to another in another node; likewise, the FCM can be considered as a set of rules, where the input nodes are interconnected with the output ones and whose value corresponds to the consequent rule, and that data You can be represented in a knowledge matrix so that they are trained to obtain new values, all of this represented FCM as seen in **Figure 1**.

Fuzzy logic has been used in multiple areas with multiple benefits for humanity. In the field of health, the help of this logic is shown by reducing the complexity of calculating the degree of similarity that may exist between diabetic patients who require different follow-up plans and proposing fuzzy decision trees that help the accuracy of this classification and thus improve the recovery step of case-based reasoning [24]. In addition, Fuzzy Logic has been used in contemporary designs by

Hard value (classical logic)	Fuzzy value	Linguistic variable
1	1.0	Very hot
0	0.8	Hot
0	0.6	Warm
0	0.0	Very cold

Source: prepared by the authors.

Table 2.
Fuzzy values.

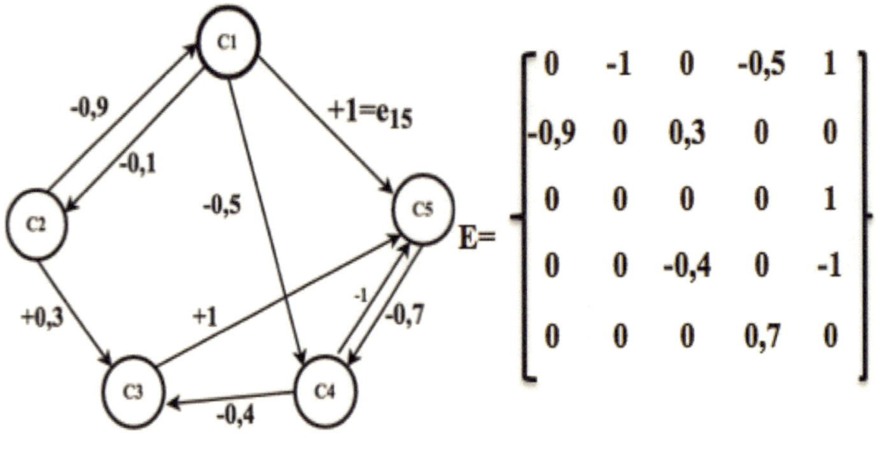

Figure 1.
Fuzzy cognitive map. Source [23].

companies such as Eaton Industrial Controls, Motorola, NCR, Intel, Rockwell, Togai, and Nasa Gensym, among others, that use linear and nonlinear control, data analysis, pattern recognition, operations research, and financial systems [25].

The representation of the FCM has been done as shown in **Figure 2**, where a hybrid FCM is displayed to make time series forecasts, where it is observed that the input nodes are connected to a black box that improves the prediction rate and corrects the outputs and produces a better degree of confidence, based on metaheuristics.

In chemical processes, they have also been applied [27] to regulate the 3-valve liquid mixtures and thus obtain the best.

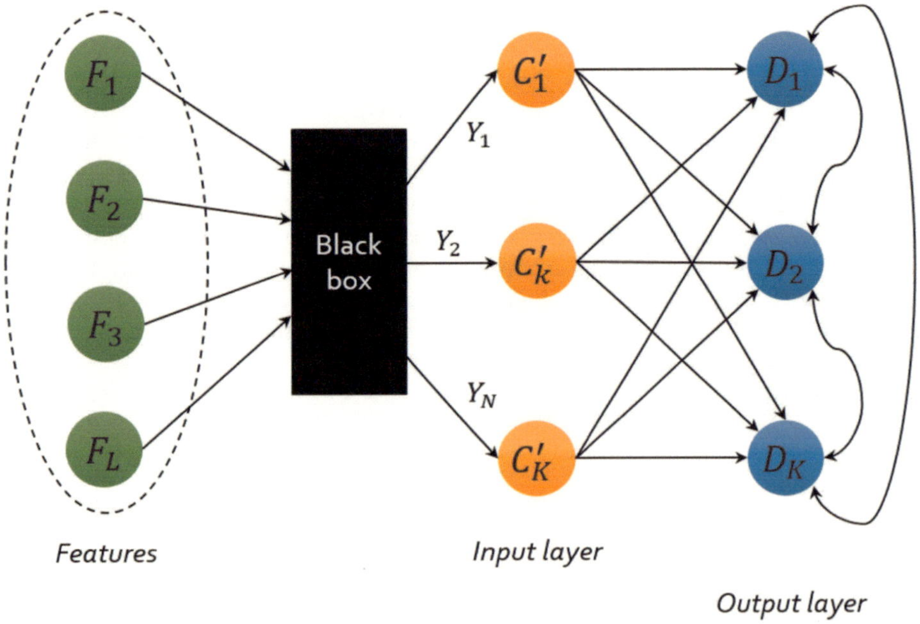

Figure 2.
Hybrid classifier based on FCM type 1. Source [26].

In other contexts, fuzzy logic has also been very beneficial for decision-making, applying it in social, governmental, or production fields through FCM. In social areas, FCMs have been used to analyze and solve problems related to the prediction of the socioeconomic consequences of privatization at the company level, where the opinions and expectations of the employees of the Nevşehir Alcoholic Beverage Factory of the General Directorate of Tekel, with the highest capacity in the Turkish distilled alcoholic beverages sector, in "If-Then" scenarios, to make predictions of variable interactions [28].

In this same vein, the FCM was also applied in case studies involving a complex phenomenon of poverty eradication and socioeconomic development strategies in rural areas under the DAY-NRLM (Deendayal Antyodaya Yojana-National Rural Livelihoods Mission) in India to be able to help policymakers to obtain precise results from proposed policies that address social resilience and sustainable socioeconomic development strategies [29].

3. Methodology

The project was implemented in a manufacturing company, and based on its problems analyzed through FCM, strategies were obtained that were implemented and adjusted to investigate their causes and effects. The description of the company and its issues are mentioned below to serve as a basis for the fuzzy analysis that was carried out.

3.1 Analysis

The Protexjd company is a company with 2 years of life, which belongs to the SMEs category, its business activity is the manufacture of uniforms for other companies, it currently has 20 workers, and its problems are basically with administration and production, the same which are mentioned subsequently:

1. There is no record of monitoring inputs, outputs, and processes of the manufactured materials and garments.

2. The staff makes manufacturing errors because they need to remember what is explained to them regarding product preparation.

3. The characteristics of the garments are not stored, so you have to start by explaining their manufacture each time a garment arrives, even if it has already been done.

4. They do not have production monitoring to know how the production processes are going.

5. Lack of uniformity in staff training.

6. Perceptions must be checked, so they must know the money flow.

An FCM was structured for the company to obtain possible implementation strategies, obtaining the one shown in **Figure 3**.

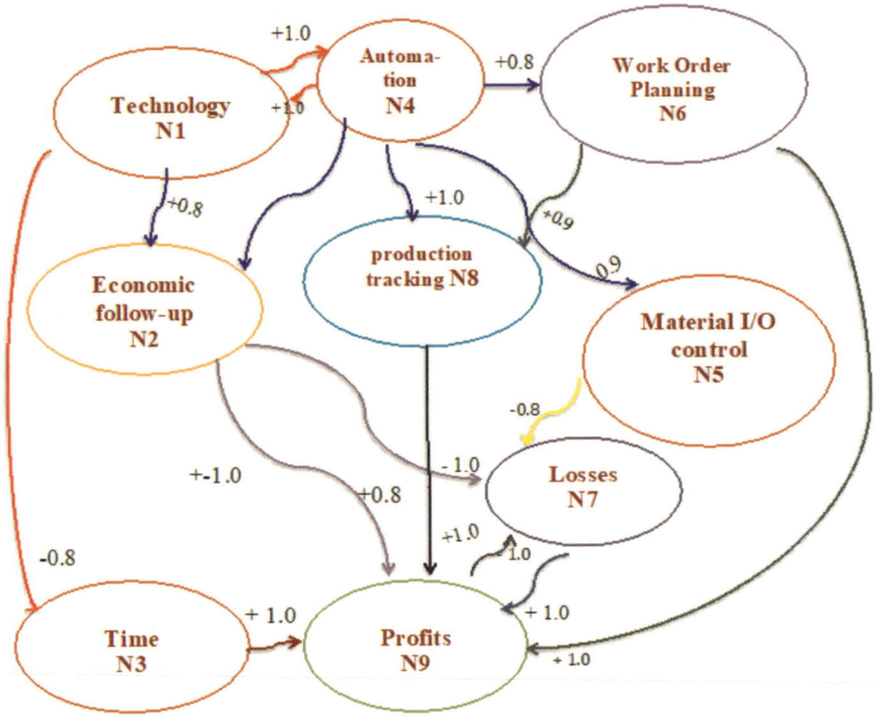

Figure 3.
FCM of a manufacturing company. Source: [30].

After establishing the FCM, the causes and effects were analyzed, determining the following strategies so that the company can give a better performance.

If the technology is increased, then:

- Perceptions increase.
- Production and management time is reduced.
- The time of the inventory management process is reduced.
- The repository of competencies and specifications is expanded.
- Reduction of losses.
- Production monitoring is increased.
- Profits are increased.

From the strategies, the items that would serve as solution factors were determined, establishing as solution variables: Production time, management time, production profits, and management profits, which gave rise to the other base variables, which are essential to be able to analyze and forecast established benefits, as described in **Table 3**, which makes a relationship between strategies and solution items with fuzzy variables:

	Fuzzy value	Production	Management time	Utilities
With technology	1.0	High	Low	High
	0.7	Half	Half	Half
	0.3	Low	High	Low
Source: prepared by the authors.				

Table 3.
Relationship of fuzzy values with solution strategies in linguistic terms.

3.2 Design

Based on the data in **Table 3** and by the FCM in **Figure 3**, the degree of belonging to each set was determined, as observed in **Table 4**, where values were assigned to the linguistic variables to have parameters of measurement in the evaluation and forecasts of the operation of the company.

To know if the above is being handled properly and to determine forecasts for the use of technology, an analysis was made applying the fuzzy theory, precisely the Mandamni technique, which consists of having an antecedent and a consequent that is specified in the function:

If a is A1 and b is B1 then c is C1.

If a is A2 and b is B2 then c is C2.

Subsequently, the data in **Table 3** were coded in Python, where the low, medium, and high values were established in production, time, and profit, which can be seen in **Figure 4a–c**, respectively. All this is according to the data given by the employer.

Afterward, the fuzzy rules based on Mandamni, shown in **Figure 5**, were applied to determine the base behavior of the variables. In the figure, it can be seen that the antecedent in rule 1 is "low production," "high time," and they have a consequence of "low profits"; in rule 2, "high production" and "low time" are antecedents of "high profits" which is consequent; and finally, rule 3, "average production" and "average time," produce "average profits."

Item	Amount	Linguistic variable
Products	0–150	Low
	100–220	Half
	180–400	High
Time	0–3	Low
	2–4	Half
	3–6	High
utilities	0–2000 *(Mexican pesos)*	Low
1800–8000 *(Mexican pesos)*	Half	
	4500–14,500 *(Mexican pesos)*	High
Source: prepared by the authors.		

Table 4.
Linguistic variables of the system.

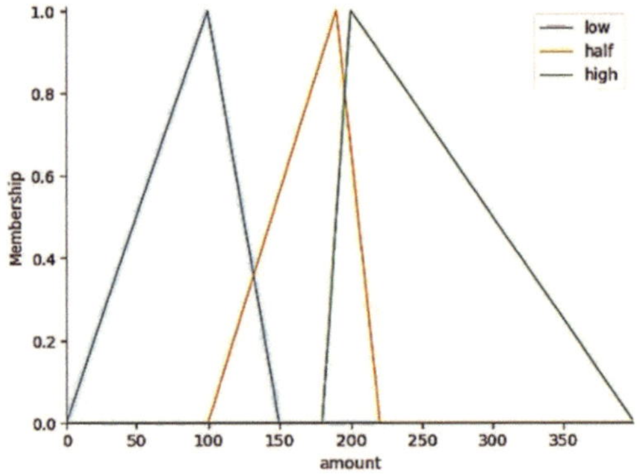

a)

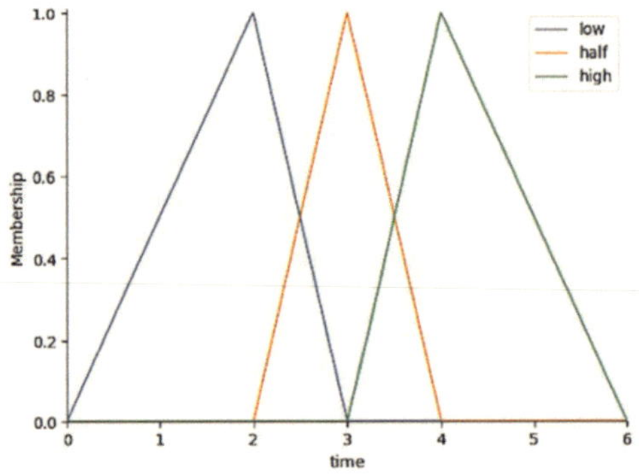

b)

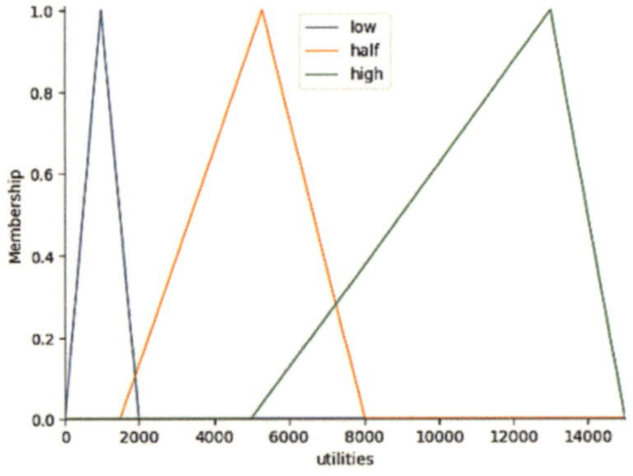

c)

Figure 4.
Fuzzy representation of the linguistic data of (a) production, (b) time, and (c) utilities. Source: Prepared by the authors.

After applying the rules, the analysis reflected that with the technology in the company, the production levels are "low," and consequently, its profits as well, and obviously, the production and management time was categorized as "high." The chart in **Figure 6** shows that the initial profit level was about 1500 in 6 days, which gives a membership of 1.0, which is low.

```
[ ] rule1 = ctrl.Rule(amount['low'] & time['high'], utilities['low'])

[ ] rule2 = ctrl.Rule(amount['high'] & time['low'], utilities['high'])

[ ] rule3 = ctrl.Rule(amount['half'] | time['half'], utilities['half'])
```

Figure 5.
Fuzzy system rules. Source: Prepared by the authors.

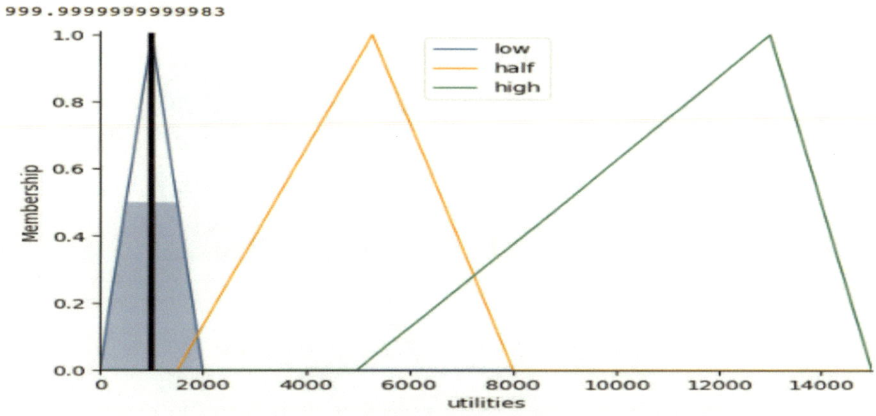

Figure 6.
Fuzzy graph generated at the beginning of the company analysis. Source: Prepared by the authors.

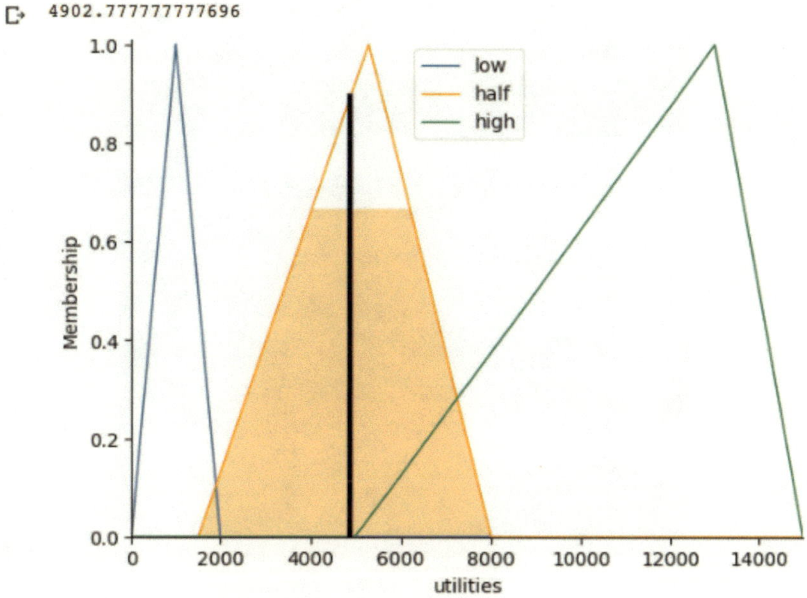

Figure 7.
Fuzzy graph resulting from the implementation of computerized machines. Source: Prepared by the authors.

With this panorama of data and to verify the innovation forecasts in the company, technology based on embedded systems was added, which consisted of the insertion of two intelligent sewing machines to improve profits to 4900, see **Figure 7**.

Finally, technology based on production management systems was added, which controls the flow of products, orders, and deliveries. The design shows the basic operations of insertion and consultation of the products, which are added to the products that enter the company (see **Figure 8a**). In addition, the system shows the

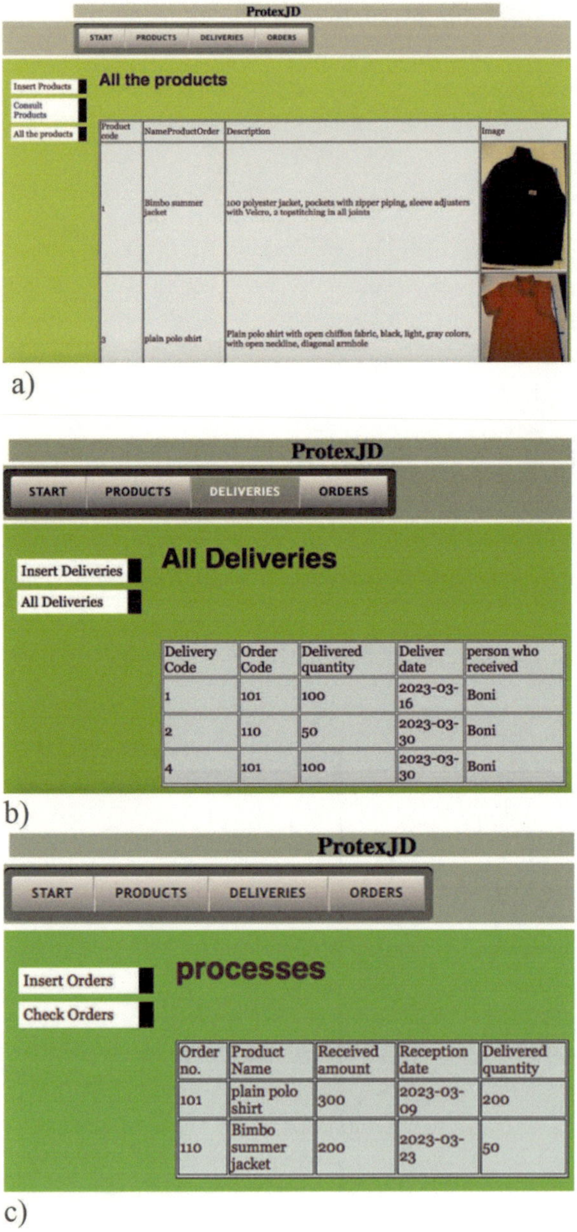

Figure 8.
Management information system. (a) Insertion of products (b) inputs and outputs of products (c) processes. Source: Prepared by the authors.

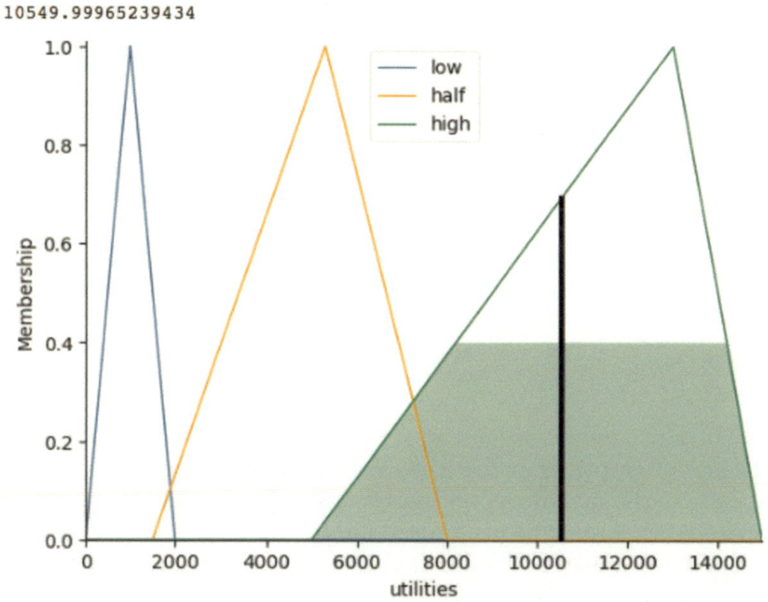

Figure 9.
Fuzzy graph resulting from the implementation of computerized machines and production management system. Source: Prepared by the authors.

production orders along with their control data, which allows the current number of garments to be reflected and displays the result of the arithmetic operation of the inputs and outputs of products (see **Figure 8b**); in addition, the numbers that are stored in the product deliveries section are those that are displayed as final products to update the number of garments that remain to be delivered (see **Figure 8c**). This information system is essential for monitoring production management.

With this latest technology, the profits increased to 10,550 pesos in 6 days, as shown in **Figure 9**, which is marked with the black line, where you can see that the membership was approximately 0.7.

4. Results

The company's technology benefits are summarized in **Table 5**, which shows the state of the profits.

Table 5 shows the fuzzy logic analysis forecast, which suggests that the more significant the technological increase in the company, the more production and profits increase. That seems logical, but it is necessary to show business people how much the benefit of the increase could be so that it serves as a reference.

Concerning time, it decreases the initial quantities produced; that is, if 100 pieces were made at the beginning in 6 days, with technology, the production of those same products over time was reduced by 30 percent.

With the implementation of the first technology, production increased considerably by 120, and it is logical because these machines generate fewer errors fewer excess threads, and each process is done automatically.

They increased those of the second phase by more than 50% and, although it seems that it does not coincide with the products generated, which were 100 more, it is

Phase	Production quantity	Time	Utilities (Mexican pesos)	Membership	Linguistic Variable
Start	100 products	6 days	$1500	1.0	Low
With embedded technology	220 products	6 days	$4900	0.8	Half
With information systems	320 products	6 days	$10,550	0.7	High

Source: prepared by the authors.

Table 5.
Analysis of the production process with fuzzy logic.

understandable, since the management of the system monitors production, and thus prevents the loss of garments or that they are paid twice. In addition, it controls the entries and exits of the inventory, both products and materials, derived from calculating the material that must be used based on the number of garments in the process. It helps save and avoid waste or theft. In the end, profits increased with a high membership of 0.7.

5. Discussion

The fuzzy logic establishes threshold data; in this study, it can be observed that the low membership is 1.0 for 80 products, but if the company produces from 0 to 150, they are in a low range. As the products increase, the "low" membership decreases to become "medium." Analogically, in all phases (low, medium, and high), the same happens with all items of products, time, and profits.

In this way, it is known that if the production was 220 products, its membership was 0.8, that is, to be closer to being within the "high" production set.

In the profits, and considering these data, if the profits were 10,550, he had a membership of 0.8, which is regarded as "high." In a hypothetical case, if the profits had been 7000, the membership would be approximately 0.3, considered high, but less than 0.8.

It is necessary to clarify that there is still a lack of technology to be implemented, which could not only improve profits but could even decrease the human emotional problem generated by production errors, but this analysis, valued in fuzzy logic, provides the basis for it to be used as a methodology to evaluate a company and forecast benefits based on parameters of each company.

6. Conclusions

SMEs support the economy around the world; therefore, looking for strategies to obtain the best results in different aspects is essential. In this case, the innovation occurred in manufacturing and production management. Manufacturing is one of the activities where there are microenterprises that collaborate with a larger company, and it is here where emphasis should be placed on manufacturing processes since their limitations are more significant when it comes to small companies, considering that they are companies formed generally by people who do not know much about technology, nor its benefits and obviously, nor how it could help them have better profits and fewer problems.

Fuzzy logic is proposed in this research chapter as a method that evaluates and validates the manufacturing processes of a company presented as an object of study. The technology incorporated into the company evaluates and validates the results, foreseeing that it can be further improved with the integration of more technology, which makes the company increasingly mature.

The fuzzy methodology was established through rules that manage degrees of uncertainty called "high," "medium," and "low," selected by ranges of data that relate them to the variables "products," "time," and "utilities" that generate their variations.

The use obtained in each implementation stage was reflected in the analysis of the manufacturing process, comparing its results without and with the implementation of technology. It may be logical to know that technology brings benefits, but measuring the certainty of the company's growth is necessary.

Fuzzy technology provides vagueness in the data, which provides certainty that it is within established parameters and gives entrepreneurs an idea of what the technology is doing for their businesses.

With embedded systems technology, one could have the idea that it serves to generate greater production and consequently greater profits, but it is necessary to determine how much the benefit is, in this case, in terms of products, time, and profits. With the information management system, it is not so easy for people to see its benefits, which, in this case, is less time to review the monitoring of production and the input and output of products. It seems simple, but having this knowledge generates less anxiety for microbusiness leaders since they always have in view the number of garments that remain to be delivered, those that have entered the company, and those that are still in production.

Fuzzy analysis clarifies data in the manufacturing process, showing benchmarks in production, time, and profits through languages understood by workers and measured in a language that provides an objective perspective to workers. Saying that production is low, time is short, and profits are high gives leaders a better idea of what they need to adjust in their processes.

The first time the company analysis data was obtained, a company with "low" profits was observed. When the fuzzy analysis of the second stage was carried out, where embedded systems were implemented through automated machines, the results showed graphs with an increase in profits that classified them as "medium." In the third stage, when the information system for production management was implemented, profits reached the "high."

For all of the above, it is concluded that systems analysis using fuzzy logic can show forecasts of the quantities involved, and this can help in planning and, consequently, in decision-making.

Finally, with this method, entrepreneurs could plan and invest in their companies with the certainty that they will be able to obtain profits in a certain time, generating confidence in their investments.

It is important to mention that based on the strategies generated by the analysis with the fuzzy cognitive map, it is necessary to increase the implementation of technology, but this way of measuring progress in the company provides entrepreneurs with the best expectation of the development of their company.; This model may vary from one company to another, but it is a reference for other companies, which, although they will have different data and technology, the results could occur in a similar way.

As already mentioned, SMEs are very important financial entities for the economic development of countries, and this diffuse method could help them grow to have more and better companies and, what is better, help companies survive.

Acknowledgements

Marisol Hernández-Hernández would like to express his appreciation for the support provided by the Technological Institute of Higher Studies of Ixtapaluca through its program of national postdoctoral stays coordinated by CONAHCYT (National Council of Humanities, Sciences, and Technologies).

Author details

Marisol Hernández-Hernández[1]*, Luis Alfonso Bonilla Cruz[2] and Lizbeth Cobián-Romero[2]

1 Autonomous Mexico State University, State of Mexico, Mexico

2 Technological of Higher Studies of Ixtapaluca, Mexico

*Address all correspondence to: mhernandezh@uaemex.mx

References

[1] Alting L. Manufacturing Engineering Processes. In: Boothroyd G, editor. 2nd edition. Londres, Inglaterra: CRC Press; 2020

[2] Inegi. demografía de los establecimientos mipyme en el contexto de la pandemia por covid-19. 2022. Available from: from https://www.inegi.org.mx/contenidos/saladeprensa/aproposito/2022/EAP_Demog_MIPYME22.pdf

[3] García MLS, Uribe JJ. Flujo de efectivo para las pymes: una propuesta para los sectores automotor y de tecnologías de la información en México. Revista Finanzas y Política Económica. 2018;**10**(2):287-308. DOI: 10.14718/revfinanzpolitecon.2018.10.2.3

[4] CAF, Índice De Políticas PYME: América Latina Y El Caribe. 2019. Available from: https://www.caf.com/es/actualidad/noticias/2019/04/indice-de-politicas-pyme-america-latina-y-el-caribe-2019/

[5] World Bank SME Finance: Development News, Research, Data, World Bank, World Bank, s. f. Available from: https://www.worldbank.org/en/topic/smefinance

[6] Organization for Economic Co-operation and Development. SME and Entrepreneurship Outlook 2019. Paris Cedex, Francia: Organization for Economic Co-operation and Development (OECD); 2019

[7] Estrada S, Cano KAF, Joao Aguirre J. Cómo se gestiona la tecnología en las pymes? Diferencias y similitudes entre micro, pequeñas ymedianas empresas. Contaduría y Administración. 2018;**64** (1):72. DOI: 10.22201/fca.24488410e.2019.1812

[8] Villavicencio, Daniel, y Mónica Casalet. VIII. Desarrollo tecnológico en las pequeñas y medianas empresas. Aproximaciones al caso de México. In: Calvo, Thomas, y Bernardo Méndez. Micro y pequeña empresa en México: Frente a los retos de la globalización. México: Centro de estudios mexicanos y centroamericanos; 1995. pp. 191-217. Available from: http://books.openedition.org/cemca/2668

[9] Data México. Industrias Manufactureras: Salarios, producción, inversión, oportunidades y complejidad [Internet]. Data México, México. 2023. Available from: https://www.economia.gob.mx/datamexico/es/profile/industry/manufacturing

[10] Alfonso BM, Eusebio MOC, Flavio MOJ. Manufactura: Conceptos y aplicaciones. Ciudad de México: Grupo Editorial Patria; 2019

[11] Favela-Herrera MKI et al. Herramientas de manufactura esbelta que inciden en la productividad de una organización: modelo conceptual propuesto. Revista lasallista de investigación. 2019;**16**(1):115-133

[12] Feng L, Zhang X, Zhou K. Current problems in China's manufacturing and countermeasures for industry 4.0. EURASIP Journal on Wireless Communications and Networking. 2018; **2018**:1-6

[13] Katiyar JK, Sahu RK. Modern Manufacturing Technology: Spotlight on Future [Internet]. Londres, Inglaterra: Taylor & Francis; 2021. DOI: 10.1201/9781003203162

[14] Andres CR. International commercial logistics. Colombia: Universidad del Norte; 2021

[15] Socconini LV. Lean Company. Más allá de la manufactura. Barcelona: España: Marge Books; 2019

[16] Medina La Plata EH. Consideraciones para implementar exitosamente Business Intelligence. In: Business Intelligence Una guía práctica. Lima, Perú: Universidad Peruana de Ciencias Aplicadas (UPC); 2012

[17] Garrido Á. Los avances de la Inteligencia Artificial. Madrid, España: Dykinson; 2020

[18] Zadeh LA. Fuzzy logic. In: Encyclopedia of Complexity and Systems Science. New York, NY: Springer; 2009. pp. 3985-4009

[19] Luis Izquierdo y Luis Izquierdo, Mamdani fuzzy Systems for Modelling and Simulation: A critical assessment, Journal of Artificial Societies and Social Simulation. 2018;**21**(3):2. DOI: 10.18564/jasss.3660

[20] Rout SS, Misra BB, Samanta S. Competency mapping with Sugeno fuzzy inference system for variable pay determination: A case study. Ain Shams Engineering Journal. 2017;**9**(4): 2215-2226. DOI: 10.1016/j.asej.2017.03.007

[21] Suharjito D, Yulyanto NA. Mobile expert system using fuzzy Tsukamoto for diagnosing cattle disease. Procedia Computer Science. 2017;**116**:27-36. DOI: 10.1016/j.procs.2017.10.005

[22] Buckley JJ, Eslami E. An Introduction to Fuzzy Logic and Fuzzy Sets. Vol. 13. Springer Science & Business Media; 2002

[23] Vaščák J et al. Means of IoT and fuzzy cognitive maps in reactive navigation of ubiquitous robots. Electronics. 2021;**10**(7):809

[24] Benamina M, Atmani B, Benbelkacem S. Diabetes diagnosis by case-based reasoning and fuzzy logic. IJIMAI. 2018;**5**(3):72-80

[25] Peckol JK. Introduction to Fuzzy Logic. Nashville, TN, Estados Unidos de América: John Wiley & Sons; 2021

[26] Felix G et al. A review on methods and software for fuzzy cognitive maps. Artificial Intelligence Review. 2019;**52**: 1707-1737

[27] Papageorgiou EI, Salmeron JL. Methods and algorithms for fuzzy cognitive map-based modeling. In: Fuzzy Cognitive Maps for Applied Sciences and Engineering: From Fundamentals to Extensions and Learning Algorithms. Berlin, Heidelberg: Springer Berlin Heidelberg; 2013. pp. 1-28

[28] Çoban O, Seçme G. Prediction of socio-economical consequences of privatization at the firm level with fuzzy cognitive mapping. Information Sciences. 2005;**169**(1–2):131-154

[29] Papageorgiou K et al. Fuzzy cognitive map-based sustainable socio-economic development planning for rural communities. Sustainability. 2019; **12**(1):305

[30] Marisol HH, Cruz LAB, Olmos PS. Technology and innovation in organizations using fuzzy systems. TEM Journal. 2022;**11**:4

Chapter 4

Europe's Raw Materials Supply Chain: Front-End Considerations

Antje Wittenberg, Daniel de Oliveira, Tom Bide, Julie Hollis, Siim Nirgi, Gorazd Žibret, Håvard Gautneb, Martiya Sadeghi, Rafael Navarro Domínguez and Boris Malyuk

Abstract

Supply chains are linked for specific purpose and by something. Hence, the respective links of the chain must be hooked in the right place, sufficiently strong, and have to start somewhere. This chapter looks at the raw materials supply chain as the first link in a commodity supply, from the European Union (EU) perspective. Aspects of the raw material potential of critical or strategic mineral resources in Europe, its further exploration, and the concept of modifying factors are considered, and reporting systems of resources and reserves are described, underpinned by examples of mineral potentials in different regions of the EU. Thus, targeted exploration of raw materials, especially within the framework of national geological research, serves to support a sustainable and resilience supply chain. EU projects, such as GeoERA and Geological Service for EU, assist in shaping the tailor-made exploration programs fit for providing mineral data publicly available through EuroGeoSurveys' European Geological Data Infrastructure. In the future, raw materials may be seen as global public goods required to address many challenges, from the climate crisis to geopolitical instability; therefore, the society could conceptualize them in a new way, from a dominant investment returns-oriented viewpoint to one linked to delivering global objectives.

Keywords: exploration, raw materials, sourcing, strategic, critical, potential, Europe, resource management, UNFC

1. Introduction

Supply chains may be defined as including all stages involved in producing and delivering a final product, including managing supply and demand, sourcing raw materials and parts, manufacturing and assembly, and warehousing and inventory. They are essential for maintaining and improving the well-being of societies worldwide [1]. Mineral and energy raw materials are of particular importance, for example, [2, 3] in many supply chains, because they provide the basis for products, as well as they are essential for the supply of energy [4, 5]. Mineral raw materials can be divided into primary raw materials, which are extracted from the Earth's

IntechOpen

crust, and secondary raw materials, which are produced in the process of recycling. This chapter will focus on primary inorganic raw materials of natural origin and in particular on metals and metalliferous minerals (e.g., Fe, Cu, Pb, Zn, Au), and industrial minerals (e.g., salt, clay, barite, fluorite, limestone), while construction minerals (e.g., sand, gravel, marble, granite, basalts) are only touched upon. Primary raw materials are the starting point of the complex supply chains in Europe and beyond [6].

Primary raw materials pass through extraction, beneficiation, and transport processes before being introduced into the manufacturing process of various goods. Different regions and countries are involved in these actions. Numerous players with different interests and objects have to play together, including producers and manufacturers, suppliers, traders, and customers, ensuring the flow of goods and products on the global markets as much as in the local one. Establishing global relationships by upstream and downstream industries, including the primary raw material production, is part of common strategies [7, 8]. The functioning of supply chains is also influenced by the collaboration, innovation, trade relationships, and relationships among various disciplines and stakeholders, up to foreign affairs.

Europe's key industries, including automotive, electronics, and pharmaceuticals, need a steady flow of essential goods made from minerals and metals [9], and the requirement is not limited to them. Moreover, economy is highly dependent on reliable and timely supply of raw materials and semifinished or finished goods [10, 11]. Geographic considerations have been a key component for building up raw materials supply chains for centuries when manufacturing facilities, for example, were established in proximity to raw material sources and related refinement facilities to minimize logistical challenges, including transportation costs. Nowadays, geographic location is of less importance since many supply chains are globalized [12, 13]. The belief in a fair and open market was high, while in Europe raw material prospection, exploration, and mining were often considered as unfavorable [14]. Yet, many downstream industries in Europe have withdrawn their direct engagement in mining since 1990, while new players arrived on the global market. During this time, the demand for commodities has increased significantly and with it the competition for the available resources [15].

The plentiful crises of the last decade have pointed out the importance of undisrupted raw materials supply chains, highlighted also by headlines of daily news [16–20]. Events that are not only difficult to influence, such as natural disasters, political instabilities, or changes in trade policy, but also labordisputes and the like can lead to significant bottlenecks, price fluctuations, or delays that disrupt the entire raw materials supply chain [21–24]. Any market distortion or failure has its consequences, some of which have hit Europe's economy unexpectedly hard [25].

Thus, modern supply chain planning benefits from a good knowledge of primary raw material deposits, the local conditions, where they are mined and processed, and the framework conditions under which the partners in the supply chain perform [26, 27]. Such planning enables companies to anticipate potential supply shortages, assess risks, and develop strategies to secure a stable and reliable supply of raw materials. At the same time, sustainability practices, such as responsible sourcing, ethical labor practices, and minimizing the environmental footprint associated with raw material extraction, are becoming increasingly important [19, 27–29]. This is due to both the need to meet production demands and consumer concerns about the associated environmental and social impacts [30–32].

Hence, it is currently widely recognized that functional supply chains serve our societies through the functioning of our economies by providing jobs and high living standards. This holds at least for developed and industrialized countries. Thus, building up resilient supply chains has become as much of strategic importance by governments [21, 22, 33–38] as by industry [38–40] and is a matter of many supply risk studies in the twenty-first century [41–44].

2. The raw materials supply chain front-end approach

Over the last decades, Asia has become an important player on the global market. China, in particular, has demonstrated strength in all parts of the raw materials value chain. It continues to build its position with strategic activities abroad, for example [42, 45–48]. Supported by strategic exploration programs, China is systematically improving its knowledge of national resources and acquiring competencies in the most preferred technologies [44, 45, 49, 50]. Other countries, such as Saudi Arabia and Indonesia, for example, are gaining more and more market dominance on raw materials such as nickel, cobalt, gold, and their related supply chain. The increasing global competition and the very fragile supply chains call urgently for actions and smart strategies by companies and governments [51, 52]. Strategic thinking starts often only at the extraction stage [1, 22, 53]. Yet, all of the supply chain stepping-stones are more or less obviously related to mining. In contrast, the very first step—the exploration of potential resources—is often overlooked, while the general principles still hold [8]. Thus, a first step toward greater resilience by promoting import independence is knowledge about one's own raw material deposits (potentials), especially their distribution, quantities, and qualities (see 3.2). The regional and National Geological Survey Organizations (NGSOs) and their European umbrella organization "EuroGeoSurveys" act particularly, but not exclusively, in the first segments of the supply chain that sets the raw material value chain in motion (**Figure 1**).

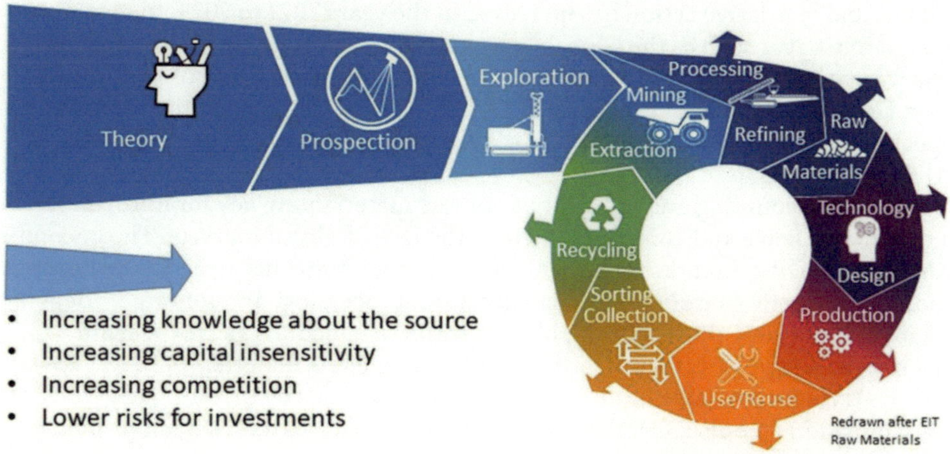

Figure 1.
The supply and value chain of raw materials shows the importance of the first segments of the supply chain—From theory (e.g., geological modeling) to exploration—To turn the wheel of a (circular) economy, redrawn after ref. [54]. The smaller arrows indicate the inevitable loss of resources associated with the respective segment of chain link, making mining indispensable even in the best possible circular economy.

2.1 The political dimension of exploration and mining data in the raw material supply chain

Europe is the only populated continent that has seen a decline in mining production by 31% in the period 2000–2021 [55]. Lack of investment in European exploration, mining, and processing is a key reason for the EU's current raw materials supply chain weakness. For example, the supply chain squeezes on magnesium [56], gallium and germanium [57, 58], illustrates China's dominance on several commodities along the value chain. Europe's weak position is also caused by limited focus on international raw materials strategic partnerships and diversification of sourcing over the same period.

This vulnerability has not gone unnoticed in the EU. As far back as 2008, the European Commission established the raw materials initiative, which set the framework for the future EUs raw material supply security. The initiative consists of three pillars: (i) access to raw materials on world markets at undistorted conditions, (ii) foster sustainable supply of raw materials from European sources, and (iii) reduce the EU's consumption of primary raw materials [59, 60], followed by the European Innovation Partnership (EIP) on raw materials, the raw material alliance, strategic partnerships on raw materials and not yet adopted Critical Raw Materials Act (CRMA) [33]. Within the Act European Commission defined a) critical (CRMs) and b) strategic raw materials (SRMs) as a) materials of high importance to the economy, while the supply is associated with a high risk of disruption; b) crucial to technologies important to Europe's green and digital ambitions and for defense and space applications, while being subject to potential supply risks in the future [58, 59]. The European Commission updates periodically its list of CRMs. The list of 2023's contains a total of 34 individual raw materials or groups of raw materials [61].

Unfortunately, such EU actions have been overtaken by subsequent events that heavily impacted European raw materials supply chains, including the COVID-19 pandemic, the Russian war in Ukraine, and the international race for mineral security to meet the ambitions of the required green transition. As a result, the pace of EU strategic and legislative action has increased in the years 2021 to 2023, for example, through initiatives such as the Global Gateway [62] and InvestEU [63], as well as implementation of the European Climate Law [64], REPowerEU Plan [65], the Green Deal Industrial Plan [66], the Chips Act [67, 68], the Corporate Sustainability Reporting Directive [69, 70], as well as the recently proposed Net Zero Industry Act [71] and CRMA [33].

Sustainable sourcing and efficient use of raw materials are key for Europe's long-term resilience and competitiveness in the face of global markets. The upcoming CRMA sets the benchmarks for annual consumption of raw materials in the European Union for domestic sourcing through extraction, processing, and for import dependencies from a single third country. Moreover, these benchmarks are the main objective of Europe's strategy on critical and strategic raw materials [43]. Moreover, the EU is trying to increase its knowledge on raw materials by investing in geoscience data acquisition (see also 3.1). Estonia, for example, focuses its "General principles of Earth's crust policy until 2050" on the collection of geological information and the use of the national resources the most profitable way for the country [72]. At national level, several countries, including Austria, Finland, France, Germany, Sweden, and more recently Norway and Spain, have developed or updated strategic initiatives, such as the "Roadmap for the Sustainable Management of Mineral Raw Materials" [73–75]. Some strategic actions have been devised to stimulate the industrial sectors related to mineral raw materials, thereby ensuring access to essential mineral resources. These initiatives include the implementation of diverse types of instruments: a) regulatory mechanisms that align mining legislation with the European Union's action plans, b) sector-specific tools that secure the principles of the circular economy, knowledge enhancement, and ensure regulatory compliance, c) cross-cutting instruments to foster public-private collaboration and enhance citizen involvement in decision-making, as well as risk finance instruments to stimulate capital investments, and d) an impetus toward research spanning the entire value chain (from cradle-to-gate [76]). The NGSOs play a key role in examining the geological potential of individual countries. This is why the CRMA sets a precedent in identifying the NGSOs, for the first time in EU legislation, as central point to provide required geoscientific data and expert advice to drive domestic exploration investment, which is currently a limiting factor in maintaining the uninterrupted raw materials supply chains (point 1, above). Such strategic approach has been successfully applied in China and led to its economic boom in the 21st century, for example [77].

2.2 Elements of a strong raw materials supply chain

Building strong, reliable supply chains that fulfil the concept of sustainability is the golden rule. Like investments, this requires a good governance structure, reliable political and legal frameworks, fair tax systems, and transport and tariff regulations [78, 79]. It also requires good working conditions, such as high work safety and low risk of labor disputes, as well as low risks for natural disasters (e.g., weather, earthquakes, landsides) that can affect the functioning of a supply chain [10, 80, 81].

Key elements of a robust raw materials supply chain are as follows:

- Access to reliable exploration data and mineral resource databases of primary and secondary raw materials.
- Access to primary production, from mining to processing of the ores and concentrates of the raw material demanded.
- Access to secondary production, from collection to recovery and refining.
- Access to the downstream production of the finished or semifinished products.

Chemical elements are not equally abundant nor equally distributed on the Earth's crust [82]. Mineral resources must be extracted where they occur, and this will affect the environment where they are exploited. What sounds like a truism, however, sets the framework where, how, when, and by whom these resources can be used at all. Ideally, these key elements take place in a setting, free of geopolitical risk and with access to water, (green) energy, infrastructure, and similar.

3. How exploration and extraction fits in the supply chain

The supply chain for minerals is fed by continuous investment into investigations over the location and properties of minerals found in the Earth's subsurface. The importance of exploration to the mineral supply chain is highlighted by several reports [83–85]. This is conducted at a wide variety of scales and levels of details (i.e., from remote sensing surveys and regional airborne geophysics to site-level detailed exploration drilling) by different actors from public research organizations to private companies and investors. While it will always be commercial entities that are responsible for bringing mineral projects into production, state agencies, such as NGSOs provide an important role in creating and providing data and knowledge through exploration on the geological potential for resources. Their unbiased assessment of geological potential helps guide exploration and mining activities by identifying areas that are most likely to yield economically viable deposits. These assessments can be used to target specific regions for more detailed commercial exploration, determine the best drilling locations, and inform decisions related to resource extraction and state aid level as on company level.

3.1 Geological data and information

Geological data and information underpin key elements of a robust raw materials supply chain. Data from NGSO's, on a national and regional scale, provide information on the structure and composition of the Earth's subsurface that influences the likelihood of mineral deposit occurrences. Due to new technologies, changes in demand, and new environmental regulatory requirements there is a constant need to keep geological data up to date. This importance is acknowledged in the CRMA Article 20 [33].

Assessments and forecasts on the national potentials for raw materials and the related industry are done by many NGSOs. These lay down the treasure trove of national raw materials, where in Europe commodities relevant for infrastructure and construction, such as aggregates, sand, and gravel, are the top commodities in terms of quantities, while in terms of value industrial miners (e.g., potash) and metals play an important role, for example [86]. While there is no geological shortage for many raw materials, there might be a shortfall in the availability and access to the treasure deposits. Moreover, resource inventories form the basic data critical for underpinning decision-making relating to resource management for a wide range now widely implemented, or upcoming policies from national government such as security of supply, decarbonization, circular economy, etc. [87].

The NGSOs have developed the European Geological Data Infrastructure (EGDI, www.europe-geology.eu) applying the FAIR (Findable, Accessible, Interoperable, Reusable) data principles that provide open access on maps and aggregated national data on production, trade, resources, reserves, and exploration at commodity level.

Since establishment of the 2008 Raw Materials Initiative, the European Commission has acknowledged the key role of research, development, and innovation in driving investments in and advancement of the European raw material sector and the role of collaborative science. Underpinning funding instruments (e.g., the current Horizon Europe program, EIT-Raw Materials, ERA-MIN) stimulate research and innovation in the field of raw materials and cooperation among and between various research institutions, educational institutions, public bodies, NGSOs, and industry. The projects ProMine, ORAMA, GeoERA, SCRREEN (1-3), FutuRaM, and GSEU are good examples of such cooperations [14].

Notably, many of such projects involve or involved NGSO as coordinators or partners. The importance of NGSOs in collaborative pan-European projects that aim to deliver an European perspective on CRMs stems from their national mandates to collect, archive, and deliver geoscientific data and knowledge. As a collaborative network of NGSOs, linked through the umbrella organization EuroGeoSurveys, this has brought EU-level benefits in the form of a committed approach to data harmonization and delivery of EU-scale products. Such contributions have been progressively built through projects such as EGDI Scope, which developed the framework for a common open subsurface data infrastructure, followed by GeoERA, which delivered multiple pan-European harmonized datasets related to minerals, energy, and groundwater. Currently, the NGSOs and other key partners collaborate through the Geological Service for Europe (GSEU) project, which takes data collection, harmonization, and delivery further, developing the EGDI into a knowledge hub, while preparing and delivering extensive data products, including CRM data. Such data and data products can then inform policy makers, expert and layman and allowing the assessment, evaluation and interpretation of genetic and prospectivity aspects of selected commodities for example [88, 89].

3.2 Reporting codes and standards

To understand raw material supply chains, it is important to use exploration data to conceptualize and quantify, where resources are and of which quality. There are many different types of data and metrics regarding these aspects of mineral exploration and extraction, but the most fundamental commonly used of these is the concept of "resources" and "reserves."

The most widely accepted definition published by the Committee for Mineral Reserves International Reporting Standards (CRIRSCO) is in simple terms and reserves are that part of an identified resource that could be economically extracted at the time of the assessment [90]. The determination of mineral resources and reserves is the means by which deposits that are currently economically extractable (reserves) are distinguished from those where economic extraction of a commodity is potentially feasible (resources).

This estimation comes along with uncertainties. Stepwise, these uncertainties are minimized to increase the likelihood of success. Those steps are verifying the basic conceptual idea of the location of a mineral occurrence in the field. That includes a) converting exploration results from a prospective area into a quantitative estimate of the amount, quality, and distribution of the target mineral (e.g., by drilling, assaying, and preliminary laboratory testing to determine if the mineral can be effectively separated from its host rock) and b) detailed evaluation of all aspects of geological confidence, technical feasibility, environmental, social factors, etc., and may take several years to complete. The vast majority of reconnaissance exploration projects are abandoned without ever verifying the presence of a discovered resource because one or more of these factors limit the financial viability of the project in the market. The next step is the determination of the technological setup that makes mining and process feasible and includes a) comprehensive technical investigations to confirm the size and grade of the deposit, b) determination of geological and physical constraints that may affect how a mine needs to be designed and constructed, how the extraction can take place technicality and how the extracted material need to be treated to liberate the target materials. In conjunction with further modifying factors (MF), a mineral reserve is then defined with a full financial analysis to confirm economic viability, usually associated with a bankable feasibility study. However, this reserve is valid only at a particular point in time (as market, regulatory, political, and social conditions can vary significantly over sometimes even short time scales) and is best regarded as a working inventory of the amount of minerals available to extract at the time the assessment was made. The work required to calculate resources and

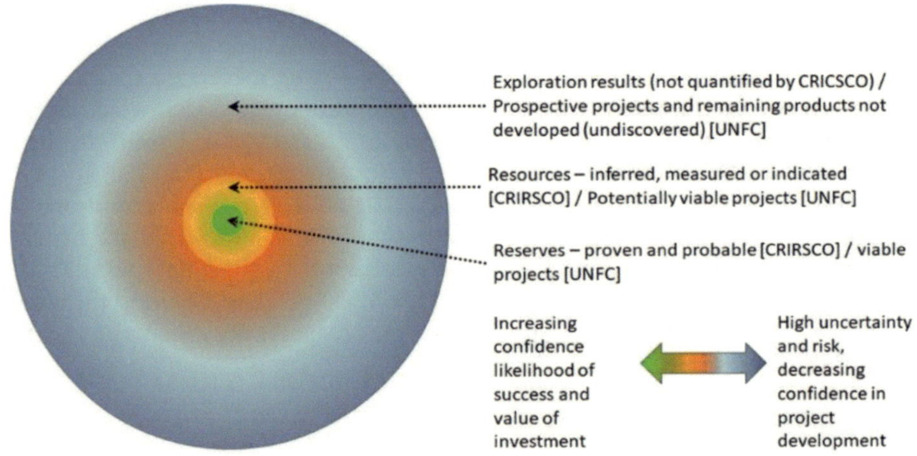

Figure 2.
Schematic representation of the relative size of the quantities represented by the terms resources and reserves (not to scale) and how the most commonly used definitions fit within this.

reserves is very costly and, as such, project operators typically only define resources and reserves to the level that it will be possible to obtain further investment. Thus, the quantity of undiscovered resources is almost always very much larger than that of discovered resources, which, in turn, is much larger than that of reserves, often by many orders of magnitude [91]. Each successive class is associated with an increasing level of confidence, corresponding to the increasing amount of data required for its classification (**Figure 2**). Forecasting with the assumption that "all we known is all there is" (e.g., [92]) has been shown to be incorrect by, for example [93].

At the very early stage of exploration, the quality and accessibility of data and information sets the course for future resource availability. This pre-production part of the supply chain must continue to provide data on regional prospectivity through to actual resources. This will allow the necessary exploration investment to flow and sustain the activity required for a small percentage of exploration projects to be successful.

3.3 Modifying factors

The application of the modifying factors (MF) constitutes an integral part of the mineral reserve estimation process (mineral reserves are mineral resources that are economically exploitable under current technological and market conditions). Such adequate consideration during the estimation and reporting of mineral reserves is crucial [94]. Hence, the MF are acknowledged by all international standard codes for reporting (see 3.2). Commonly, the following key MF are considered in alphabetic order [94–96]:

- Beneficiation (e.g., metallurgical recoveries).
- Economic (e.g., raw materials quality, royalties, exchange rates, transport costs, final product, and its market conditions).
- Environmental (i.e., Environmental Impact Assessment (EIA), by mining, mining residuals, and after mines lifetime).

- Infrastructural (e.g., physical access, energy, water supply, labor, and facilities).
- Legal (e.g., permitting procedures—duration, reliability for exploration, and mining rights).
- Marketing and market developments (e.g., price and demand forecasts).
- Mining (technical and geological aspects, e.g., mining losses and dilution).
- Social and governmental (establishing trust and getting acceptance and the license to operate).

Ideally, these key MF are considered adequately and reported in a transparent and understandable format to allow a comprehensive risk assessment on all aspects. All of these MF will probably also be considered in reserve estimations for secondary raw materials in the future.

3.4 Comparability of reporting codes and standards

Development of potential exploration projects requires risk estimation, including expectations on volumes, cost, and other associated risks. The mineral industry typically needs these estimates to communicate with stock exchanges and investors. The majority of industry data adheres to the International Reporting (ITR) template in CRIRSCO style, an internationally accepted standard designed specifically for the reporting of results to stock exchanges and investors to ensure a consistent standard is applied [90]. As a result, any reported "reserves" should not be considered as physical stocks, but as economic entities that have a realistic chance of being extracted in the foreseeable future (typically within 3–5 years). While these international reporting standards are a mandatory requirement by international stock exchanges, there is a lack of requirement to use them in Europe outside the financial sector.

National governments and regional bodies conversely require data that may be more focused on long-term strategic planning and less on short- to medium-term investment decisions. As a result, many countries have their own specific way of recording such information. The wide variety of definitions can lead to incompatible data being aggregated and misunderstandings about what data points represent, which can lead to poor policy decisions [93, 97].

To establish interoperability of data from different reporting standards, the United Nations Economic Commission for Europe (UNECE) has developed a code, namely the United Nations Framework Classification (UNFC), bridging differences between different standards; thus, the UNFC allows a comparable representation of data, **Figure 3** [98].

The importance of clear, reliable, and comparable data is noted in the CRMA, which calls for an obligatory use of an international standard the United Nations Framework Classification (UNFC) for reporting resource data of projects considered strategic in the EU. New research, development, and innovation projects under EIT Raw Materials are already evaluated according to the UNFC on the basis of their economic, technical, social, and environmental feasibility for resource production [98–100]. The various classification criteria are set up in three categories based on a) *environmental-socioeconomic viability* (E-category), b) *project status and feasibility* (F-category), and c) *degree of confidence in the estimates* (G-category), **Figure 3** [98].

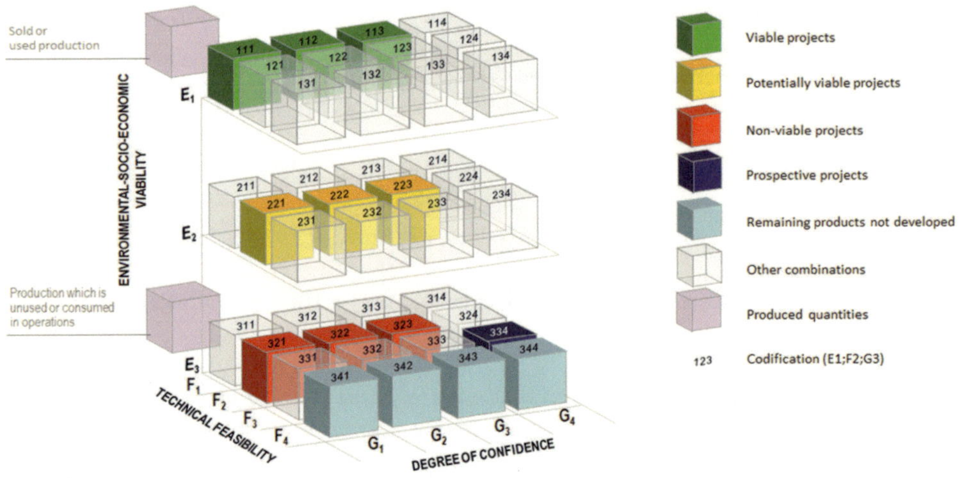

Figure 3.
The UNFC classification system. From United Nations framework classification for resources updated 2019, UNECE, © (2022) United Nations. Reprinted with the permission of the United Nations [98].

3.5 The use of raw material reporting data in understanding supply chains

Exploration activity and subsequent data reported by industry will be focused on maximizing economic value for investors. This may cause issues with knowledge gaps around commodities where they may be a mismatch between economic returns to the extractive industry and the strategic needs of a country or region. For instance, with regard critical raw materials, these are often produced as by- or co-products of other primary mineral production (cobalt as by-product of nickel production or rhenium, tellurium, gold, and selenium as by-products of copper extraction, as examples) [101–103]. These may not be of primary interest to investors as they may have a small contribution to economic feasibility of a mining project. Similarly, critical minerals, which may occur in minor amounts in deposits or those that might occur in mining residuals (heaps and tailings), are often even not analyzed or reported.

This can be at odds with the intense focus on CRMs by national governments. However, it can also counteract opportunities for transdisciplinary—or niche – solutions, as well as new business models. The UNFC may provide an advantage here by providing easy understandable and comparable information for different projects and/or commodities, including those that are currently not economically extract, meeting the wider [104]. According to UNFC, details on MF like ecological, social, technical, and financial aspects can be outlined in a comparable way and allows comparison of projects of different nature for decision-making. Significant barriers in terms of technical, environmental, or societal constraints can be identified and monitored assisting governments and companies to develop suitable measurements to overcome such barriers for projects of general interest (e.g., projects required for the energy transition). Countries, such as Finland, Sweden, Norway, Hungary, and Ukraine, for example, provide or plan to provide standardized and harmonized, UNFC and INSPIRE-compliant mineral data to the pan-European digital platforms on the whole range of minerals with a special emphasis on strategic minerals [105].

Moreover, the UNFC reporting is flexible enough to include data on quantities of material that are considered currently noneconomic. This data, often collated in national inventories by NGSs and mining authorities, is critical for understanding the pipeline of available minerals over decadal times or longer, as well as minerals that may currently be uneconomic to extract now but may be in the future. Currently, there are a couple of projects for mining critical and strategic raw materials in the pipeline that build on such data treasures that form the bulk of mineral potential on national and regional scales. In the cases of Zinnwald Lithium Project at the Czech-German border, for example, adding new data using modern technologies will provide answers to questions on what may currently be in production and what may be produced over the next five or so years. Yet, at the moment, it is impossible to answer many questions currently asked by those with concerns over supply chains, such as, where indigenous production of certain minerals is possible over longer timescales or what the geological availability may be if certain policy decisions were implemented or economic barriers significantly changed. Regardless of the shortfalls, the UNFC system is still best suited to resource reporting and aggregation of resource quantities at national and regional scales, thereby facilitating decision-making on large-scale, long-term, and resource management.

4. Europe's geological potential

The European territory contains some areas, which are favorable for finding the occurrences of mineralization. Geological studies of such areas facilitate genetic studies of ore deposits, putting emphasis on their metallogenetic relationships in space and time, which are fundamental for determining new mineral exploration targets. The geological evolution of the European terrains identified several favorable conditions for the formation of a variety of mineral deposits. These deposits are unevenly distributed geographically because they formed in a various epoch of the Earth history and can form regional clusters. These clusters or areas are called metallogenic provinces or districts [106]. An active interface with all types of subsoil resources, their location, mining or oil-gas status, related reserves, possibilities of use, needs of each industrial sector, and also risks impact that their exploitation would have on the environment and is a starting point for drawing up viable and long-term strategies by lowering the uncertainties and assisting in fostering the raw material resilience [107].

As the geological potential is an expert estimate or interpretation based on available data and knowledge at a given time, it rather provides an indication of where exploration efforts may be more promising [108]. However, it can also be impacted by additional MF, including company strategies, data maturity and reliability, commodity prices, geopolitical issues, and future market outlooks.

The mineral potential of Europe has been investigated at all levels from small exploration companies to government. It can be seen as an indicator of various parameters, such as a) known deposits occurrences, b) share on public revenue, c) share on gross domestic product (GDP), d) public acceptance, e) competing commercial sectors interested to use the same space, or f) technical readiness, for example.

Potential is, therefore, a function of the geological setting, the physical accessibility, and the level of detail of geological information. In the case of Europe, seven mineral-hosting metallogenic belts/areas/provinces are recognized, **Figure 4**.

Each mineral commodity is distributed in specific geographical locations that contain similar geological structures, including host rocks, state of rock alteration, and similar structural domains, as detected by the GeoERA project on Forecasting

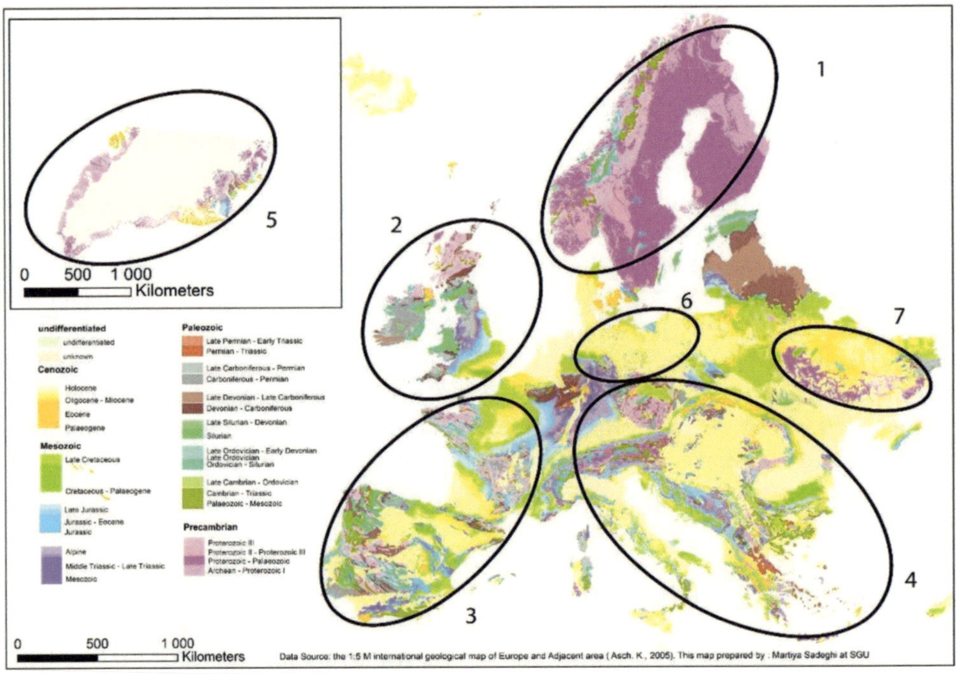

Figure 4.
An overview of major metallogenic belts and endowment of Europe and Greenland modified after refs. [105, 106, 109] And the main metallogenetic areas in Europe listed according to their most common abundance. 1: Fennoscandian shield with potential for Fe, Cu, Zn, Pb, Ni, Cr, Ti, Au, Ag, Te, Se, Mo, Co, Li, graphite, Be, REE, Sc, Si, V, Sb, Bi, Nb, Ta, In, Ge, PGM; 2: Britain and Ireland with potential for Zn, Pb, Ag, Sn, Cu, Ni, Mo, Au, barite, fluorspar, Li, Co, Be, Sb, W, PGM; 3: Iberian-Variscan belt with potential for Cu, Zn, Pb, Ni, Au, Ag, Al, Se, Mn, Li, Co, Si, W, In, Ta, Nb, Be, Bi, Ga, fluorspar, barite; 4: Tethyan/Carpathian-Balkan with potential for Cu, Zn, Pb, Ni, Al, Cr, Mo, Au, Ag, Re, Se, Li, Co, Mn, Sb, W, Bi, REE, PGM, Sc, Ge, V, Nb, Ta, Mg, graphite, magnesite, fluorspar, barite, borate; 5: North Atlantic/Greenland with potential for Fe, Cu, Zn, Ni, Cr, Ti, Zr, Sn, Ag, Au, REE, Nb, Ta, W, Co, PGM; 6: Fore-Sudetic with potential for Cu, Zn, Ni, Sn, In, Ag, Co, Li, W, Mo, Au, Se, Re, PGM; 7: Ukrainian shield with potential for Fe, Mn, Ni, Co, Ti, Au, Li, U, Be, REE, Sc, V, Nb, Ta, Zr, graphite.

and Assessing Europe's Strategic Raw Materials Need (FRAME) for example [106, 110, 111]. These differences are expressed in **Figure 5** that shows (A) the lithium metallogenic belts that differ significantly to those of (B) cobalt metallogenic belts. For further details, see https://data.geus.dk/egdi/?mapname=egdi_geoera_frame#baslay=baseMapGEUS&extent=1139240,1,345,340,7,499,790,4,120,660&layers = frame_li_occurrences_deposits,frame_lithium_metallogenic_areas [88].

4.1 Paving the way for exploration activities in Europe

Exploration is a constant task for all actors given the fact that needs by industry is developing as well as technologies used to discover and to mine unknown deposits and to process ores. Chemical elements, which are now important to our economies, have been of low interest for centuries, and hence rather a target of academic interest only. Systematic exploration for these elements and for deep-seated deposits has started rather recently. Thus, in Europe, many mineral/metal potential maps are based on data that has been collected within the last century. Further progress depends on: the improvements in exploration methods and technologies (from geophysics to drilling technologies), more efficient and environmentally sustain mining

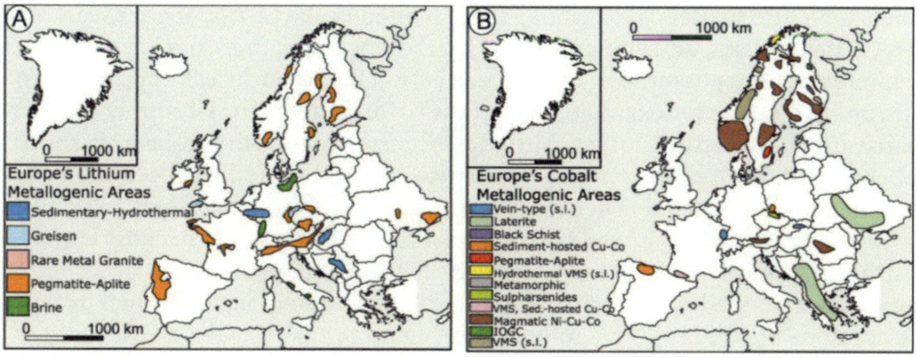

Figure 5.
Metallogenic belt maps for lithium (A) and cobalt (B). Modified after refs. [106, 112].

process and minerals processing technologies, on the global price market of the target raw materials (see Section 3.3), and on the ability of geologists to identify new potential areas for greenfield exploration, which means the exploration in the areas of no known historical mining or exploration activities.

The incoming CRMA calls on members states to set up National Exploration Programmes, which will become a mandatory task as stated in CRMA Article 18 [33]. The exploration potential of Europe can be demonstrated in various forms: be they from recent success stories of new mineral finds in both brownfield and greenfield areas, by innovation regarding new sources of minerals, or by advanced mathematical means. One example combining many forms in advances is the discovery of the Kiruna rare earth elements (REE) deposit owned by the state company LKAB in Sweden, which is said to contain one million metric tons of rare earth oxides. This discovery could pave the way for REE to start being mined in Europe is such a successful example of brownfield exploration. Yet, REEs deposits are not scarce but requires smart technological solutions to be further processed and separated. Hence, the REE-bearing ores (and tailings) of Kiruna will be separated by a new chromatography-based technology developed by REEtec (https://ree-map.com/). This has the potential to be a game changer. The separated individual REE in oxide form, which will, in turn, be converted to metal by the British Less Common Metals Ltd. (LCM). In addition, the rare earth processing factory in nearby Estonia (https://www.silmet.ee/) that produces a variety of high-purity rare earth materials from mixed REE feedstock. Products include neodymium-praseodymium (NdPr) oxide as one of its kind in the European Union being currently the only industrial-scale rare earth separation plant in full-scale operation in Europe. Moreover, a sintered rare earth permanent magnet factory is being built in the same location that will certainly contribute to the global supply chain. Further down the supply chain companies as the German Vacuumschmeltze GmbH (VAC) will use these materials to produce permanent magnets and magnetocaloric alloys, all needed for the energy transformation of the society. With these links connected and all placed in Europe a step toward resilient supply chains in a cradle-to-gate scenario similar to the battery challenges is made [113].

A huge driver for innovative research is the efforts to meet the UN sustainable development goals, which also pushes the development of innovative ways to extract lithium from European geothermal fluids sourced from geothermal and hydrocarbon drill holes [112], which is a potential nontraditional source of this metal. Similar leached-type lithium deposits (salars) are exploited in the Li-triangle at the borders of Argentina, Bolivia, and Chile [114–117]. In recent years, there has been considerable interest for the potential of lithium extraction from southwest England, France, Spain, and Germany, for example, to feed the battery raw material supply chain from both hard rock and brine sources. Although occurrences of lithium-bearing minerals and brines have been noted previously, no detailed exploration had been undertaken due to the previous low value in lithium and a lack of historical interest, a situation, which has dramatically changed in recent years. This has resulted in considerable investment in new drilling and geological evaluation and qualification of resources in two projects as well as new technology for the processing of geothermal brines to be developed [118, 119]. This activity is being undertaken against a backdrop of increased interest in metal mining in southwest England for a variety of other metals due to the current focus on critical raw materials. Southwest England has a long mining history and was once a global mining hub. To ensure that any future development makes this renaissance of metals mining a success for everyone in Cornwall, researchers have been collaborating with policymakers and the industry using the UNFC to help regional stakeholders consider the whole range of sustainable development actions, which are needed for well-being of all. This is done by first using the UNFC to classify projects in the area with the intention to understand the development stage they are in and the barriers they may face. Furthermore, these are integrated with the United Nations Resource Management System (UNRMS) to give a strategic view of environmental impacts and how they can be linked with regional initiatives, to ensure that a social licence to operate is maintained and incorporated geoscience data into the decision making process [120]. Contrary, the discovery of the one of the largest lithium deposits in the world in western Serbia attracted interests from the global mining companies to extract this commodity, in particular the Rio Tinto Group, which planned to start mining operations in 2023. However, the project faced severe public opposition and has many environmental concerns, so the project has been canceled so far. In a similar situation is the Valdefores project in Cáceres (Spain), operated by the company Infinity Lithium, which has encountered strong opposition from the public opinion and local politicians. This opposition primarily stems from the proximity to the city and the potential environmental impact on the territory. These examples point out that the socioeconomic factors can be of equal, if not of greater importance than geological or technological ones.

EU projects, such as exploration and information systems (EIS, https://eis-he.eu/tool/), develop innovative exploration tools that push the limits in earth observation further while using artificial intelligence (AI) for curation of huge datasets. Using digitalized information for statistical approaches and different GIS techniques to deliver maps showing favorable areas referring to a specific commodity is becoming a common praxis described elsewhere [121, 122]. Such methods allow prospectivity mapping of the favorability of occurrences of a nonrandom phenomenon and quantitative evaluation to highlight areas of known mineralization and delineate targets for further investigation.

Mineral exploration presents a set of unique challenges, which vary from place to place, including working in remote and inaccessible locations, cost and capital requirements, geological complexity, technological limitations, legal and regulatory hurdles, market volatility, depth of exploration, limited success rates, environmental and social considerations (the so-called "social license to operate"), health and security, and political instability. These are all part of MF considerations [123].

The latter two are the most difficult to overcome and predict and they affect almost all exploration activities. Whereas the public acceptance of mining is usually negative in Europe, there is a great need for completely transparent population-engaging mechanisms in place from the very beginning. One such example can be found in Estonia, where a deposit of the critical raw material phosphorite that had been thoroughly investigated and already mined during the twentieth century was disapproved due to the public outcry because of several reasons, that is. demographic, environmental, and political issues. Hence, new exploration activities by the local NGSO are being carried out openly and include environmental and groundwater research in the initial phases, which result in having at the outset, the public's acceptance. One example of the political instability issue is the current Russian war in Ukraine. Despite Ukraine's significant mineral potential [105], the outcome of this war is still not known, while the first steps to link Ukraine's raw materials potential to the European supply chain have already been made before the invasion started [124, 125].

5. Outlook/uptake

Europe has been among the leading regions in the raw materials supply sector for thousands of years, with the introduction of copper, bronze, and iron products, and later on, with the mining of many other various elements, such as silver, gold, lead, tin, and mercury. The largest renaissance in mining dates back to medieval ages when Georgius Agricola completed his cutting-edge opus magna "De Re Metallica" that paved the way for modern science-based fieldwork, exploration, mining technology, metallurgical work, and many more [126]. Europe's long tradition in mining has added significantly to the raw material stock in the value chain. Still, there is a potential even for critical and strategic minerals from primary and secondary resources. Based on existing knowledge and data, target areas can be identified, while modern and more detailed exploration campaigns using the most advanced technologies will assist in discovering yet hidden resources. Additional information on a possible exploration target will help reduce the risk of failure, whether being of economic, environmental, or social aspects. These risks associated with the development of any kind of a project can be expressed in a comparable format proposed by UNECE. Hence, the UNFC can support reliable supply chain decision-making as options can be compared on an equal basis [16, 120, 127]. The NGSOs will be required to play a key role regarding the required national programs for the general exploration of critical raw materials if the CRMA comes alive (Art 18 CRMA). The recent networking project GSEU - A Geological Service for Europe might serve as a stepping-stone and the Nordic Countries as a model to unlock Europe's raw material potential.

6. Conclusions

Europe is not a resource-poor region albeit access to known resources is limited and the knowledge on its raw material deposits is still a matter for improvement. Most of the potential sites for mining are small in size compared to the frontrunners on the global market. However, to improve Europe's raw material resilience, all sites that can be developed in line with the sustainable development goals count. To classify a potential raw material deposit as an exploitable mineral reserve, which can be put on the market, modifying factors, including geological, technical, economic, environmental, and societal ones, must be considered. Setting up the right network between National Geological Survey Organizations for the general mineral potential assessment and exploration companies, miners, processing units, final customers, local population, environmental organizations, decision makers, and other important players down the value chain is a stepping-stone for success. The European Union recognized the importance of uninterrupted mineral raw material supply for the economy already in 2008 when establishing the Raw Materials Initiative, stimulating raw material supply from global markets, supply from European sources, and reducing the EU's consumption of primary raw materials. This initiative was followed by various actions, including EU's strategic partnerships, various collaborations, and research projects on raw materials. The foreseen adoption (as in September 2023) of the European Critical Raw Materials Act sets the frame to decrease the European dependency for raw materials imports. European national geological surveys will play a key role in doing that. They will be crucial for preparing national exploration plans, new geological, geochemical and geophysical data acquisition, data storage, and service to enable the diverse and sustainable supply chains that are required. First steps have already been made by setting up the European Geological Data Infrastructure, and by successful implementation of the Geological Service for Europe project funded by the Horizon Europe financial mechanism. This would not be possible without the umbrella organization, EuroGeoSurveys, which is connecting the national geological surveys of Europe.

Acknowledgements

This chapter is based on research by GeoERA Raw Materials project that has received funding from the European Union's Horizon 2020 research and innovation program under grant agreement No 731166. Any information published in this paper reflects only the authors' view.

The authors thank the GeoERA Raw Materials Team, the EuroGeoSurveys Mineral Resources Expert Group Members (MREG), and the NGSOs. We are grateful for the constant support, valid sharing of information and data on resources and reserves occurring in the very country, and the ongoing cooperation possible.

Conflict of interest

The authors declare no conflict of interest.

Appendices

See **Table A1**.

Raw Material	Global production, 2021 [t]	EU27, UK, NO mining production, 2021 [t]	EU27, UK, NO global share [%]	countries potential hosting primary deposits [country code]
Antimony	9724	n.d.	n.d.	AT, CZ, FR, IT, RO, PT, SI, SP
Barite	6,795,998	127,921	1.88	AT, BG, CZ, DE, GR, IE, IT, PL, PT, RO, SE, SI, SK, SP, UK, UA
Bauxite	380,131,540	157,490	0.04	AT, FR, GR, IT, HU, HR, RO, SI
Beryllium	6805	n.d.	n.d.	FI, FR, NO, PT, SE, UA
Borate	6,897,867	n.d.	n.d.	DE, IT
Cobalt*	131,766	1084	0.82	DE, FI, IT, PL, SE, SP, UA
Fluorspar	8,417,382	215,155	2.56	BE, BG, DE, FR, GR, IT, NO, PL, RO, SE, SP
Natural Graphite	1,159,618	6574	0.57	AT, CZ, DE, FI, IT, NO, SE, SP, UA
Phosphate†	74,316,730	363,720	0.49	EE, FI, FR, PL, SE, SP, UA
Strontium	583,586	281,535	48.24	CY, IT, SP, UK
Tantalum*	1319	n.d.	n.d.	FI, NO, SE, SP, PT, UA

*Note: * given in tonnage of yield; † as P_2O_5; n.d. no data available or not significant; source of data [128].*

Table A1.
Critical elements for which the high supply risk already exists in the mining phase are shown with the global annual production for 2021 compared to the production in the EU27, the UK, and Norway (NO). Apart from strontium, where Spain plays an important role globally, Europe contributes only a very small part to global production from primary deposits. The geology and knowledge of former mining of these raw materials are further indications of a possible raw material potential in these countries.

Author details

Antje Wittenberg[1*], Daniel de Oliveira[2], Tom Bide[3], Julie Hollis[4], Siim Nirgi[5], Gorazd Žibret[6], Håvard Gautneb[7], Martiya Sadeghi[8], Rafael Navarro Domínguez[9] and Boris Malyuk[10]

1 BGR - Federal Institute for Geosciences and Natural Resources, Hannover, Germany

2 LNEG - The National Laboratory of Energy and Geology, Amadora, Portugal

3 BGS - British Geological Survey, Nottingham, UK

4 EGS - EuroGeoSurveys, Brussels, Belgium

5 EGT - Geological Survey of Estonia, Rakvere, Estonia

6 GeoZS - Geological Survey of Slovenia, Ljubljana, Slovenia

7 NGU - Geological Survey of Norway, Trondheim, Norway

8 SGU - Geological Survey of Sweden, Uppsala, Sweden

9 IGME-CSIC - Geological and Mining Institute of Spain, Granada, Spain

10 BRGM - The French Geological Survey, Orleans, France
(formerly at SRDE "Geoinform of Ukraine")

*Address all correspondence to: antje.wittenberg@bgr.de

References

[1] Beamon BM. Supply chain design and analysis: Models and methods. International journal of production economics. 1998;**55**(3):281-294

[2] European Commission. Europe's Future Well-Being-Proposal for a European Innovation Partnership on Raw Materials. Brussels: Publications Office of the European Union; 2012

[3] Pavel C, Tzimas E. Raw Materials in the European Defence Industry. JRC Science for Policy Report. Luxembourg: Publications Office of the European Union; 2016. 126 p. DOI: 10.2790/509931

[4] Nuss P, Graedel TE, Alonso E, Carroll A. Mapping supply chain risk by network analysis of product platforms. Sustainable Materials and Technologies. 2016;**10**:14-22. DOI: 10.1016/j.susmat.2016.10.002

[5] Magagna D, Shortall R, Telsnig T, Uihlein A, Vázquez HC. Supply Chain of Renewable Energy Technologies in Europe: An Analysis for Wind, Geothermal and Ocean Energy. Luxembourg: Publications Office of the European Union; 2017. DOI: 10.2760/271949

[6] Cook J, DeBree K, Feroleto A. From raw materials to customers: Supply chain management in the service industry. SAM Advanced Management Journal. 2001;**66**:14-21 https://scholarworks.rit.edu/article/508

[7] Hendriksen C. Artificial intelligence for supply chain management: Disruptive innovation or innovative disruption? Journal of Supply Chain Management. 2023;**59**(3):65-76. DOI: 10.1111/jscm.12304

[8] Stadtler H, Kilger C, Herbert M. Supply Chain Management and Advanced Planning. Berlin, Heidelberg: Springer; 2014. 557 p. DOI: 10.1007/978-3-642-55309-7

[9] Alicke K, Bayazit C, Beckhoff T, Foster T, Mysore M. Supply Chains: To Build Resilience, Manage Proactively. McKinsey and Company. McKinsey Global Publishing; 2022. Available from: https://www.mckinsey.com/capabilities/operations/our-insights/supply-chains-to-build-resilience-manage-proactively

[10] Kolotzek C, Helbig C, Thorenz A, Reller A, Tuma A. A company-oriented model for the assessment of raw material supply risks, environmental impact and social implications. Journal of Cleaner Production. 2018;**176**:566-580. DOI: 10.1016/j.jclepro.2017.12.162

[11] Watzel R. Minerals for future technologies: How Germany copes with challenges. In: Smelror M, Hanghøj K, Schiellerup H, editors. The Green Stone Age: Exploration and Exploitation of Minerals for Green Technologies. London: Geological Society, Special Publications; 2023. pp. 13-24. DOI: 10.1144/SP526-2022-12

[12] Kotabe M, Murray JY. Global sourcing strategy and sustainable competitive advantage. Industrial Marketing Management. 2004;**33**(1):7-14. DOI: 10.1016/j.indmarman.2003.08.004

[13] Sauer PC, Seuring S. Sustainable supply chain management for minerals. Journal of Cleaner Production. 2017;**151**:235-249. DOI: 10.1016/j.jclepro.2017.03.049

[14] Wittenberg A, de Oliveira DPS, Flindt Jørgensen L, González J, Heldal T, Aasly KA, et al. GeoERA Raw Materials

Monograph: The Past and the Future. Hannover, Germany: GeoERA Project; 2022. 141 p. DOI: 10.25928/geoera_rawmat22_1

[15] Mateus A, Martins L. Building a mineral-based value chain in Europe: The balance between social acceptance and secure supply. Mineral Economics. 2020;**34**:239-261. DOI: 10.1007/s13563-020-00242-3

[16] Haschke M, Gielisch H, Berse R. The Impact of COVID-19 on Critical Raw Material Supplies needed for the Healthcare and Possible Mitigation Actions. Geneva, Switzerland: UNECE; 2022. 84 p. DOI: 10.13140/RG.2.2.26024.44806

[17] Alblowi R, Brydges T, Henninger CE, Heinze L, Retamal M, Parker-Strak R, et al. Exploring supply chain sustainability drivers during COVID-19- tale of 2 cities. Journal of Cleaner Production. 2022;**373**:133956. DOI: 10.1016/j.jclepro.2022.133956

[18] PWC. Impact of COVID-19 on the Supply Chain Industry. PricewaterhouseCoopers International Limited [Internet]; 2020. Available from: https://www.pwc.com/ng/en/assets/pdf/impact-of-covid19-the-supply-chain-industry.pdf [Accessed: September 7, 2023]

[19] Lèbre É, Owen JR, Corder GD, Kemp D, Stringer M, Valenta RK. Source risks As constraints to future metal supply. Environmental Science & Technology. 2019;**53**(18):10571-10579. DOI: 10.1021/acs.est.9b02808

[20] Yousaf I. Risk transmission from the COVID-19 to metals and energy markets. Resources Policy. 2021;**73**:102156. DOI: 10.1016/j.resourpol.2021.102156

[21] The White House. Building Resilient Supply Chains, Revitalizing American Manufacturing, and Fostering Broad-Based Growth - 100-Day Reviews under Executive Order 14017 [Internet]. 2021. Available from: https://www.whitehouse.gov/wp-content/uploads/2021/06/100-day-supply-chain-review-report.pdf [Accessed: August 31, 2023]

[22] Carrara S, Bobba S, Blagoeva D, Alves Dias P, Cavalli A, Georgitzikis K, et al. Supply Chain Analysis and Material Demand Forecast in Strategic Technologies and Sectors in the EU – A Foresight Study. Luxembourg: Publications Office of the European Union; 2023. 261 p. DOI: 10.2760/386650

[23] Lang O. The Dangers of Mining Around the World. BBC News [Internet]. 2010. Available from: https://www.bbc.com/news/world-latin-america-11533349 [Accessed: August 31, 2023]

[24] Sun X, Hao H, Hartmann P, Liu Z, Zhao F. Supply risks of lithium-ion battery materials: An entire supply chain estimation. Materialstoday Energy. 2019;**14**:100347. DOI: 10.1016/j.mtener.2019.100347

[25] Rabe W, Kostka G, Smith SK. China's supply of critical raw materials: Risks for Europe's solar and wind industries? Energy Policy. 2017;**101**:692-699. DOI: 10.1016/j.enpol.2016.09.019

[26] Northey SA, Klose S, Pauliuk S, Yellishetty M, Giurco D. Primary exploration, mining and metal supply scenario (PEMMSS) model: Towards a stochastic understanding of the mineral discovery, mine development and co-product recovery requirements to meet demand in a low-carbon future. Resources, Conservation & Recycling Advances. 2023;**17**:200137. DOI: 10.1016/j.rcradv.2023.200137

[27] Mancini L, Eynard U, Eisfeldt F, Ciroth A, Blengini G, Pennington D.

Social Assessment of Raw Materials Supply Chains. A Life-Cycle-Based Analysis. Luxembourg: Publications Office of the European Union; 2018. p. 94. DOI: 10.2760/470881

[28] Guarnieri P, Trojan F. Decision making on supplier selection based on social, ethical, and environmental criteria: A study in the textile industry. Resources, Conservation and Recycling. 2019;**141**:347-361. DOI: 10.1016/j.resconrec.2018.10.023

[29] Ghadimi P, Wang C, Lim MK. Sustainable supply chain modeling and analysis: Past debate, present problems and future challenges. Resources, Conservation and Recycling. 2019;**140**:72-84. DOI: 10.1016/j.resconrec.2018.09.005

[30] Azimifard A, Moosavirad SH, Ariafar S. Selecting sustainable supplier countries for Iran's steel industry at three levels by using AHP and TOPSIS methods. Resources Policy. 2018;**57**:30-44. DOI: 10.1016/j.resourpol.2018.01.002

[31] Rashidi K, Noorizadeh A, Kannan D, Cullinane K. Applying the triple bottom line in sustainable supplier selection: A meta-review of the state-of-the-art. Journal of Cleaner Production. 2020;**269**:122001. DOI: 10.1016/j.jclepro.2020.122001

[32] Luthra S, Govindan K, Kannan D, Mangla SK, Garg CP. An integrated framework for sustainable supplier selection and evaluation in supply chains. Journal of Cleaner Production. 2017;**140**:1686-1698. DOI: 10.1016/j.jclepro.2016.09.078

[33] European Commission. Proposal for a Regulation of the European Parliament and of the Council Establishing a Framework for Ensuring a Secure and Sustainable Supply of Critical Raw Materials and Amending Regulations (EU) 168/2013, (EU) 2018/858, 2018/1724 and (EU) 2019/1020 (COM(2023)160 Final) [Internet]. 2023. Available from: https://single-market-economy.ec.europa.eu/publications/european-critical-raw-materials-act_en [Accessed: August 31, 2023]

[34] UNECE. Future-Proofing the Supply of Critical Minerals for Net-Zero Emissions Summary Report, January 2022. Geneve: UNECE and UK Mission Geneva [Internet]; 2022. 5p. Available from: https://unece.org/sites/default/files/2022-01/UNECE%20UK%20Critical%20Minerals%20Report%20Jan%202022.pdf [Accessed: August 31, 2023]

[35] UK Government. Resilience for the Future: The UK's critical minerals strategy. Department for Business, E.I.S. [Internet]. 2022. Available from: https://www.gov.uk/government/publications/uk-critical-mineral-strategy/resilience-for-the-future-the-uks-critical-minerals-strategy [Accessed: August 31, 2023]

[36] Pasimeni P. Supply, or Demand, That Is the Question : Decomposing Euro Area Inflation. Luxembourg: Publications Office of the European Union; 2022. 20 p. DOI: 10.2873/301426

[37] European Commission. Communication from the Commission to the European Parliament and the Council 2022 Strategic Foresight Report Twinning the Green and Digital Transitions in the New Geopolitical Context (COM/2022/289 Final) [Internet]. 2022. Available from: https://eur-lex.europa.eu/legal-content/EN/TXT/?uri=CELEX:52022DC0289 [Accessed: August 31, 2023]

[38] IEA.Critical Minerals Market Review 2023 [Internet]. 2023. Available from:

https://www.iea.org/reports/critical-minerals-market-review-2023 [Accessed: August 31, 2023]

[39] Zanbak C. Hammaddelerin Kritikliği/Stratejikliği ve Türkiye (in Turkish, Engl. Criticality/Strategic Nature of Raw Materials and Türkiye) [Internet]. 2023. Available from: https://www.ituvakif.org.tr/hammaddelerin-kritikligi-stratejikligi-ve-turkiye [Accessed: August 31, 2023]

[40] Langley J. Third-Party Logistics Study - Back to Basics - Results and Findings of the 27th Annual Study. USA: NTT DATA; 2023. 86 p

[41] Zhou X, Zhang H, Zheng S, Xing W, Yang H, Zhao Y. A study on the transmission of trade behavior of global nickel products from the perspective of the industrial chain. Resources Policy. 2023;**81**:103376. DOI: 10.1016/j.resourpol.2023.103376

[42] Wang X, Wang A, Zhong W, Zhu D, Wang C. Analysis of international nickel flow based on the industrial chain. Resources Policy. 2022;**77**:102729. DOI: 10.1016/j.resourpol.2022.102729

[43] Månberger A. Critical raw material supply matters and the potential of the circular economy to contribute to security. Intereconomics. 2023;**58**:74-78. DOI: 10.2478/ie-2023-0016

[44] Liu W, Li X, Liu C, Wang M, Liu L. Resilience assessment of the cobalt supply chain in China under the impact of electric vehicles and geopolitical supply risks. Resources Policy. 2023;**80**:103183. DOI: 10.1016/j.resourpol.2022.103183

[45] Zuo Z, Cheng J, Guo H, McLellan BC. Catastrophe progression method - PATH (CPM-PATH) early warning analysis of Chinese rare earths industry security. Resources Policy. 2021;**73**:102161. DOI: 10.1016/j.resourpol.2021.102161

[46] Yu S, Duan H, Cheng J. An evaluation of the supply risk for China's strategic metallic mineral resources. Resources Policy. 2021;**70**:101891. DOI: 10.1016/j.resourpol.2020.101891

[47] Shuai J, Peng X, Zhao Y, Wang Y, Xu W, Cheng J, et al. A dynamic evaluation on the international competitiveness of China's rare earth products: An industrial chain and tech-innovation perspective. Resources Policy. 2022;**75**:102444. DOI: 10.1016/j.resourpol.2021.102444

[48] Ren B, Li H, Wang X, Shi J, Ma N, Qi Y. The flow of embodied minerals between China's provinces and the world: A nested supply chain network perspective. Resources Policy. 2022;**78**:102853. DOI: 10.1016/j.resourpol.2022.102853

[49] Ramahandry T, Bonneau V, Bani E, Vlasov N, Flickenschild M, Batura O, et al. Key Enabling Technologies for Europe's Technological Sovereignty. Brussels: European Parliamentary Research Service; 2021. 97 p. DOI: 10.2861/24482

[50] Zuo Z, Cheng J, Guo H, Li Y. Knowledge mapping of research on strategic mineral resource security: A visual analysis using CiteSpace. Resources Policy. 2021;**74**:102372. DOI: 10.1016/j.resourpol.2021.102372

[51] van Wieringen K. EU-China 2030: European Expert Consultation on Future Relations with China. Brussels: European Parliamentary Research Service; 2022. 46 p. DOI: 10.2861/729211

[52] Kalantzakos S. The geopolitics of critical minerals. 2019. IAI Papers.

2019;**19**:27 https://www.jstor.org/stable/pdf/resrep23660.pdf

[53] European Commission. Tackling the Challenges in Commodity Markets and on Raw Materials (COM(2011)0025 Final) [Internet]. 2011. Available from: https://eur-lex.europa.eu/legal-content/EN/TXT/?uri=celex%3A52011DC0025 [Accessed: August 31, 2023]

[54] EIT Raw Materals. Circular Economy (image) [Internet]. 2018. Available from: https://eitrawmaterials.eu/wp-content/uploads/2018/06/Circular-Economy-5.jpg [Accessed: August 20, 2023]

[55] Reichl C, Schatz M. World Mining Data 2023. Vienna: Federal Ministry of Finance; 2023. 265 p

[56] Imahashi, R. Manufacturers rue Dependence on China for Supplies of Magnesium. Market Spotlight [Internet]. 2021. Available from: https://asia.nikkei.com/Spotlight/Market-Spotlight/Manufacturers-rue-dependence-on-China-for-supplies-of-magnesium [Accessed: August 20, 2023]

[57] Liang A, Marsh N. Gallium and Germanium: What China's New Move in Microchip War Means for World. London: BBC News [Internet]; 2023. Available from: https://www.bbc.com/news/business-66118831 [Accessed: August 20, 2023]

[58] Harper GDJ. China's Gallium and Germanium Controls: What they Mean and What Could Happen Next [Internet]. 2023. Available from: https://theconversation.com/chinas-gallium-and-germanium-controls-what-they-mean-and-what-could-happen-next-209156 [Accessed: August 20, 2023]

[59] European Commission. Communication from the Commission to the European Parliament and the Council - the Raw Materials Initiative: Meeting our Critical Needs for Growth and Jobs in Europe {SEC(2008) 2741} (COM(2008)0699 Final) [Internet]. 2008. Available from: https://eur-lex.europa.eu/legal-content/EN/ALL/?uri=celex%3A52008DC0699 [Accessed: August 31, 2023]

[60] European Commission. Communication from the Commission to the European Parliament, the Council, the European Economic and Social Committee and the Committee of the Regions on the Review of the List of Critical Raw Materials for the eu and the Implementation of the Raw Materials Initiative (COM(2014)0297 Final) [Internet]. 2014. Available from: https://eur-lex.europa.eu/legal-content/EN/TXT/?uri=celex%3A52014DC0297 [Accessed: August 31, 2023]

[61] European Commission. Study on the Critical Raw Materials for the EU 2023: Final Report. Luxembourg: Publications Office of the European Union; 2023. 154 p. DOI: 10.2873/725585

[62] European Commission. Global Gateway [Internet]. 2023. Availible from: https://commission.europa.eu/strategy-and-policy/priorities-2019-2024/stronger-europe-world/global-gateway_en [Accessed: August 02, 2023]

[63] European Union. InvestEU [Internet]. 2023. Available from: https://investeu.europa.eu/index_en [Accessed: August 02, 2023]

[64] European Parliament and Council of the European Union. Regulation (EU) 2021/1119 of the European Parliament and of the council of 30 June 2021 establishing the framework for achieving climate neutrality and amending regulations (EC) No 401/2009 and (EU) 2018/1999 ('European climate

law') (PE/27/2021/rev/1). Brussels: Official Journal of the European Union. 2021;**243**:1-17

[65] European Commission. REPowerEU Plan. COM(2022) 230 final [Internet]. 2022. Available from: https://eur-lex.europa.eu/legal-content/EN/TXT/?uri=COM:2022:230:FIN [Accessed: September 7, 2023]

[66] European Commission. A Green Deal Industrial Plan for the Net-Zero Age. COM(2023) 62 final [Internet] 2023. Available from: https://commission.europa.eu/document/41514677-9598-4d89-a572-abe21cb037f4_en [Accessed: September 7, 2023]

[67] European Commission. A Chips Act for Europe - Staff Working Document PART 1/4 [Internet]. 2022. Available from: https://ec.europa.eu/newsroom/dae/redirection/document/86690 [Accessed: September 7, 2023]

[68] European Commission. A Chips Act for Europe. COM(2022) 45 final [Internet]. 2022. Available from: https://eur-lex.europa.eu/legal-content/EN/TXT/PDF/?uri=CELEX:52022DC0045 [Accessed: September 7, 2023]

[69] European Commission. Proposal for a DIRECTIVE OF THE EUROPEAN PARLIAMENT AND OF THE COUNCIL on Corporate Sustainability Due Diligence and amending Directive (EU) 2019/1937. COM(2022) 71 final [Internet]. 2022. Available from: https://eur-lex.europa.eu/legal-content/EN/TXT/?uri=CELEX:52022PC0071 [Accessed: September 7, 2023]

[70] European Parliament and Council of the European Union. Regulation (EU) 2017/821 of the European Parliament and of the council of 17 may 2017 laying down supply chain due diligence obligations for Union importers of tin, tantalum and tungsten, their ores, and gold originating from conflict-affected and high-risk areas. Brussels: Official Journal of the European Union. 2017;**130**:1-20

[71] European Commission. Proposal for a Regulation of the European Parliament and of the Council on Establishing a Framework of Measures for Strengthening Europe's Net-Zero Technology Products Manufacturing Ecosystem (Net Zero Industry Act). COM(2023) 161 final [Internet]. 2023. Available from: https://eur-lex.europa.eu/legal-content/EN/TXT/?uri=CELEX:52023PC0161 [Accessed: September 7, 2023]

[72] Ministry of the Environment, Republic of Estonia. General Principles of Earth's Crust Policy until 2050. Tallinn: Ministry of Enivronment; 2017; 11 p. https://kliimaministeerium.ee/media/907/download

[73] Ministerio para la Transición Ecológica y el Reto Demográfico. Hoja de Ruta para la gestión sostenible de las Materias Primas Minerales. Madrid: Ministerio para la Transición Ecológica y el Reto Demográfico; 2022; 72 p https://energia.gob.es/_layouts/15/HttpHandlerParticipacionPublicaAnexos.ashx?k=41163

[74] Bundesregierung. Rohstoffstrategie der Bundesregierung - Sicherung einer nachhaltigen Rohstoffversorgung Deutschlands mit nichtenergetischen mineralischen Rohstoffen. Berlin: Bundesministerium für Wirtschaft und Energie; 2020; 37 p. https://www.bmwi.de/Redaktion/DE/Publikationen/Industrie/rohstoffstrategie-der-bundesregierung.pdf?__blob=publicationFile&v=4

[75] Norwegian Ministry of Trade, I.a.F., Norwegian Mineral Strategy.

Norwegian Ministry of Trade, Industry and Fisheries. 2023. 66 p. https://www.regjeringen.no/contentassets/1614eb7b10cd4a7cb58fa6245159a547/norges-mineralstrategi_engelsk_uu.pdf

[76] European Commission. Commission recommendation of 9 April 2013 on the use of common methods to measure and communicate the life cycle environmental performance of products and organisations. Brussels: Official Journal of the European Union. 2013;**56**:1-210

[77] Zhang Z, Elshkaki A. An analysis of the supply-side factors of geological exploration in China based on provincial panel data between 1999 and 2017. Resources Policy. 2022;**76**:102589. DOI: 10.1016/j.resourpol.2022.102589

[78] Ali SH, Giurco D, Arndt N, Nickless E, Brown G, Demetriades A, et al. Mineral supply for sustainable development requires resource governance. Nature. 2017;**543**:367-372. DOI: 10.1038/nature21359

[79] Jowitt SM, Mudd GM, Thompson JFH. Future availability of non-renewable metal resources and the influence of environmental, social, and governance conflicts on metal production. Communications Earth & Environment. 2020;**1-13**:1-7. DOI: 10.1038/s43247-020-0011-0

[80] van den Brink S, Kleijn R, Sprecher B, Tukker A. Identifying supply risks by mapping the cobalt supply chain. Resources, Conservation and Recycling. 2020;**156**:104743. DOI: 10.1016/j.resconrec.2020.104743

[81] Manhart A, Vogt R, Priester M, Dehoust G, Auberger A, Blepp M, et al. The environmental criticality of primary raw materials – A new methodology to assess global environmental hazard potentials of minerals and metals from mining. Mineral Economics. 2018;**32**:91-107. DOI: 10.1007/s13563-018-0160-0

[82] Girtan M, Wittenberg A, Grilli ML, de Oliveira DPS, Giosuè C, Ruello ML. The critical raw materials issue between scarcity, supply risk, and unique properties. Materials. 2021;**14**(8):1826. DOI: 10.3390/ma14081826

[83] Fogarty JJ, Sagerer S. Exploration externalities and government subsidies: The return to government. Resources Policy. 2016;**47**:78-86. DOI: 10.1016/j.resourpol.2016.01.002

[84] Duke JM. Government geoscience to support mineral exploration: Public policy, rational and impact. PDAC. 2010:1-64. Available from: www.academia.edu/5085907/Government_Geoscience_to_Support_Mineral_Exploration_public_policy_rationale_and_impact

[85] Fogarty JJ. An Economic Assessment of the Exploration Incentive Scheme: 10 Years from 2009 to 2020, Prepared for the Department of Mines, Industry Regulation and Safety. Perth: Geological Survey of Western Australia; 2021. 48 p. https://www.dmp.wa.gov.au/Documents/Geological-Survey/EIS_Economic_Impact_report_10_years.pdf

[86] BGR - Bundesanstalt für Geowissenschaften und Rohstoffe. Deutschland – Rohstoffsituation 2021. Hannover: Bundesanstalt für Geowissenschaften und Rohstoffe; 2022; 162 p. https://www.bgr.bund.de/DE/Themen/Min_rohstoffe/Downloads/rohsit-2021.pdf;jsessionid=2BCA1AC3E15D8C9E0D8D12F4E1CF9267.internet002?__blob=publicationFile&v=4

[87] Simoni MU, Aasly KA, Eilu P, Schjøth F, Lead W. Mintell4EU Deliverable D4.1: Case Study Review with

Guidance and Examples for Applying the UNFC to European Mineral Resources. Report on Harmonization Issues, Data Gaps and Challenges, Reviewing Also the Quality of PanEuropean Aggregated Inventories for Selected Commodities. 2021. 24 p. https://repository.europe-geology.eu/egdidocs/mintell4eu/d41-mintell4eu-case-study-overview-final.pdf

[88] European Geological Data Infrastructure (EGDI) [Internet]. Available from: https://www.europe-geology.eu/ [Accsessed: June 30, 2023]

[89] Flindt, Jørgensen L, Wittenberg A, Deady E, Kumelj Š, Tulstrup J. European mineral intelligence - collecting, harmonising, and sharing data on European raw materials. Geological Society, London, Special Publications. 2022;**526**:51-67. DOI: 10.1144/SP526-2022-179

[90] CRIRSCO. International Reporting Template for the Public Reporting of Exploration Results, Mineral Resources and Mineral Reserves. Committee for Mineral Reserves International Reporting Standards (CRIRSCO). USA: International Council of Mining & Metals. Global; 2019. 78 p. http://www.crirsco.com/templates/CRIRSCO_International_Reporting_Template_October_2019.pdf

[91] Lusty PAJ, Gunn AG. Challenges to global mineral resource security and options for future supply. In: Jenkin GRT, Lusty PAJ, McDonald I, Smith MP, Boyce AJ, Wilkinson JJ, editors. Ore Deposits in an Evolving Earth. London: Geological Society; 2015. pp. 265-276. DOI: 10.1144/SP393.13

[92] Meadows DH, Meadows DL, Randers J, Behrens WW III. The Limits to Growth; a Report for the Club of Rome's Project on the Predicament of Mankind. New York: Universe Books; 1972. p. 205 https://www.clubofrome.org/publication/the-limits-to-growth/

[93] Meinert DL, Robinson RG, Nassar TN. Mineral resources: Reserves, peak production and the future. Resources. 2016;**5**(1):14. DOI: 10.3390/resources5010014

[94] Rupprecht SM. SAMREC CODE 2016 - the application of modifying factors. In: Proceedings of the SAREC/SAMVAL Companion Volume Conference Emperors Palace; 17-18 May 2016. Johannesburg: Southern African Institute of Mining and Metallurgy; 2016. pp. 187-194

[95] Winterstetter A, Laner D, Rechberger H, Fellner J. Evaluation and classification of different types of anthropogenic resources: The cases of old landfills, obsolete computers and in-use wind turbines. Journal of Cleaner Production. 2016;**133**:599-615. DOI: 10.1016/j.jclepro.2016.05.083

[96] Henley S, Allington R. PERC, CRIRSCO, and UNFC: Minerals reporting standards and classifications. European Geologist. 2013;**36**:49-54

[97] Bide T, Brown TJ, Gunn AG, Mankelow JM. Utilisation of multiple current and legacy datasets to create a national minerals inventory: A UK case study. Resources Policy. 2020;**66**:101654. DOI: 10.1016/j.resourpol.2020.101654

[98] UNECE. United Nations framework classification for resources update 2019. In: UNECE Energy Series 61. Geneva: United Nations; 2019. 28p. https://unece.org/sustainable-energy/publications/united-nations-framework-classification-resources-update-2019-ece

[99] EIT RawMaterials. Developing Raw Materials into a Major Strength

for Europe [Internet]. Availible from: https://eitrawmaterials.eu/ [Accessed: September 7, 2023]

[100] Bide T, Brown TJ, Gunn AG, Deady E. Development of decision-making tools to create a harmonised UK national mineral resource inventory using the United Nations framework classification. Resources Policy. 2022;**76**:102558. DOI: 10.1016/j.resourpol.2022.102558

[101] Nassar NT, Graedel TE, Harper EM. By-product metals are technologically essential but have problematic supply. Science Advances. 2015;**1**(3):e1400180. DOI: 10.1126/sciadv.1400180

[102] Afflerbach P, Fridgen G, Keller R, Rathgeber AW, Strobel F. The by-product effect on metal markets – New insights to the price behavior of minor metals. Resources Policy. 2014;**42**:35-44. DOI: 10.1016/j.resourpol.2014.08.003

[103] Campbell GA. The role of co-products in stabilizing the metal mining industry. Resources Policy. 1985;**11**(4):267-274. DOI: 10.1016/0301-4207(85)90044-3

[104] UNECE. UNFC GUIDANCE EUROPE. In: Chanes R, Hokka J, Eilu P, Heiberg S, Jones A, Falck H, Kral U, editors. Guidance for the Application of the United Nations Framework Classification for Resources (UNFC) for Mineral and Anthropogenic Resources in Europe. Geneva: UNITED NATIONS ECONOMIC COMMISSION FOR EUROPE; 2022. 66 p. https://unece.org/sites/default/files/2022-10/Revised_UNFC_Guidance_Europe_as_of_19.October.2022.pdf

[105] Mykhailov VA, Malyuk BI, de Oliveira D, Wittenberg A, et al. Strategic Minerals of Ukraine and their Investment Attractiveness [in Press]. Orleans: BRGM; 2023. p. 293

[106] Sadeghi M, Pereira A, Bertrand G, Arvanitidis N, de Oliveira D, Decrée S, Sievers H, Quental L, Bergman T, Hallberg A, McGrath E, Lynch E, Delgado Arenas P, Timón Sanchez SM, Teran K, Munreanu M, Horváth Z, Gtorok K, Jonson E, Salgueira R, Kovács G, Vigh C, González J, Marino E, Somoza L, Medialdea T, Blasco I, Kuhn T, Ferreira P, Magalhães V, Malyuk B. Providing a data platform, digital version of metallogenic map and related description report highlighting the endowment and exploration potential of CRM in Europe. FRAME Deliverable 3.2 Report [unpublished]. 2020. p. 29

[107] Anastasiu N. Resursele minerale – un potențial uitat! 2015. Bucharest, Romania: Academiei Române; 2015. p. 12

[108] Makkonen HV, Halkoaho T, Konnunaho J, Rasilainen K, Kontinen A, Eilu P. Ni-(Cu-PGE) deposits in Finland – Geology and exploration potential. Ore Geology Reviews. 2017;**90**:667-696. DOI: 10.1016/j.oregeorev.2017.06.008

[109] Asch KE. The International Geological Map of Europe and Adjacent Areas 1:5000000, IGME 5000: More than Just a Map - a Multinational GIS Project. Hannover: BGR; 2005. p. 1

[110] Bertrand G, Sadeghi M, de Oliveira D, Tourliere B, Arvanitidis N, Gautneb H, et al. Mineral PROSPECTIVITY mapping for critical raw materials AT the EUROPEAN scale with the CBA method. Special Paper - Geological Survey of Finland. 2021;**57**:79-82

[111] Bertrand G, Sadeghi M, Arvanitidis N, de Oliveira D, Gautneb H, Gloaguen E, et al. Prospectivity maps of critical raw materials in Europe. FRAME DELIVERABLE. 2021;**D3**(5):68 www.frame.lneg.pt

[112] Sanjuan B, Gourcerol B, Millot R, Rettenmaier D, Jeandel E, Rombaut A. Lithium-rich geothermal brines in Europe: An up-date about geochemical characteristics and implications for potential Li resources. Geothermics. 2022;**101**:102385. DOI: 10.1016/j.geothermics.2022.102385

[113] Thomitzek M, Cerdas F, Thiede S, Herrmann C. Cradle-to-gate analysis of the embodied energy in lithium ion batteries. Procedia CIRP. 2019;**80**:304-309. DOI: 10.1016/j.procir.2019.01.099

[114] Cabello J. Reservas, recursos y exploracion de litio en Salares del Norte de Chile (reserves, resources and lithium exploration in the salt flats of northern Chile). Andean Geology (Online). 2022;**49**(3):297-306. DOI: 10.5027/andgeov49n2-3444

[115] Cabello J. Lithium brine production, reserves, resources and exploration in Chile: An updated review. Ore Geology Reviews. 2021;**128**:103883. DOI: 10.1016/j.oregeorev.2020.103883

[116] Munk LA, Hynek SA, Bradley DC, Boutt D, Labay K, Jochens H, et al. Lithium brines: A global perspective. In: Verplanck PL, Hitzman MW, editors. Rare Earth and Critical Elements in Ore Deposits. Boulder: Society of Economic Geologists; 2016. pp. 339-365. DOI: 10.5382/Rev.18.14

[117] Sarchi C, Lucassen F, Meixner A, Caffe PJ, Becchio R, Kasemann SA. Lithium enrichment in the Salar de Diablillos, Argentina, and the influence of Cenozoic volcanism in a basin dominated by Paleozoic basement. Mineralium Deposita. 2023;**58**:1351-1370. DOI: 10.1007/s00126-023-01181-z

[118] Lithium in Geothermal Waters - GeoCubed [Internet]. Available from: https://cornishlithium.com/projects/lithium-in-geothermal-waters/geocubed/ [Accsessed: September 7, 2023]

[119] Cornish Lithium Announces Maiden JORC Resource For The Trelavour Project [Internet]. Availible from: https://cornishlithium.com/company-announcements/cornish-lithium-announces-maiden-jorc-resource-for-the-trelavour-project/ [Accsessed: September 7, 2023]

[120] Met4Tech. UNRMS: A Cornwall Case Study [Internet]. 2023. Available from: https://met4tech.org/unrms-a-cornwall-case-study/ [Accessed: September 7, 2023]

[121] Carranza EJM, Zuo R. Introduction to the thematic issue: Analysis of exploration geochemical data for mapping of anomalies. Geochemistry, Exploration, Environment, Analysis. 2017;**17**(3):183-185. DOI: 10.1144/geochem2017-901

[122] Carranza EJM. Geochemical anomaly and mineral Prospectivity mapping in GIS. Handbook of Exploration and Environmental Geochemistry. 2008;**11**:368

[123] Bilham NT. Responsible mining and responsible sourcing of minerals: Opportunities and challenges for cooperation across value chains, In Di Capua G, Bobrowsky PT, Kieffer SW, Palinkas C, editors. Geoethics: Status and Future Perspectives, Geological Society, London, Special Publications. 2020;508. DOI: 10.1144/sp508-2020-130

[124] Gurskiy DS. Conceptual Principles of the State Mineral Resources Policy on the Use of Strategically Important Minerals for the Country's Economy. Lviv, Ukraine: ZUKC; 2008. p. 192

[125] Malyuk BI. Ukraine: Mineral Policy. In: Tiess G, Majumder T,

Cameron P, editors. Encyclopedia of Mineral and Energy Policy. Berlin: Springer-Verlag GmbH; 2023. pp. 798-804. DOI: 10.1007/978-3-642-40871-7_49-1

[126] Hoover HC, Hoover LH. GEORGIUS Agricola de RE Metallica - Translated from the First Latin Edition of 1556. New York: Dover Publications Inc; 1950. p. 638

[127] Horváth Z, de Oliveira D, Aslaksen Aasly K, Simoni M, Flindt Jørgensen L, Whitehead D, et al. UN Framework Classification - a Tool for Sustainable Resource Management. Utrecht, The Netherlands: GeoUtrecht; 2020. p. 2020. DOI: 10.48380/dggv-dakj-bn91

[128] BGR Budesanstalt für Geowissenschaften und Rohstoff. Fachinformationssystem Rohstoffe, BGR. without date: Hannover. [not public]

Chapter 5

Road Haulier Competition: Implications for Supply Chain Integration

Benedikte Borgström, Susanne Hertz and Leif-Magnus Jensen

Abstract

Road freight competition is playing out in deregulated markets. The EU single market is a market with abundant responses in terms of haulier strategic actions. This chapter situates the crucial role of road haulier strategies in the logistics service supply chain and industrial supply chain to achieve sustainability. Competitive and sustainable transport depends on effective transport services, vehicles and transport infrastructure, and conditions that foster the development of transport and logistics services. By examining how four case firms develop competences and make use of available resources we develop insights into road haulier competition and its implications. The chapter contributes to understanding how road hauliers are part of logistics service chains as well as industrial supply chains and how the many links and relationships increase the magnitude and implications of hauliers' performances.

Keywords: supply chain management, transport services, road haulage, competition, supply chain integration

1. Introduction

In this chapter, we analyze how competitive road hauliers influence the industrial supply chain performance. Road transportation is by far the most important mode of inland transportation in Europe accounting for roughly 77% of ton-kilometers (Eurostat Statistics). Competition in the basic trucking or transport sector is increasingly fierce and international. The road hauliers themselves are challenged by this fierce competition and some respond by trying to cut costs equally fiercely. In this chapter, however we see that there are several other competitive responses which depend on the creative use of resources including connections to the industrial supply chains and specialist competence. We argue that changes in the road transport business influence users of transport services, such as industrial supply chains. However, very little is written about road hauliers' pivotal role in the flows and even less about their role in industrial supply chains. This is surprising since the demands for higher integration and transparency of supply chains due to sustainability should not exclude the physical flow and what is happening in the logistics chain. Integration is a process over time where parties provide significant inputs into the service production process thus co-creating value in the relationships [1].

Seeing the supply chain as a network of firms that coordinate their activities to deliver the final product according to customer demands means the logistics firms and network play a key role [2]. Including transport actors such as road hauliers in the understanding of inter-organizational networks, integrated chains and the process of integration is increasingly relevant as a supply chain management topic, since it influences not only financial performance, but also environmental and social outcomes. The basic prerequisites for the integration process are inter-organizational collaboration and coordination of the flows of the whole supply chain. The road hauliers' role in the supply chain might be critical and is little investigated. Despite that most definitions do not even see these as part of the supply chain, they will have large effects on both firms and flows [3]. Logistics firms in general are performing a large part of the whole physical flow as suppliers of services in the industrial supply chain and are a direct link between the firms in the industrial supply chains [4].

2. Literature

2.1 Road hauliers for efficient, safe, secure and environmentally friendly transport in the industrial supply chain

The EU is a single market in which competition, from an economics perspective, should create sustainable road transportation that is efficient, safe, secure and environmentally friendly. In the road transportation sector, the opportunity for effective competition is strongest in road freight transportation, i.e., trucking or road haulage [5]. Still, in different countries the enforcement of EU legislation differs, which creates different competitive conditions. Leading market actors argue the fragmentation of the transport industry and other inefficiencies hinder healthy competitiveness [6]. The fragmentation implies that conditions decided by the EU are used for "gray" advantages in transportation. There are legal and less legal ways of dealing with rules on access to the profession and the market, these involve standards for working time, driving time and resting periods, the use of vehicle taxes, tolls and costs related to using infrastructure [7]. The standard economics perspective does not apply well to understanding road haulier competition, because of the industry characteristics of heterogeneity and dynamics [8]. The complex web of different types of interfirm linkages, networks, and alliances determine to a large extent the competitive conditions. For that reason, we need to understand road haulier competition from the point of view of strategic development [9].

From a logistics and supply chain management perspective Christopher [2] develops the competitive understanding in three c: customers, company and competitors. Competition is how these actors create value sought by customers. The company and the competitor have different resources to utilize, which render cost differentials. Thus, a competitive advantage might be gained by service and costs in different customer segments.

OECD [5] subdivided the road freight sector into truckload and less-than-truckload, and national and international trucking. Recent studies elaborate that road haulier competitiveness depends on its procedures in calculating costs and transport prices [10], and on the optimization of driving and rest periods of drivers and their routes [11]. Also, a survey of 300 customers of Hungarian transport services combined with five qualitative interviews explored competitive problems and opportunities [11]. Strengths of Hungarian hauliers are explained in terms of reliability, customer-friendly attitude, punctuality, flexibility and speed. Customers indicated that they would only change haulier if their usual partner lacked capacity or if it was an intra-organizational decision of their centralized procurement to change hauliers. Important haulier resources are employees, such as drivers, dispatchers, clerks and customer service personnel who are often in contact with customers [1, 11].

Christopher [2] argues that supply chains compete with supply chains rather than company with company, which means that the value of offers is strongly dependent on the combined effect of an integrated supply chain. All types of road haulier business, truckload and less-than-truckload, and national and international trucking are normally part of the supply chain processes. The industrial supply chain depends on its logistics service processes for effectiveness.

2.2 Performance of poorly integrated links

The industrial supply chain procurement function is driving supply network development by demands and control functions regarding costs, environment and social aspects. The supply chain coordination is of indisputable relevance in terms of low costs, responsiveness and sustainability. There seems to be a difference when it comes to the procurement of logistics services. Are the services procured customized services or generic transportation between two locations? The same logistics providers offer both types of services with similar resources, which creates doubts among the purchasers [12]. Most often the customer knows little about the logistics operations that are bought and the complex coordination that is needed for customized operations [12, 13]. Much literature investigates the competitive advantage of logistics providers (see e.g. [14]) rather than the sustainable advantage of the integrated relationship.

Wagner and Sutter [15] focus on the relationship and depict it in the degree of integration and degree of commitment. More specifically, relationships range from single transaction, repeated transaction, partnership agreement, third-party agreement and integrated logistics service agreements. Poor knowledge of the other's operations and a low degree of commitment imply a low degree of integration. A higher degree of commitment, obligations, mutual information exchange and customization involves higher integration. But such highly committed and integrated relationships are rare. Wolf and Seuring [13] argue that buying decisions are made on price, while environmental performance is seen as a basic requirement and cooperation is minimal (in line with Mortensen and Lemoine [16]).

Sustainable development is increasingly expected by society as is seen in regulations, economic policy instruments and media. Individual firms in the business network, production firms as well as logistics firms, relate to sustainability in their strategic visions. This is not necessarily because of competitive reasons, but because "of a corporate desire to do the right thing" ([17], p. 526). Transport and logistics firms are influenced by their organization, finances (savings), customer demand, government support and regulatory pressure, and technology in their decisions to develop sustainable performances [18]. Regularly, industrial supply chain firms audit their supply network, in order to enforce their supply chain codes of conduct [6, 19]. Outsourced logistics services are seen as the responsibility of the logistics providers, they have to do a trade-off between low costs and environmental and social performances. Opportunities related to higher commitment and integration are mostly unrealized [16]. Such opportunities are learning and innovation, improved logistics service quality and supply chain effectiveness and performance [15].

The links between the supply chain and the logistics providers have problems (Makelin and Vepsalainen, 1990 in [12]). Regardless of whether the service offer is complex or simple the relationships with customers tend to be similar [20]. Customers think they have to pay too much for simple operations while they mistrust the complex services. The closer relationships in these links are important to logistics service providers that build competitive advantage by customer orientation [14].

On the one hand, logistics service providers need to understand customer's business in order to be competitive, e.g., by knowledge of supply chain and customers' operations, to offer shorter lead time, and to offer multiple integrated logistics services [14]. On the other hand, industrial actors outsource the responsibility of complex transport business [16]. But small independent actors are vulnerable to both long-term contracts and take-it-or-leave-it contracts, because of the price pressure. They have to take the risk of increased costs, despite minimal margins. To avoid losing money, they might increase speed or overload, which negatively influences safety, working conditions and environment ([5], p. 114).

In any industrial supply chain road hauliers' performances are a part of total economic, environmental and social performances. This is the case to an increasing degree, because of the trend of global production and marketing in which the role of logistics in industrial supply chains is intensified. Transporters' activities are both in upstream and downstream supply chain processes. They are involved in the supply chain processes so many times that their impact, economic, environmental and social most likely is underestimated. Despite this buyer demands are operational, rather than strategic. Further, third-party logistics (TPL) providers most important short-term sustainability challenge is in "balancing sustainability efforts with customer expectations for low-priced services" ([17], p. 529).

2.3 A complex web of customers

Road hauliers might be seen as embedded in interfirm cooperative logistics networks [8] that take shape in a logistics service supply chain for a long-term or short-term contract. The industry has specific competitive dynamics compared to other mature industries. The Danish trucking industry did not end up in only big companies, as was expected, due to economies of scale [8]. In Denmark, the industry was involving some large hauliers, some smaller specialized and flexible hauliers relying on their network linkages, and many small hauliers and independent owner-operators serving the industrial supply chain customers as well as other hauliers [8]. This is in line with Cui & Hertz [4] outlining the logistics service supply chain to include hauliers, logistics intermediary and TPL firms.

Existing logistics literature mainly distinguishes logistics firms in terms of service offerings. Hauliers provide routine transport services, moving material from point A to point B [4, 12]. Logistics intermediary firms perform standard freight forwarding services and their major roles are consolidating flows [21]. TPL firms provide a bundle of customized services including warehousing, transportation and value-added activities for effectiveness and efficiency in industrial supply chains [9, 22–25].

However, the existing literature seldom focuses on the many complex interactions of the industrial supply chain and the logistics firm network. The many and simultaneous interactions imply huge effects of how transportation is executed [26]. The logistics firm network is in flux as different types of logistics firms invest their resources in different areas and develop their capabilities in various ways. Logistics firms mostly outsource part of the physical performance to other firms in the network. For example, TPL firms normally outsource the performance of their transport and consolidation to different destinations to intermediaries like freight forwarders while the freight forwarder in turn normally outsource to road hauliers [4]. The many different types of inter-firm linkages, networks, and alliances create specific competitive dynamics based on the need for complex coordination [8]. Thus, the customer of the road haulier might be a freight forwarder, a TPL firm, or an actor of the industrial supply chain. Outsourcing logistics often implies better performance through specialization in the supply chain. However, worse performance that influences both the logistics supply chain and shippers in the industrial supply chain may occur.

The high-quality transport services are characterized with:

a. Availability and completeness of services rather than damage from incomplete services [27].

b. Customer information service level based on complete awareness of customers' and the properties of services [27].

c. Reliability and uninterrupted operation of transport [27].

d. Delivery speed and avoidance of excessive delivery time [27].

e. Cargo safety during transportation [27].

f. Observance of traffic safety requirements [27].

g. Eco-friendliness of transportation avoiding environmental degradation [27].

In this way transport services in the logistics service supply chain and the industrial supply chain will impact the supply chain performance.

2.4 Road hauliers in the logistics service chain

There is a recent interest in the value-creation of TPL firms' offers to the industrial supply chain [9, 25] and in the competitive advantages of road hauliers [10, 11, 27, 28]. A typical challenge for competitive high-quality transport services reported from Central Asia, such as Uzbekistan are the necessity of regional cooperation to manage border disputes, common infrastructure, trade and communications, and security concerns that are regulated in agreements. The agreements are however not complied with and involved actors are treated as instruments serving political interests of member states rather than the interest of businesses [27].

Outsourcing important resources such as vehicle fleets and drivers enables and influences Croatian road hauliers' differentiation strategies such as differentiation of services, price differentiation, image differentiation, technological differentiation, and staff differentiation [28]. Yarashova and Hoshimov argue that the effective competitive transport system depends on high-quality transport services, high-performance safe vehicles and transport infrastructure, and conditions that foster the development of transport services [27].

Different logistics firms are categorized based on capabilities in operating a logistics service system in the logistics service chain [4]. The road hauliers main capability is seen as efficiency in moving products from one location to another in the physical flow. Their most important resources based on costs are often drivers, fuel and trucks.

Drivers are an important resource for the haulier [29]. They are meeting the customers or customers' customers and are ensuring both the timely delivery and the quality of the services. They also meet the authorities, such as customs and traffic police. Drivers' competence about how to drive influence fuel consumption, accidents, and environment [5, 30].

Haulier firm competence is to a large extent in coordinating drivers, trucks and service activities. They strive to improve driver retention, cost structure, and profitability [23]. They cooperate with each other and other logistics providers horizontally and vertically [8, 31, 32]. Logistics firms' efficiency is related to their use of trucks and other logistics resources, and effectiveness is related to their belonging in a transportation network, in a supply chain and in the wider business network.

Freight forwarders and TPL firms coordinate, such as consolidating several physical flows for a full truck to a destination and back home from that destination [4]. Freight forwarders and TPL firms' most important resources include relationships, warehouses, information and competence required to integrate resources, in order to integrate an efficient logistics service system [14]. A strategic perspective of TPL providers is defining TPL providers as value-cocreating relationships that can help manage the complexities of logistics services [1, 25].

Road hauliers might be differentiated in terms of their competences [33]. From low abilities in general and in problem-solving, a type of transaction-orientated relationships for low-cost objectives to a high general ability and problem-solving competence, which is needed in customer solutions. Innovative services towards fewer customers in intense working customer relationships are paid higher rates per mile [34]. The more innovative services are about developing complementary services for customers, adapting to specific customers and insourcing their logistics activities, and developing customer logistics operations.

2.5 Research questions

Figure 1 illustrates the complex web of interconnections between the industrial supply chain and the different layers of the logistics network that are of importance in an analysis of how competitive road hauliers influence the industrial supply chain performance. There are two different networks of firms, one is the industrial supply chain and the other is the network of logistics service firms performing the services needed for the industrial supply chain to operate effectively. Road haulier customers are partly from the supply chain and partly from the logistics service network. The transport markets are regulated in multiple dimensions such as working hours, safety and technical standards. Changes in conditions, rules and regulations influence the competition between the different logistics firms. Based on road hauliers, their conditions, and their direct and indirect business relationships, we might now elaborate the purpose how competitive road hauliers influence the industrial supply chain performance in three research questions:

- *RQ 1 How do competitive actors in road transportation affect integration and competence in the logistics services chains?*

Based on the theoretical framework, less integration is likely in low-committed relationships where the parties have little knowledge of the others' operations [15]. Then also the ability of problem solving and competence to adapt to customers and develop customer solution will decrease and services offered are routine and standard services [12, 29]. Rules involve access to the profession and the market, standards for working time, driving time and resting periods, vehicle taxes, tolls and costs related to using the infrastructure.

- *RQ2 What are the implications of competitive actors in road transportation on effectiveness and efficiency in the logistics services chain in terms of sustainability?*

  The effectiveness and efficiency of a logistics service supply chain require specific competence in customer's operations [8, 14] and an orientation towards sustainability including ways to balance environment and social concerns with low costs service deliveries [15, 17, 23]. Integration implies that involved actors have organizational ambitions to develop sustainability (economic, environmental and social performance) [6, 10, 11, 17–19].

- *RQ3 What are the implications of competitive actors in road transportation on integration and sustainability in industrial supply chains?*

  The industrial supply chain actors' supply chain codes of conduct take responsibility for also the logistics service chain [6, 19]. Integration in between these different chains is a process over time where parties provide significant inputs into the service production process thus co-creating value in the relationships [1]. Road haulier performance can be expected to influence not only financial performance, but also environmental and social outcomes.

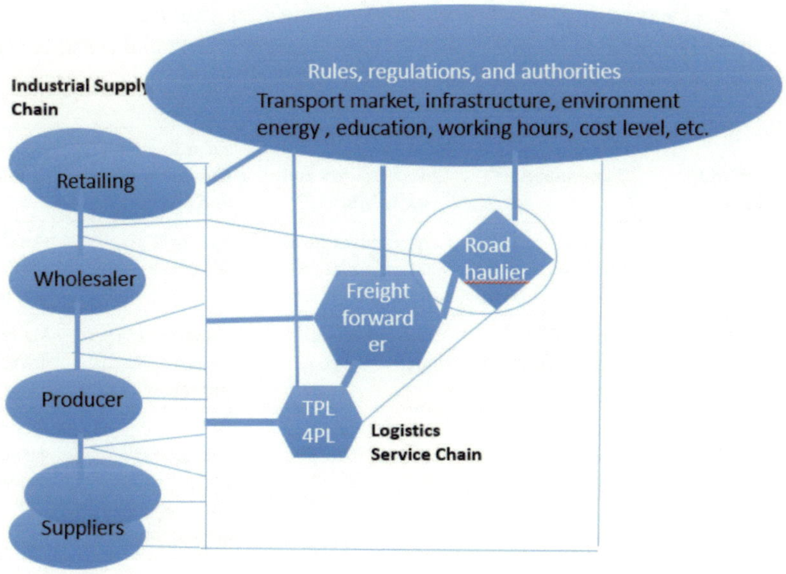

Figure 1.
The industrial supply chain and the logistics service chain.

3. Method

The connection between competition in the logistics network and the final performance of the industrial supply chain is necessarily complex, difficult to trace and subject to numerous other influences. This is not a subject that has been studied extensively placing us in a context of discovery.

The empirical material in this paper is based on a large collaborative project with a heavy vehicle manufacturer giving access and opening doors to logistics supply chain actors' business. This is a fit with the purpose since we are in an explorative setting and aim for useful interpretation rather than testing, ending with suggestions and proposals rather than final conclusions. The project ran from 2012 until the end of 2016, however we have continued researching logistics service firms.

Primary data is from two different markets, Sweden and Poland; focusing on the operations of the logistics firms and is the basis for Firms 1–4 (**Table 1**). In total 39 semi-structured interviews have been carried out with managers from the vehicle manufacturer, dealers, freight forwarders and buyers of the trucks. The majority of the interviews have been recorded and then transcribed. Where this was not possible notes were taken during and directly after the interviews and completed by other researchers present for the interviews. Interpretations and initial findings have been presented back to a workshop of industry participants for discussion and re-interpretation.

We introduce four illustrative case firms from the empirical material, in order to analyze how competitive road hauliers influence the industrial supply chain performance. All four firms represent a stable and growing business and they have been chosen because of their different strategic actions.

The strength of the study is the width of empirical data and different sources enabling us to cover substantial ground of the complex phenomenon, further discussed in Näslund et al. [35] on the basis of quality criteria from Lincoln and Guba [36]. The number of cases has had to be balanced to give some variation but cannot reasonably cover all the different varieties of road hauliers. However, a crucial point for the present

Cases: Differentiation by the firm	**Firm 1: Customization**	**Firm 2: Customization and sustainability**	**Firm 3: Customization and low costs**	**Firm 4: Service development**
Ownership/size	Private, 2 employees	Large multinational, 500 trucks and 750 drivers	Family firm, 105 drivers	Family firm, 170 drivers, 60 semitrailer, 60 lorries.
Customers	Drive full trucks for one customer	Many customers, some very large	Connected to a large freight forwarder	Many big customers in Western Europe
Industry	Water/ sanitation	Construction, pharmaceutical and others	Bulk transports, petrochemical, construction as second market	Automotive parts, various special transports to Russia

Table 1.
Case studies.

chapter is that we do not claim strong connections or conclusions but rather open up for proposals and observations that must be explored further in subsequent research.

4. Case firms

4.1 Firm 1—Customization

This Swedish family business with long experience in road haulage concentrates on distribution for one single customer in Sweden. The customization is to a water and sanitary wholesaler and retailer with special demands on time for deliveries, transparency and a crane as special equipment. There is a close relationship is to the final customer. The customer has high demands on delivery precision as they deliver to the construction industry. Much of what is delivered is bulky. The customer demands are that the firm should be environmentally friendly but is not willing to pay extra for it. They have an index clause to safeguard them against large increases in costs.

Managers at Firm 1 schedule the deliveries following Swedish rules on working hours. They are aware of the importance of driver's competence. The drivers are trained in how to drive and behave. Management has regular check-ups with the drivers. The firm is facilitated in its customization by a relatively close contact with the truck supplier and use premium brand trucks only. The contact is even closer to the serviceman in the workshop of the truck supplier.

4.2 Firm 2—Customization and sustainability

This large multinational firm does TPL, freight forwarding and trucking services, but the three services are separated organizationally. All services are discussed in terms of sustainability. The domestic trucking organization in Sweden has a close relationship with a few dominating customers. One is a big wholesaler for the construction industry and the other is a drug wholesaler distributing to pharmacies. There is a need not only for fixed routes and specific handling. There are higher demands for quality and precision in deliveries. The drivers for the new trucks are trained both in how to handle the different types of goods such as drugs with specific demands on temperature-controlled transports, safety and the condition of the trucks. There are specific rules and regulations for the transport that the customer, trucking organization and drivers have to follow.

The differentiation in terms of customization and sustainability is facilitated by a good relationship with the supplier of trucks. The majority of maintenance and repair is done by the brand workshop. The latest trucks are of high brands, more eco-friendly and sustainable new models. They have also bought special training programs for their trucks and drivers to be sustainable. The company is ISO 14001 certified.

4.3 Firm 3—Customization and low costs

The firm is a Polish road haulier which is growing fast and is ISO certified. The firm specializes in bulk transport. The majority i.e., 75% of their customers are national within the construction industry and 25% are international transports for a petrochemical producer, who delivers to the west coast of Sweden. The petrochemical customer requires that the Polish firm is certified for transporting (both truck and equipment) their goods i.e., understanding the necessary conditions for the goods and the truck. This gives the trucking firm a closer relationship to the petrochemical producer but also their two partners in Sweden and Norway since the whole chain has to be certified for handling this type of goods. As for the domestic construction industry customers demand lower costs but settle for older trucks and specialized bulk equipment.

Through the certification the driver has to have competence about the process and the certification including cleaning, control, etc. The Polish haulier has fleet management programs which enables management of how the transports are performed. Furthermore, to get the driver to perform in a better way they go through programs learning how to drive, in order to reduce fuel. Most of the drivers have worked for over 10 years in the firm.

The firm has a close relationship with a premium brand supplier of trucks from which they lease the trucks on a five-year basis. The new trucks are used for the petrochemical industry. When the trucks are paid off they are used for the construction industry at a much lower cost. Thus, the firm combines customization to one segment and low costs to another. Special discounts through the freight forwarders give them a reduction on costs for fuel on the European market. The customer of petrochemicals specifically has high demands on the environment and safety specifically since the effects of accidents or loss of control can be costly and serious.

4.4 Firm 4—Service development

The Polish firm has developed from a trucking firm to include also a freight forwarder part. In the last three years they have started to outsource several services to other firms. For example, they use six different small trucking firms, which has the advantage that these use less workshop capacity. They have their own workshop with 25 mechanics. Most of the employees have worked for the firm a long time.

Their main market is transports to Russia in which risks and uncertainties are seen as high. Many of their Western European customers including freight forwarding firms are using them specifically for their quality and knowledge about the Russian market. The firm has ISO qualifications (such as 9001 and 14001). They also have 24-hour supervisory staff and are monitored by a security agency to guarantees safekeeping of goods. Due to the risks insurance is a big problem. The firm offers certain guarantees to their customers (up to 300.000 dollars). It has recently set up a new subsidiary in Germany to facilitate the transports to Russia in order to continue to develop the Russian service. The specialization of transports to Russia was studied before the war of 2022.

The drivers are very important, 30% are from Belarus or Ukraine and the remainder are Polish. They have special demands on the drivers that drive to Russia. They have to be able to handle both money, communication in Russian and to negotiate. It takes time to train a new driver for this type of assignment. Not only do they have to know about customers' demands, handle security but also to learn about customs, different types of border crossing problems. Experienced drivers do not need the services of dispatchers. The drivers get awarded with IRU certificate of merit if they have driven over a million km and 10 years without accidents.

An advantage of driving in Russia is the lower cost of fuel (about 50% of the Polish costs). They have a relatively close relationship with the suppliers of trucks. They have a KPI on fuel consumption. They are now upgrading their fleet of trucks, which gives higher sustainability.

DOI: http://dx.doi.org/10.5772/intechopen.112994

4.5 Road hauliers as competitive actors

Case firms show costs and service differences, i.e., value differences in their service offerings by making use of resources and competences. The market is heterogeneous with standardized or customized services on domestic or international routes. Dynamics are an important characteristic in that logistics and transport cannot fully be controlled, because of weather and congestion. The complexity is another important characteristic of the services offered, not only because of the heterogeneity and dynamics but because the cost of a trip depends not only on miles but on how the trip fits with other jobs.

The EU market is competitive in that many firms offer their services at an extremely low cost. Differences in salaries, working conditions and fuel between the Western and Eastern EU countries can be more than 50%. Therefore, these firms can compete with lower costs, skilled drivers and high competence of the firm.

Low costs can also be achieved by violating rules, tax crimes, theft of fuel, etc. Even though buyers of transport services demand high-quality services their control and insight are limited.

Table 2 summarizes the differences of the cases of differentiation strategies. The competitive variables we use are high, medium, and low. High implies they are pro-active in that variable, medium implies they are re-active in that variable, and low implies adverse. Firms 2, 3, and 4 are interesting in that they combine customization with precise specializations.

Customer-specific demand relieves price pressure. We found that smaller hauliers in Europe adapt to the customer in terms of equipment, delivery times, behavior, competence demands and service level. The road haulier can be successful in spite of fierce competition, because of drivers, competence and specific advantages. The customer is prepared to pay for differentiated services. The most common situation is when customers have special requirements and cannot use the standard selection of trucks. Customer investment is increasing integration in the value co-creating relationships. This also implies that the road haulier takes on part of the freight-forwarder or TPL role.

Common characteristics of the four differentiation examples firms are coping with the problematic competition and are stable or growing. They all have loyal personnel

	Firm 1: Customized	**Firm 2: Customized/ sustainability**	**Firm 3: Customized/ low cost**	**Firm 4: Service developer**
Customer relationship	high	high	high/low	medium
Supplier relationship (equipment)	medium	high	high/low	medium
Driver competence	high	high	high/low	high
Sustainability	med	high/medium	high/medium	high
Domestic/ International	Dom	Dom	Int/dom	Int

Table 2.
Competitive actors' differentiated customer solutions.

and have been in business for a relatively long time. Knowledge seems to be important both for management and drivers. They take good care of their vehicles and have close relationships with their customers. Sustainability is important especially as a cost saving of fuel consumption or if the customer so demands. However, it seems that customers and drivers are of key importance for customer satisfaction.

5. Analysis and discussion

5.1 Competitive road hauliers affecting the integration and competence in the logistics services supply chains

It seems that rather than move towards higher integration there is a continual adaptation of integration to fit prevailing conditions. There are small hauliers in Europe that combine offerings of e.g. standardized services at low costs, adaptive or developing innovating solutions. Integration is low and especially in the short-term market relationships seem to be more transactional. To a large extent these relationships seem to be connected to other logistics firms buying their services. The integration is low between them and the industrial supply chain.

For competence in the logistics supply chain, we can make use of the differentiation of standardized and developing solution offerings of road hauliers [29]. In the cases we follow it seems to be more of a combination of the standardized offering based on low cost and efficiency and a more developed innovative approach. They seem to use part of their business for adaptive or innovative services. Hauliers make use of the advanced new trucks in the first years in an adaptive or even innovative way. Then they use the older trucks already paid for standardized low costs assignments. Competence is also increasing for chosen differentiation strategies such as particularly demanding customers, specific markets or new services such as freight forwarding or even TPL. The logistics service chain has more fluid roles than the industrial supply chain.

5.2 Implications of competitive actors in road transportation on effectiveness and efficiency in the logistics services chain in terms of sustainability

Logistics supply chain actors that act as service developer and customer developer, i.e., Firm 4 and Firm 2 are pro-active to develop services and relationships. These are important actors for industrial supply chain effectiveness. In order to be sustainable, the industry has to make sure all suppliers in their supply chain work in a sustainable way, which is problematic for anonymous transport providers from far away. Logistics firms outsource to a large extent to each other in what can be described as a complex web [3, 8]. Low commitment among industrial actors and low degree of competence of different logistics competences hinder effective solutions. Even if demands on environmental and social standards are included in contracts it is the logistics providers that need to operationalize and balance these demands in relation to costs (in line with [17]).

In the differentiation examples the hauliers have close customer relationships and loyal drivers, much in line with what Voss et al. [30] explain to be survival techniques. The integration of the firm in the logistics service supply chain is high. The final customer knows them and their drivers. The integration is high between the logistics chain and the industrial supply chain. Summarizing differentiated

DOI: http://dx.doi.org/10.5772/intechopen.112994

solutions, drivers are not allowed to sacrifice road safety, and their own working conditions, in order to deliver goods on time. Regardless of legal responsibility, the moral concerns of big industrial actors (transport buyers) are written in codes of conduct but supplier development programs that are common in their network of product suppliers are not implemented towards logistics providers. Professional and ethical transport service suppliers attract equally professional and ethical buyers which in turn leads to a more sustainable logistics service chain because demands from customers, legal authorities and even employees are more likely to be fulfilled [1, 6, 19].

5.3 Implications for integration and sustainability on industrial supply chains

Supply chain interdependencies connect the industrial and the logistics supply chains. The chain is not stronger than its weakest link. The degree of integration and supply chain orientation determines supply chain effectiveness. Yet supply chain management scholars have not elaborated on the lack of integration in between the supply chain network and the logistics chain network (in line with [3]). Supply chain management practitioners are hesitant to engage in strategic relationships with logistics service providers. The logistics service providers collaborate with other logistics providers and governmental agencies because the customers want to avoid close relationships [17].

Several of our cases improve environmental performance by agreeing with customers that the fleet shall be eco-efficient. The hauliers have better opportunities to keep and attract good drivers because of investments in modern vehicles. The hauliers' customization activities foster sustainability in the service production process [1]. Hauliers service development for example developing freight forwarder services foster social sustainability in the network of the logistics service chain.

A basis for developing value creation of transport services is the relationship. The consequential benefits of the relationship are in the recognition of the importance of logistics and transport and its role in supply chain sustainability. **Figure 1** illustrates the magnitude of links and relationships in the total industrial supply chain where the logistics service chain is connected. Customer demands are more deeply understood when there is direct contact with the industrial customers, this might be in terms of vehicles, schedules or ways of operating. In this way integration increases the sustainability of the industrial supply chain. The competence of transport buyers is a vehicle to leverage sustainability. Competence needed is in challenges and opportunities related to e.g., performance of vehicle fleets, recycling, energy conservation, and reduction of carbon footprint [17].

6. Conclusion and further research

Successful and growing road hauliers contribute to improved sustainability in the logistics supply chain as well as the industrial supply chain. In the present study, we see how four road hauliers differentiate their service offers. The differentiation influences industrial supply chain performance directly in terms of price, cost, and service, as seen in the relationship's links in **Figure 1**. The impact of the services adds up because they are offered in different steps of the industrial supply chain. Where sustainability audits are carried out consistently, performance also improves through better engines, driver training and EU working hour regulations.

Figure 1 shows the main connections between the industrial supply chain and the logistics chain. The findings of this study illustrate some of the possible strategic moves for hauliers, but also the complexity and flexibility of some of the roles especially in the logistics chain.

Future research about road hauliers can depart from their role in the logistics service supply chain and also their role in the industrial supply chain. One future research question could be how road hauliers increase competitiveness and grow by combining their existing services through adding services of a freight forwarder or a TPL. They are making use of their existing knowledge as a road haulier of a specific market. It would be of interest to study how could this influence the other roles of the logistics service supply chain. In turn, what are the consequences of such dynamics in the logistics service chain for the industrial supply chain?

Another topic of interest for future studies is how a road haulier can successfully offer both low-cost standardized services and at the same time offer highly advanced services demanding high competence of drivers and personnel and close customer contacts? One of the firms studied met the competition by offering both advanced bulk services and highly competent drivers and offering low-cost standardized services by making use of their older equipment. What are the effects of such a combined strategy on differentiation, for example in terms of image?

Acknowledgements

We thank Vinnova for funding the project: Market Making of a High-value Business Model in Low Cost Markets.

Author details

Benedikte Borgström[1*], Susanne Hertz[2] and Leif-Magnus Jensen[3]

1 Malmö University, Malmö, Sweden

2 Jönköping University, Jönköping, Sweden

3 University West, Trollhättan, Sweden

*Address all correspondence to: benedikte.borgstrom@mau.se

References

[1] Borgström B, Hertz S, Jensen L-M, Kaneberg E. Third-party logistics (TPL) providers' strategic development in Sweden: Learning from a crisis. Journal of Transport and Supply Chain Management. 2022;**16**:838-850

[2] Christopher M. Logistics and Supply Chain Management. 4th ed. Harlow, England: Prentice Hall; 2011

[3] Fabbe-Costes N, Jahre M, Roussat C. Supply chain integration: the role of logistics service providers. International Journal of Productivity and Performance Management. 2009;**58**(1):71-91

[4] Cui L, Hertz S. Networks and capabilities as characteristics of logistics firms. Industrial Marketing Management. 2011;**40**(6):1004-1011

[5] OECD. Competition issues in road transport. OECD Journal: Competition Law and Policy. 2003;**4**(4):35-133

[6] Sternberg HS, Hofmann E, Overstreet RE. Perils of road freight market deregulation: Cabotage in the European Union. The International Journal of Logistics Management. 2020;**31**(2):333-355

[7] EU. Road Transport: A Change of Gear. Luxemburg: European Commission; 2012

[8] Sornn-Friese H. Interfirm linkages and the structure and evolution of the Danish trucking industry. Transportation Journal. 2005;**44**(4):10-26

[9] Borgström B, Hertz S, Jensen L-M. Strategic development of third-party logistics providers (TPLs): "Going under the floor" or "raising the roof"? Industrial Marketing Management. 2021;**97**:183-192

[10] Poliak M, Poliaková A, Svabova L, Zhuravleva N, Nica E. Competitiveness of price in International Road Freight Transport. Journal of Competitiveness. 2021;**13**:83-98

[11] Szander N, Albert G. The Competitive Position of Hungarian Hauling Companies in the Road Freight Transportation Sector. Business Logistics in Modern Management. Croatia: Josip Juraj Strossmayer University of Osijek; 2021

[12] Bask AH, Juga J. Semi-integrated supply chains: Towards the new era of supply chain management. International Journal of Logistics: Research and Applications. 2001;**3**(1):5-23

[13] Wolf C, Seuring S. Environmental impacts as buying criteria for third party logistical services. International Journal of Physical Distribution & Logistics Management. 2010;**40**(1/2):84-102

[14] Wong CY, Karia N. Explaining the competitive advantage of logistics service providers: A resource-based view approach. International Journal of Production Economics. 2010;**128**(1):51-67

[15] Wagner SM, Sutter R. A qualitative investigation of innovation between third-party logistics providers and customers. International Journal of Production Economics. 2012;**2012**(140):944-958

[16] Mortensen O, Lemoine OW. Integration between manufacturers and third party logistics providers? International Journal of Operations &

Production Management. 2008;**28**(4): 331-359

[17] Lieb KJ, Lieb RC. Environmental sustainability in the third-party logistics (3PL) industry. International Journal of Physical Distribution & Logistics Management. 2010;**40**(7):524-533

[18] Jovanovic N, Zolfagharinia H, Peszynski K. To green or not to green trucking? Exploring the Canadian case. Transportation Research Part D: Transport and Environment. 2020;**88**:102591

[19] Borgström B. What is fair in the fair transport concept? In: Paper Presented at the 33rd EGOS Colloquium 2017. Copenhagen, Denmark; 2017. Available from: https://research.cbs.dk/en/publications/what-is-fair-in-the-fair-transport-concept

[20] Bask AH. Relationships among TPL providers and members of supply chains – A strategic perspective. Journal of Business & Industrial Marketing. 2001;**16**(6):470-486

[21] Stefansson G. Collaborative logistics management and the role of third-party service providers. International Journal of Physical Distribution & Logistics Management. 2006;**36**(2):76-92

[22] Berglund M. Strategic Positioning of the Emerging Third-Party Logistics Providers. Linköping: International Graduate School of Management and Industrial Engineering; 2000

[23] Rajahonka M, Bask A, Lipponen M. Modularity and customisation in LSPs' service strategies. International Journal of Services and Operations Management. 2013;**16**(2):174-204

[24] Rajahonka M, Bask A. The development of outbound logistics services in the automotive industry a logistics service provider's view. International Journal of Logistics Management. 2016;**27**(3):707-737

[25] Marchet G, Melacini M, Sassi C, Tappia E. Assessing efficiency and innovation in the 3PL industry: An empirical analysis. International Journal of Logistics Research and Applications. 2017;**20**(1):53-72

[26] Hertz S. Domino effects in international networks. Journal of Business to Business Marketing. 1998;**5**(3):3-31

[27] Yarashova V, Hoshimov A. Comprehensive assessment methodology of the competitiveness of freight transport services. Transport Problems. 2021;**16**:187-198

[28] Naletina D, Petljak K, Rožić T. Outsourcing as a challenge for achieving competitive advantage in road freight industry – The case of Croatia. Promet – Traffic&Transportation. 2020;**32**:127-139

[29] Kennedy JW. Truck Driver Determinants of Service Quality as Perceived by Commercial Cargo Recipients. Fort Lauderdale-Davie: H. Wayne Huizenga School of Business and Entrepreneurship Nova Southeastern University; 2010

[30] Taylor GS, Garver MS, Williams Z. Owner operators: Employing a segmentation approach to improve retention. International Journal of Logistics Management. 2010;**21**(2):207-229

[31] Cruijssen F, Dullaert W, Fleuren H. Horizontal cooperation in transport and logistics: A literature review. Transportation Journal (American Society of Transportation & Logistics Inc). 2007;**46**(3):22-39

[32] Mason R, Lalwani C. Mass customised distribution. International Journal of Production Economics. 2008;**114**:71-83

[33] Hertz S, Alfredsson M. Strategic development of third party logistics providers. Industrial Marketing Management. 2003;**32**(2):139-149

[34] Voss MD, Cangelosi JD Jr, Rubach M, Nadler SS. An examination of small motor carrier survival techniques. International Journal of Logistics Management. 2011;**22**(1):87-103

[35] Näslund D, Kale R, Paulraj A. Action research in supply chain management—A framework for relevant and rigorous research. Journal of Business Logistics. 2010;**31**(2):331-355

[36] Lincoln YS, Guba EG. Naturalistic Inquiry. Newbury Park: Sage Publications; 1985. p. 416

Chapter 6

Resilient Supply Chain in United Arab Emirates

Shankar Subramanian Iyer and Ameeta Rawool

Abstract

Supply chain disruption refers to any event or occurrence that interrupts the flow of goods or services from suppliers to customers. This disruption can have a significant impact on businesses and can lead to delays, shortages, and increased costs. To mitigate the impact of supply chain disruptions, businesses can take several steps. These include diversifying their supplier base, maintaining safety stock levels, investing in technology to improve supply chain visibility, and developing contingency plans for dealing with disruptions. In addition, businesses can work with their suppliers and customers to build stronger relationships and improve communication and collaboration. This can help to identify potential issues early and allow for more effective problem-solving when disruptions do occur. Overall, supply chain disruption is a significant challenge for businesses, but with careful planning and proactive measures, it is possible to minimize the impact and maintain business continuity. The mixed methodology used in the research to capture the expertise opinions and the stakeholder's expectations of the Supply chain and its necessity to be resilient.

Keywords: supply chain, resilience, business continuity, UAE logistics, integrated transportation

1. Introduction

A resilient supply chain is one that is able to withstand and quickly recover from disruptions or unexpected events. It is a supply chain that has been designed to be flexible, agile, and adaptable, with the ability to quickly respond to changes in demand, supply, and market conditions. A resilient supply chain is able to continue functioning even in the face of unexpected events such as natural disasters, economic disruptions, or geopolitical changes. This is achieved through a combination of strategies such as redundancy in supply sources, inventory management, contingency planning, and communication and collaboration with suppliers, customers, and other stakeholders. The ability to quickly adjust to changes in demand, supply, or market conditions. The presence of multiple sources of supply or inventory to mitigate the impact of disruptions. The ability to track and monitor the movement of goods and materials throughout the supply chain [1]. Close communication and collaboration with suppliers, customers, and other stakeholders to identify potential risks and develop contingency plans. The ability to quickly adapt to changes in the business environment and to implement new processes or systems as needed. By building a resilient supply chain, businesses can minimize the impact of disruptions and maintain business continuity, even in the face of unexpected events. A resilient supply chain depends on several factors to ensure its effectiveness. Having multiple suppliers, manufacturing facilities, or distribution centers can help mitigate disruptions. If one location or supplier is affected, alternative options can be utilized to maintain the flow of goods [2]. A supply chain should be adaptable to changing circumstances. For example, having multiple suppliers for essential components or maintaining extra inventory levels can help ensure a continuous flow of materials and minimize the risk of disruption. This includes being able to quickly adjust production levels, switch suppliers, or modify transportation routes when necessary. This includes having alternative sourcing options, agile production capabilities, and the ability to quickly reconfigure distribution networks [3]. By being flexible, organizations can quickly adjust their operations to mitigate disruptions and maintain customer satisfaction. Having real-time visibility into the entire supply chain allows for better tracking and management of inventory, orders, and shipments. This helps identify potential bottlenecks or risks, allowing for timely actions to be taken [4]. Real-time data and analytics enable organizations to proactively identify potential disruptions and take appropriate actions to mitigate their impact. Building strong relationships and partnerships with suppliers, customers, and other stakeholders is essential. Collaborative efforts can lead to improved communication, shared information, and collective problem-solving during disruptions. Identifying and evaluating potential risks is crucial in building a resilient supply chain. Assessing both internal and external risks, such as natural disasters, geopolitical issues, or market fluctuations, helps in developing effective mitigation strategies [5]. By working together, organizations can leverage each other's strengths and resources, enhancing overall supply chain resilience. Leveraging technology solutions like advanced analytics, artificial intelligence, and automation can enhance supply chain resilience. These tools provide valuable insights, streamline processes, and enable faster decision-making. A resilient supply chain requires constant evaluation and enhancement. Regularly reviewing performance, analyzing past disruptions, and learning from them can help identify areas for improvement and lead to more robust operations. By considering and implementing these factors, businesses can build a resilient supply chain that can withstand various challenges and ensure continuity of operations and organizational resilience relies heavily on role-modeling behaviors [6]. This includes proactive risk assessment, implementing risk mitigation measures, and establishing contingency plans. Effective risk management enables organizations to anticipate and address potential disruptions before they occur. Most Employees are encouraged by a few credible and high-profile individuals in a company demonstrating resilient behaviors. Supply chain disruption can occur due to a variety of factors, including natural disasters, political instability, labor strikes, transportation issues, and supplier bankruptcy. In recent years, the COVID-19 pandemic has also caused significant supply chain disruptions, with many businesses struggling to source raw materials and finished products due to factory closures and shipping delays. Resilient supply chains prioritize a culture of continuous improvement, embracing innovation, and adapting to changing market dynamics. Technology integration refers to the incorporation of digital tools and technologies to enhance the efficiency, visibility, and agility of supply chain operations. This includes the use of advanced analytics, automation, Internet of Things (IoT), artificial intelligence (AI), and cloud computing. Technology integration enables organizations to streamline processes, improve decision-making, and respond quickly to disruptions in real-time. These factors work together to enhance the ability of organizations to withstand disruptions, recover quickly, and maintain operations while ensuring customer satisfaction [7].

Resilience can be nurtured through various individual behaviors. One important aspect is the ability to persevere in the face of adversity, showing determination to overcome challenges. It's also beneficial to exert effort and practice regularly, as these actions contribute to personal growth. Additionally, cultivating self-helping thought patterns and offering support and mentoring to others can enhance resilience. Leading with integrity, engaging in open communication, and demonstrating decisiveness further contribute to building resilience [8].

1.1 Research scope

The research scope for the study on "Resilient Supply Chain" will focus on analyzing the factors and strategies that contribute to the development and implementation of resilient supply chains. The study will explore various industries and sectors to understand the challenges faced and the best practices employed to ensure supply chain resilience. It will also investigate the role of technology and collaboration in enhancing supply chain resiliency.

1.2 Research questions

1. What are the key factors influencing the resilience of supply chains in different industries?

2. How does technology integration contribute to the development of resilient supply chains?

3. What are the challenges and barriers faced by organizations in implementing resilient supply chain practices?

1.3 Research objectives

1. To identify and analyze the factors that contribute to the resilience of supply chains in different industries.

2. To investigate the role of technology integration in enhancing supply chain resilience.

3. To explore the challenges and barriers faced by organizations in implementing resilient supply chain practices.

2. Literature review

Individual level factors such as mindset, commitment, family background, competencies, education, and technology savvy play a crucial role in influencing a resilient supply chain. Having a resilient mindset involves being adaptable, flexible, and possessing a positive attitude towards challenges. Individuals with a growth mindset are more likely to embrace change, learn from failures, and find innovative solutions to problems. This mindset encourages individuals to view disruptions as opportunities for growth and improvement, thereby contributing to a resilient supply chain. Resilience requires commitment from individuals to prioritize and invest in the necessary resources and actions to withstand and recover from disruptions [9]. This commitment involves a strong dedication to continuous improvement, risk management, and the willingness to go the extra mile to ensure the smooth functioning of the supply chain. Family background can shape an individual's resilience by providing a supportive environment that fosters resilience-building qualities such as perseverance, determination, and problem-solving skills. Growing up in a family that values resilience and encourages learning from setbacks can enhance an individual's ability to withstand disruptions and contribute to a resilient supply chain. Individual competencies, including technical skills, problem-solving abilities, and decision-making skills, are crucial for building resilience in the supply chain. Competencies such as effective communication, critical thinking, and collaboration enable individuals to proactively identify and address potential risks, make informed decisions, and work together effectively during times of disruption [10]. Education plays a significant role in developing the knowledge and skills needed to navigate complex supply chain challenges. Individuals with a strong educational background in supply chain management, logistics, risk management, and related fields are better equipped to understand the dynamics of the industry, anticipate potential disruptions, and implement proactive measures to mitigate risks. In today's digital era, being technologically savvy is vital for a resilient supply chain. Individuals who are familiar with emerging technologies, such as artificial intelligence, Internet of Things, and data analytics, can leverage these tools to monitor and analyze supply chain data, identify vulnerabilities, and implement proactive measures to enhance resilience [11]. Technology-savvy individuals can also adapt quickly to digital transformations and leverage digital platforms for effective communication and collaboration during disruptions. In summary, individual level factors such as mindset, commitment, family background, competencies, education, and technology savvy all contribute to building a resilient supply chain. By fostering these qualities and investing in continuous learning and improvement, individuals can play a critical role in ensuring the resilience and long-term success of the supply chain [12].

Organizational level factors, including organization culture, technology infrastructure, top management involvement, resources availability, collaboration and partnership, and competitive advantage, significantly influence a resilient supply chain. A resilient supply chain requires an organizational culture that promotes adaptability, agility, and a proactive approach to risk management. A culture that values continuous learning, innovation, and collaboration encourages employees to embrace change, identify potential disruptions, and implement necessary measures to mitigate risks promptly [13]. Robust technology infrastructure is essential for building a resilient supply chain. This includes implementing advanced supply chain management systems, data analytics tools, and other digital technologies that enable real-time monitoring, predictive analytics, and effective communication across the supply chain. A reliable technology infrastructure ensures transparency, improves decision-making, and enables quick responses to disruptions. The involvement and support of top management are crucial for establishing and maintaining a resilient supply chain [14]. When top management is actively engaged in risk assessment, decision-making, and resource allocation, it signals the importance of resilience throughout the organization. Their commitment and leadership help drive a culture of resilience and ensure that necessary resources and strategies are in place to handle disruptions effectively. Adequate resources, including financial, human, and technological resources, are vital for building and maintaining a resilient supply chain. Sufficient financial resources enable investments in technology, training, and risk mitigation strategies [15]. Human resources with the right skills and expertise are essential for identifying and managing risks effectively. Availability of advanced technology and tools helps in monitoring and responding to disruptions promptly. Collaboration and partnerships with suppliers, customers, and other stakeholders are crucial for building a resilient supply chain. Collaborative relationships facilitate the sharing of information, resources, and best practices, enabling a collective response to disruptions. Partnerships can also help in diversifying the supply base, sharing risks, and accessing alternative sources during disruptions. Building a resilient supply chain provides a competitive advantage in the market [16]. Organizations that prioritize resilience can effectively manage disruptions, reduce downtime, and recover faster, thereby maintaining customer satisfaction and loyalty. A resilient supply chain allows organizations to capitalize on market opportunities and gain a competitive edge over competitors who may struggle to adapt during disruptions. By focusing on these factors, organizations can enhance their ability to withstand disruptions, maintain operational continuity, and thrive in a rapidly changing business environment [17].

National level factors, including policies, trade agreements, threats, national initiatives, and international commitments, play a significant role in influencing the resilience of a supply chain. National policies related to trade, transportation, logistics, and risk management have a direct impact on the resilience of supply chains. Policies that promote transparency, collaboration, and risk mitigation measures can enhance the resilience of supply chains. For example, regulations on supply chain transparency and traceability can help identify and address vulnerabilities, while policies that promote investment in infrastructure and technology can improve the overall resilience of supply chains. Trade agreements between countries can affect the resilience of supply chains. Agreements that facilitate the movement of goods, reduce trade barriers, and promote stable and predictable trade relations can enhance the resilience of supply chains [18]. By reducing trade restrictions and promoting cooperation among nations, trade agreements can enable organizations to access diverse markets, suppliers, and resources, reducing dependency on a single source and enhancing resilience. National-level threats, such as natural disasters, political instability, terrorism, and pandemics, can significantly impact the resilience of supply chains. Governments play a crucial role in managing and mitigating these threats by implementing risk management strategies, providing emergency response plans, and supporting recovery efforts. Effective government interventions and preparedness can help minimize the impact of threats on supply chains and facilitate faster recovery [19]. National-level initiatives aimed at fostering resilience in supply chains can have a positive impact. Governments may launch initiatives to promote research and development, invest in critical infrastructure, and provide financial incentives for businesses to adopt resilient practices. Such initiatives can encourage organizations to proactively invest in risk management strategies, strengthen their supply chains, and build resilience. International commitments, such as agreements related to sustainability, climate change, and disaster management, can influence the resilience of supply chains. Organizations that align their strategies with international commitments and guidelines are more likely to prioritize resilience and adopt sustainable practices. By participating in international efforts, countries can share best practices, exchange information, and collaborate on building resilient supply chains. These factors can enhance the resilience of their supply chains, minimize disruptions, and foster sustainable economic growth [20].

The environmental level of integration of global systems, COVID times, lack of alternatives, carbon footprint, CSR initiatives, and overdependence on China all have significant impacts on the resilience of a supply chain. The interconnectedness of global systems, including transportation, communication, and technology networks, has both positive and negative implications for supply chain resilience. On one hand, global integration allows for efficient movement of goods, access to diverse markets, and availability of resources. However, it also increases vulnerability to disruptions. For example, a disruption in one part of the world can quickly propagate through global supply chains, affecting multiple countries and industries [21]. Therefore, the level of integration in global systems can significantly influence the resilience of supply chains. The COVID-19 pandemic has demonstrated the vulnerability of supply chains to unexpected shocks. Lockdowns, travel restrictions, and disruptions in production and transportation have severely impacted global supply chains. The pandemic highlighted the need for agility, flexibility, and risk mitigation strategies in supply chain management. Organizations have been compelled to reassess their sourcing strategies, diversify suppliers, and invest in digital technologies to ensure continuity and resilience in the face of future crises. A lack of alternatives in terms of suppliers, transportation routes, or sourcing options can reduce the resilience of a supply chain. Relying heavily on a single supplier or a specific region increases the risk of disruptions [22]. For example, if a natural disaster or political instability occurs in that region, it can lead to shortages and disruptions in the supply chain. Having alternative suppliers, transportation modes, and sourcing options can help mitigate such risks and enhance supply chain resilience. The carbon footprint, or the amount of greenhouse gas emissions produced in the supply chain, is an important consideration for resilience. Climate change and environmental concerns have led to increased regulations and consumer demands for sustainable practices [23]. Organizations that fail to reduce their carbon footprint may face reputational damage, legal consequences, and supply chain disruptions. Embracing sustainable practices, such as using renewable energy, optimizing transportation routes, and reducing waste, can enhance the resilience of supply chains in the long run. Corporate social responsibility (CSR) initiatives, including ethical sourcing, fair labor practices, and community engagement, can impact supply chain resilience. Organizations that prioritize CSR initiatives are more likely to build strong relationships with suppliers, communities, and stakeholders. This enhances trust, collaboration, and the ability to respond effectively to disruptions. In contrast, organizations that neglect CSR may face reputational risks, legal challenges, and disruptions due to social or environmental issues in their supply chains [24]. Many global supply chains have become heavily reliant on China as a major manufacturing hub. While China offers cost advantages and a vast supplier base, overdependence on a single country can create vulnerabilities. Disruptions such as trade disputes, political tensions, or natural disasters in China can have widespread consequences for supply chains worldwide. Diversifying sourcing strategies, exploring alternative manufacturing locations, and building redundancy in the supply chain can help reduce the overdependence on any single country and enhance supply chain resilience. Organizations need to consider these factors and take proactive measures to build robust and adaptable supply chains that can withstand disruptions, ensure sustainability, and maintain continuity in an ever-changing global landscape [25].

Indeed, seamless shifting, flexible systems, business continuity norms, business pressures, and opportunities are all factors that influence the resilience of a supply chain. The ability to seamlessly shift operations, resources, and production processes in response to disruptions is crucial for building a resilient supply chain. This involves having contingency plans, alternative suppliers, and backup facilities in place. When disruptions occur, organizations that can quickly and efficiently shift production, sourcing, or distribution to minimize downtime and maintain continuity are more likely to have a resilient supply chain. Flexibility is a key characteristic of a resilient supply chain. This includes having agile manufacturing processes that can easily adapt to changes in demand or disruptions in the supply chain [26]. Flexibility also extends to inventory management, transportation, and logistics. By having flexible systems in place, organizations can quickly adjust to unexpected events, such as sudden changes in customer preferences, supply shortages, or transportation disruptions. Establishing business continuity norms and practices is essential for ensuring the resilience of a supply chain. This involves identifying potential risks, developing contingency plans, and regularly testing and updating these plans. By having a well-defined business continuity strategy, organizations can minimize the impact of disruptions and recover quickly when unexpected events occur. This includes having backup systems, redundancy in critical operations, and clear communication channels to ensure the smooth flow of information and decision-making during disruptions [27]. External business pressures, such as market dynamics, competition, and customer demands, can significantly influence the resilience of a supply chain. Organizations that operate in highly competitive industries or face rapidly changing market conditions need to be agile and adaptable to maintain supply chain resilience. The ability to quickly respond to market shifts, changes in customer preferences, or new industry regulations is crucial for sustaining a resilient supply chain amidst business pressures [28]. Opportunities can also shape the resilience of a supply chain. This includes identifying and capitalizing on new market trends, emerging technologies, or potential collaborations. Organizations that actively seek and leverage opportunities can enhance their supply chain resilience by diversifying their customer base, exploring new markets, or adopting innovative technologies. By staying proactive and open to new possibilities, organizations can strengthen their supply chains and position themselves for long-term success. Organizations that prioritize these factors can adapt quickly to disruptions, maintain continuity, and seize opportunities for growth in an ever-evolving business environment [29].

The Integrated Multi-level Resilience Theory clearly depends on the Individual level, Organization level, National level, and Environmental level to ensure a Resilient Supply chain. The conceptual model and the Hypotheses formulated as shown in the **Figure 1** and have sub variables that influence this relationship. This conceptual model portrays a relationship which needs to be confirmed by Experts through semi-structured Interviews and the stakeholder's expectations through questionnaire survey. Therefore, Mixed Methodology will be used to establish the validity and reliability of this model [30].

2.1 Data analysis

The researcher used various descriptive statistical tools, such as (mean, median, mode, and standard deviation), and statistics for inference (correlation and regression analysis), to analyze the data collected from the questionnaire or survey. This allowed them to understand the responses and explore the relationships between different variables. Quantitative research techniques were used to analyze a large amount of data efficiently. However, a limitation was the inability to provide detailed explanations for participants choices. To address this, open-ended questions were included in the questionnaire to allow for more detailed feedback [31].

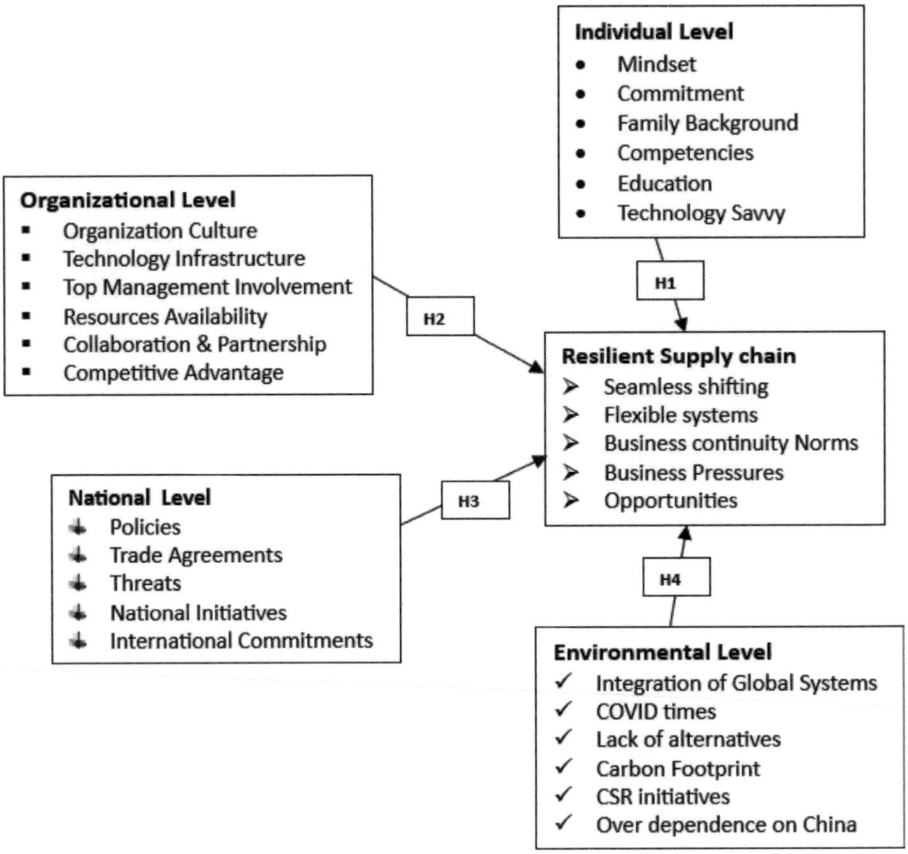

Figure 1.
Conceptual model—An integrated multi-level resilience theory. H1: The individual level factors have significant influence on the resilient supply chain; H2: The organization level factors have significant influence on the resilient supply chain; H3: The resilient supply chain depends on the national level factors; H4: There is significant relationship between the environmental level factors and the resilient supply chain.

To minimize bias, the study had a diverse and representative sample size of 432 participants from different countries. The questionnaire was well-structured, covering all relevant aspects of the research topic with clear and concise questions. The study combined qualitative and quantitative research techniques to gain a comprehensive understanding of the topic. Qualitative data provided detailed insights, while quantitative data allowed for statistical analysis [32].

Thematic analysis was used to analyze the data obtained from interviews. The researcher transcribed and reviewed the responses for accuracy. Main themes and sub-themes were identified by coding the data and reviewing them based on similarities. The findings were effectively presented using **Table 1**, which summarized the main themes and sub-themes found in the study.

Overall, this research study employed appropriate and effective methodologies to achieve the research objectives and obtain valid and reliable results [58].

The expert opinion on building a resilient supply chain and charting the path forward. Technology plays a vital role in generating innovative ideas, products, and services for supply chains. It's crucial for the logistics sector to keep up with the latest

Interviewee no, (years of experience), designation, location	Main comments on resilient supply chain (other interviewees comments in agreement)
1. (13) Vice President Logistics Sector, Dubai	• Growing up in an environment that values resilience and perseverance can instill these qualities in individuals. • A supportive family can also provide a strong foundation for personal and professional growth, which can contribute to building resilient supply chains. • Having the necessary skills and competencies is crucial for managing and maintaining a resilient supply chain. • By leveraging technology, individuals can make data-driven decisions, identify potential risks, and implement effective strategies to enhance the resilience of the supply chain (Interviewee 3, 8, 13) [33]
2. (12), CEO, Transportation Company, Abu Dhabi	• A positive and resilient mindset helps individuals navigate challenges and find solutions to disruptions effectively. • Commitment to the goals and objectives of a resilient supply chain is essential. • Individuals need to be dedicated and willing to put in the effort required to overcome obstacles and ensure the continuity of operations. • This commitment can be seen in employees' willingness to go the extra mile, take ownership of their responsibilities, and collaborate effectively with others (Interviewee 4, 6, 12) [34, 35].
3. (16), Senior Vice President, Logistics solution Company, Dubai	• Continuous education and learning are vital for building resilience in the supply chain. • Staying updated on industry trends, new technologies, and best practices allows individuals to adapt their knowledge and skills to changing circumstances. • Education also helps individuals develop critical thinking abilities, which are essential for making informed decisions during disruptions. • Technology plays a significant role in achieving a resilient supply chain. • Advanced technologies, such as artificial intelligence, blockchain, and data analytics, enable real-time visibility, predictive analytics, and streamlined communication and collaboration (Interviewee 2, 8, 14) [36, 37].
4. (16) CEO, Logistics Company, Fujairah	• resilient supply chain requires individuals to have a proactive and adaptable mindset, open to change, embracing innovation, and being willing to learn and adapt to new technologies and processes. • Family background can have an impact on an individual's resilience. • Individuals can contribute to building and maintaining a robust and adaptable supply chain. • This includes technical skills, such as data analysis and logistics management, as well as soft skills like communication, problem-solving, and decision-making. • Competent individuals can effectively respond to disruptions, mitigate risks, and find innovative solutions to challenges (Interviewee 1, 10, 15) [38].
5. (11) HR Manager Technology sector, Dubai	• A strong organizational culture that emphasizes adaptability, openness to change, and continuous improvement fosters a resilient supply chain.

Interviewee no, (years of experience), designation, location	Main comments on resilient supply chain (other interviewees comments in agreement)
	• By promoting a culture of innovation and risk-taking, organizations can better respond to disruptions and quickly adapt their supply chain strategies. • Sufficient resources, including financial, human, and technological resources, are essential for building a resilient supply chain. • A resilient supply chain can provide a competitive advantage to organizations. • By effectively managing disruptions, minimizing downtime, and maintaining customer satisfaction, companies can differentiate themselves from competitors (Interviewee 7, 8, 10) [39, 40].
6. (12) Public sector Administration Manager, Sharjah	• An efficient and robust technology infrastructure enables effective communication, visibility, and real-time data sharing across the supply chain. • This allows organizations to proactively identify and address potential disruptions, improve coordination, and make informed decisions to maintain supply chain resilience. • This advantage allows organizations to attract more customers and thrive in dynamic market conditions. • Organizations can enhance their ability to withstand and recover from disruptions effectively • Building strong collaborative relationships and partnerships with suppliers, customers, and other stakeholders is critical for a resilient supply chain (Interviewee 3, 8, 12, 15) [41].
7. (6) General Manager Cargo Services, Sharjah	• The involvement of top management in supply chain decision-making is crucial for resilience. • When leaders prioritize and actively participate in supply chain risk management, they can allocate necessary resources, establish clear goals, and provide guidance to ensure resilience strategies are implemented effectively. • Adequate investment in infrastructure, personnel training, and technology advancements enables organizations to respond swiftly to disruptions, recover quickly, and maintain consistent supply chain operations. • Through collaborative efforts, organizations can share information, jointly develop contingency plans, and support each other during disruptions, thereby enhancing overall supply chain resilience (Interviewee 6, 9, 13) [42].
8. (8) Head of University IT Operations, Dubai	• Policies that promote stability, transparency, and investment in infrastructure can enhance the resilience of supply chains. • International trade agreements impact supply chain resilience by facilitating trade and reducing barriers. • By providing a favorable trade environment, organizations can access diverse markets, suppliers, and resources, thereby enhancing their resilience. • Government initiatives to support and promote supply chain resilience can have a positive influence. • Adequate preparedness and response mechanisms can help organizations minimize the impact of such threats on their supply chains (Interviewee 4, 7, 11, 13) [43].
9. (9) International Consultant, Abu Dhabi	• National-level threats, such as natural disasters, political instability, terrorism, or economic crises, can significantly impact supply chain resilience.

Interviewee no, (years of experience), designation, location	Main comments on resilient supply chain (other interviewees comments in agreement)
	• Governments need to assess and mitigate these threats through proactive measures like risk assessment, infrastructure development, and contingency planning. • For example, policies focused on disaster preparedness, risk management, and supply chain security can help organizations mitigate potential disruptions and recover quickly. • Overdependence on a single country, such as China, for manufacturing and sourcing can pose risks to supply chain resilience. • These commitments drive organizations to adopt sustainable practices, promote responsible sourcing, and build more resilient supply chains in the face of environmental and social challenges. • Organizations need to identify alternative sources, develop contingency plans, and establish relationships with multiple suppliers to mitigate the risks associated with a lack of alternatives (Interviewee 2, 9, 13) [44].
10. (7) Commercial Vice President Airport Services ITC, Dubai	• Government policies play a crucial role in shaping the overall business environment and supply chain resilience. • These agreements can lead to more stable and predictable supply chains by promoting cross-border cooperation, harmonizing regulations, and reducing trade restrictions. • National initiatives that focus on fostering collaboration, knowledge sharing, and capacity building can also strengthen the overall resilience of supply chains. • Corporate Social Responsibility (CSR) Initiatives • Commitments made by nations at an international level, such as climate change agreements or sustainable development goals, can indirectly impact supply chain resilience • A well-integrated global system enables efficient coordination, visibility, and responsiveness across the supply chain network, enhancing its ability to withstand disruptions and recover quickly (Interviewee 1, 8, 9, 12) [45, 46].
11. (6) Vice President, Environmental Agency, Dubai	• The COVID-19 pandemic has exposed vulnerabilities in global supply chains due to disruptions in transportation, trade restrictions, and shortages of essential goods. • The pandemic has prompted organizations and governments to reassess supply chain strategies, invest in resilience-building measures, and diversify sourcing and manufacturing locations to reduce dependence on a single region. • Supply chains that rely heavily on a single source or location for critical components or raw materials are more vulnerable to disruptions. • A lack of alternatives can lead to bottlenecks and delays in the supply chain when that source is disrupted. • The integration of global systems, such as transportation networks, communication technologies, and information sharing platforms, plays a crucial role in supply chain resilience. • Organizations are under pressure to reduce their carbon footprint and adopt eco-friendly practices (Interviewee 1, 4, 8, 10, 12) [47, 48].
12. (10) Senior Executive, Corporate Services, Sharjah	• By having agile processes and systems in place, businesses can swiftly respond to unexpected events and maintain uninterrupted operations.

Interviewee no, (years of experience), designation, location	Main comments on resilient supply chain (other interviewees comments in agreement)
	• By having a flexible infrastructure, businesses can effectively manage disruptions while minimizing disruptions to their supply chain. • This includes utilizing advanced technologies such as real-time tracking, data analytics, and automation to enhance visibility, optimize inventory management, and improve overall efficiency. • Resilient supply chains have the ability to adapt and shift seamlessly when faced with disruptions (Interviewee 1, 5, 6, 13) [49, 50].
13. (3) Senior Maintenance Director, Dubai	• Implementing flexible systems within the supply chain allows for quick adjustments and adaptations to changing circumstances. • This may involve optimizing processes, streamlining operations, or collaborating with suppliers and partners to enhance overall resilience. • By having clear protocols in place, businesses can swiftly recover from disruptions and maintain continuity during challenging times. • This involves proactively identifying potential risks, establishing contingency plans, and quickly implementing alternative strategies to mitigate any negative impacts (Interviewee 1, 7, 10, 14) [51]
14. (4) General Manager Healthcare Logistics Group, Sharjah	• Establishing robust business continuity involves developing comprehensive risk management strategies, creating backup plans, and ensuring the availability of alternative resources or suppliers. • Resilient supply chains consider the various pressures that businesses face, such as cost constraints, market dynamics, and customer expectations. • By continuously monitoring these pressures, businesses can identify potential vulnerabilities and proactively implement measures to address them (Interviewee 7, 10, 12, 14) [52–54].
15. (7) Startup Entrepreneur in Logistics	• Resilience is not just about surviving disruptions but also leveraging opportunities that arise. • By staying alert to market trends, emerging technologies, and new business models, organizations can identify potential growth areas and adapt their supply chain accordingly. • Embracing innovation and exploring strategic partnerships can help businesses stay ahead of the competition and seize new opportunities that contribute to a resilient supply chain (Interviewee 2, 7, 11, 15) [55–57].

Source: Developed by the Author.

Table 1.
Interview summary.

technological trends and actively experiment with new technologies to unlock their potential benefits. Moreover, the transportation industry should be mindful of the ethical implications when using technology in their operations, ensuring it aligns with their core values. While technology offers immense opportunities for supply chains, it's important to approach its implementation carefully, considering the potential risks and impacts it may bring [59].

3. Quantitative analysis using ADANCO output

3.1 Analysis of the measurement model

The study used various methods to ensure the validity of the constructs. First, it calculated the Dijkstra-Henseler's rho (ρA) coefficient and AVE values to check the convergent validity. Second, it performed discriminant validity analysis to verify that the constructs were distinct from each other. The analysis showed that the correlations within each construct were higher than those with other constructs. Third, it applied structural equation modeling (SEM) to test hypotheses and examine the relationships among the constructs. SEM is a powerful statistical technique that can handle complex models and test multiple relationships at the same time. It was suitable and useful for this study, as it helped to understand how the constructs were connected. In conclusion, the study followed reliable and proven methods to evaluate construct validity, convergent validity, and discriminant validity. The use of SEM enabled a thorough investigation of the relationships among the constructs. The results provide valuable insights into the Resilient Supply Chain (**Table 2**) [32].

In PLS path modeling, assessing construct validity often involves using indicator variables and their outer loading values. This approach is widely recognized and accepted. Typically, a standardized outer loading value of 0.70 or higher is deemed acceptable to determine the quality of a measure. This value indicates that the indicator variable effectively represents the construct it measures. In this study, **Table 3** is utilized to present the outer loading values for each indicator variable. This presentation method offers a clear and concise overview, facilitating easy understanding and interpretation of the data. It significantly contributes to the effectiveness of assessing construct validity. Overall, the appropriate and fruitful application of indicator variables and their outer loading values in this study is evident from the results, which demonstrate that the indicator variables served as reliable measures for their respective constructs, surpassing the 0.7 threshold [60].

The validity of the relationships of all p-values are well below 0.05 and well supported (**Table 4**). The results data support and authenticate all the hypotheses were authenticated [61].

	Convergent validity		**Construct reliability**	
Latent variables	**AVE > 0.50**	**ρA reliability > 0.70**	**Pc reliability > 0.70**	**Cronbach's alpha(α) > 0.70**
Individual level factors	0.5145	0.8109	0.8731	0.8731
Organization level factors	0.5234	0.8659	0.8675	0.8654
National level factors	0.5569	0.8638	0.8256	0.8355
Environmental level factors	0.5787	0.8725	0.8581	0.8498
Resilient supply chain factors	0.5468	0.8643	0.8725	0.8732

Source: ADANCO result, 2023.

Table 2.
Analysis of measurement model.

Construct	Individual level factors	Organization level factors	National level factors	Environmental level factors	Resilient supply chain factors
Individual level factors					
Organization level factors	0.8465				
National level factors	0.7253	0.8456			
Environmental level factors	0.6498	0.7857	0.8123		
Resilient supply chain factors	0.6174	0.6916	0.7932	0.8645	

Source: ADANCO results, 2023.

Table 3.
Discriminant validity heterotrait-monotrait ratio.

Effect	Original coefficient β	Standard bootstrap results				
		Mean value	Standard error	t-value	p-value (2-sided)	Hypotheses Supported
Individual level factors → Resilient supply chain factors	0.245	0.2115	0.0741	5.674	0.0021	Yes
Organization level factors → Resilient supply chain factors	0.465	0.4148	0.0904	6.793	0.0031	yes
Environmental level factors → Resilient supply chain factors	0.532	0.4821	0.0413	15.762	0.0000	Yes
Individual level factors → Organization level factors	0.1383	0.0968	0.0443	6.7643	0.0000	Yes
Environmental level factors → Individual level factors	0.2314	0.1903	0.0432	4.3345	0.0000	yes
Environmental level factors → Organization level factors	0.6542	0.5752	0.1092	11.341	0.0012	yes
National level factors → Environmental level factors	0.3613	0.2959	0.1077	4.3241	0.0041	yes
National level factors → Organization level factors	0.2114	0.1761	0.1502	12.344	0.0000	yes

Source: ADANCO results, 2023.

Table 4.
Direct effect interference.

Table 5 shows the discriminant validity measures, which indicate how much a variable is related to other variables in the structural model. The Fornell-Larcker criterion and cross-loadings are used to measure the discriminant validity. The bold figures on the diagonal are the highest in each row and column, which means that the discriminant validity is confirmed. The output from ADANCO 2.3 was used to generate the table (**Table 6**) [60].

Construct	Individual Level Factors	Organization Level Factors	National Level Factors	Environmental Level Factors	Resilient Supply Chain Factors
Individual level factors	**0.5820**				
Organization level factors	0.5761	**0.6544**			
National level factors	0.5360	0.6323	**0.7812**		
Environmental level factors	0.5254	0.6253	0.6519	**0.8278**	
Resilient supply chain factors	0.4334	0.5234	0.6231	0.7531	**0.8769**

Table 5.
Discriminant validity.

Indicator	Individual level factors	Organization level factors	National level factors	Environmental level factors	Resilient supply chain factors
(INDVF1)	0.7568				
(INDVF2)	0.7253				
(INDVF3)	0.6903				
(INDVF4)	0.7385				
(INDVF5)	0.7823				
(INDVF6)	0.8226				
(ORGF1)		0.7954			
(ORGF2)		0.7445			
(ORGF3)		0.6643			
(ORGF4)		0.8215			
(ORGF5)		0.7791			
(ORGF6)		0.7348			
(NATF1)			0.7550		
(NATF2)			0.6916		
(NATF3)			0.6505		
(NATF4)			0.7561		
(NATF5)			0.7604		
(ENVPF1)				0.6834	
(ENVPF2)				0.8754	
(ENVPF3)				0.6610	
(ENVPF4)				0.7261	
(ENVPF5)				0.7660	
(ENVPF6)				0.7828	
(RSCF1)					0.6843

Indicator	Individual level factors	Organization level factors	National level factors	Environmental level factors	Resilient supply chain factors
(RSCF2)					0.7636
(RSCF3)					0.7547
(RSCF4)					0.7215
(RSCF5)					0.7104

Table 6.
Loadings of indicator loadings.

Construct	Coefficient of determination (R^2)	Adjusted R^2
Individual level factors	0.6031	0.5815
Organization level factors	0.4152	0.3876
National level factors	0.3530	0.3285
Environmental level factors	0.5333	0.4932
Resilient supply chain factors	0.7654	0.7256

Table 7.
R-squared.

The cross loadings in **Table 7** shows how the variables affect each other. The construct relationship to all the constructs in the research study is explained by the coefficient of determination (R2). The construct is relevant and significant if the value of R2 is more than 0.25, which is the minimum requirement [62]. The result shows that the value of R2 of Resilient Supply chain is 0.7654, which is high and indicates that the construct is important and significant in explaining all the variables in the research.

Figure 2 shows the PLS-SEM validation framework given by the ADANCO software.

This research paper has made a useful contribution by developing and testing the above research framework for validity and reliability using PLS-SEM. The framework was based on the consensus of 432 respondents, who were stakeholders of the Supply

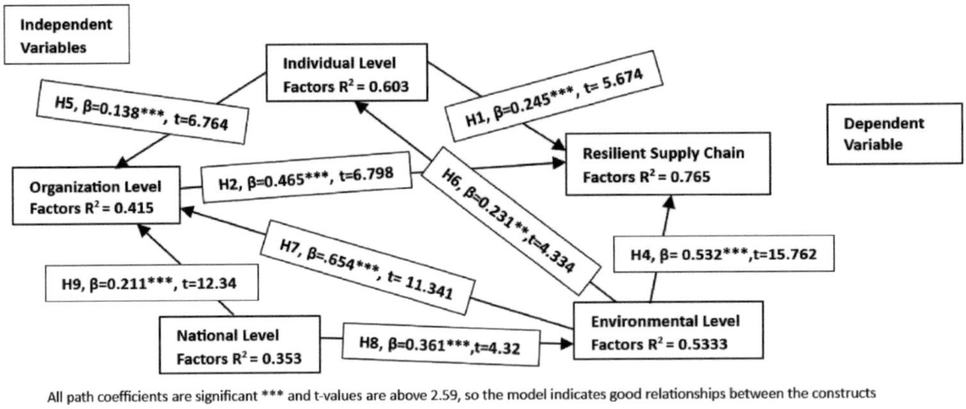

Figure 2.
PLS-SEM validation.

Hypotheses no	Construe description	β-value	t-value	Significance $t \geq 2.59$ $1.96 \leq t \leq 2.59$	Hypotheses supported or not supported
H1	Individual level factors → Resilient supply chain factors	0.245	5.674	Strong	Yes
H2	Organization level factors → Resilient supply chain factors	0.465	6.798	Strong	Yes
H3	National level factors → Resilient supply chain factors	0.00	0.00	No	No
H4	Environmental level factors → Resilient supply chain factors	0.532	15.762	Strong	Yes

Table 8.
Showing the direct relationships.

Chain and Logistics sector. The methodology followed addressed the lack of relevant data for future researchers and paved the way for further research by building on this model or similar models. The above-mentioned theories have their relevance in certain situations, such as stable economies, equal education opportunities, and infrastructure availability. However, these theories seem insufficient to explain many factors in times of recession, COVID, or sanction regimes. Therefore, a solid and research-based framework was created to contribute to further work (**Tables 8** and **9**) [63].

The next level relationships are not relevant as the β value will be well below the 0.01 levels hence not considered in this study [60].

Table 10 summarizes the Similarity in the outcomes ascertained by qualitative and quantitative methodologies.

Hypotheses No	Construe Description	β-value	t-value	Significance $t \geq 1.96$	Hypotheses Supported or not supported
H52	Individual level factors → Resilient supply chain factors through organization level factors	0.064	7.856	Strong	Yes
H61	Environmental level factors → Resilient supply chain factors through individual level factors	0.056	6.7433	Strong	Yes
H72	Environmental level factors → Resilient supply chain factors through organization level factors	0.304	6.2745	Strong	Yes
H84	National level factors → Resilient supply chain factors through environmental level factors	0.192	4.2745	Strong	Yes
H92	National level factors → Resilient supply chain factors through organization level factors	0.098	8.2745	Strong	Yes

Table 9.
Indirect relationships.

Qualitative outcomes	Quantitative outcomes
The individual level factors, the organization level factors, national level factors, and the environmental factors will influence the resilient supply chain factors.	H1—Individual level factors, $\beta_{INDVF-RSCF}$ = 0.245, t = 5.674 indicates a Strong relationship H2—Organization level factors, $\beta_{ORGF-RSCF}$ = 0.465, t = 6.798, indicates a strong relationship H3—National level factors, $\beta_{ORGF-RSCF}$ = 0.465, t = 6.798, indicates a strong relationship H4—Environmental level factors, $\beta_{ORGF-RSCF}$ = 0.465, t = 6.798, indicates a strong relationship H52—Individual level factors_organization level factors, $\beta_{INDVF-ORGF-RSCF}$ = 0.064, t = 7.856, indicates a strong relationship H61—Environmental level factors_individual level factors, $\beta_{ENVF-INDVF-RSCF}$ = 0.056, t = 6.7433, indicates a strong relationship (t > 2.59) H72—Environmental level factors_organizational level factors, $\beta_{ENVF-ORGF-RSCF}$ = 0.304, t = 6.2745, indicates a strong relationship (t > 2.59) H84—National level factors_ environmental level factors, $\beta_{NATF-ENVF-RSCF}$ = 0.192, t = 4.2745, indicates a strong relationship (t > 2.59) H92—National level factors_ organizational level factors, $\beta_{NATF-ORGF-RSCF}$ = 0.098, t = 8.2745, indicates a strong relationship (t > 2.59)
This coincides exactly with both the methodologies so; it is validated, and reliability tested to greater extent [64].	

Table 10.
Similarity in outcomes.

3.2 Differences in outcomes

The main areas of disagreement in both the methodologies are much less restrictive to the None (no direct significance) i.e., H3 in Direct relationship **Table 8** and has established indirect relationship, as seen in **Table 9**, H84 and H92 through the Environmental Level Factors and Organizational Level Factors, seen in the Quantitative methodology (proven statistically). However, the indirect relationship displays there exists a relationship. The difference in outcomes can be attributed to due to the lack of awareness of the stakeholders (Participants of the Survey) on the Resilient Supply chain in various Sector applications, whereas the top management of Logistics and Transport experts (Participants of the Interviews) have exposure to the issues. Another area is sustainability; most stakeholders only know this as Pollution, Carbon Footprint and do not understand the Green initiative values and modes that are possible [64].

4. Conclusion and recommendation

4.1 Implications of this research

Practical Implications: The research study on "Resilient Supply Chain" focuses on enhancing the durability and adaptability of supply chains in today's interconnected world. It addresses the impact of disruptions like natural disasters, political instability, and pandemics on supply chain operations. The study emphasizes proactive risk management through identifying vulnerabilities and developing strategies such as diversifying suppliers, establishing backup plans, and implementing monitoring systems. Building resilient supply chains involves quick response and adaptation, achieved through multiple sourcing options, buffer stocks, and advanced forecasting techniques. Collaboration and communication among supply chain partners are crucial for addressing disruptions and finding innovative solutions. Technology adoption, including data analytics, real-time tracking, and automation, enhances supply chain resilience. Continuous monitoring, evaluation, and improvement are emphasized to ensure long-term efficiency and resilience [65].

Social implications: The study on "Resilient Supply Chain" has social implications as it aims to minimize disruptions caused by natural disasters, political instability, and pandemics. By enhancing supply chain durability and adaptability, it ensures the availability of essential goods and services during challenging times. Identifying risks and vulnerabilities helps companies proactively manage them, preventing shortages or delays in critical products. Collaboration among supply chain partners fosters stronger relationships and coordination, benefiting society. Leveraging technology improves efficiency, reduces waste, and promotes a sustainable and socially responsible supply chain. Additionally, leveraging technology and digital tools in supply chain operations can have positive social implications. Implementing real-time tracking systems and automation technologies can improve efficiency and reduce waste, contributing to sustainable practices. This can result in cost savings and environmental benefits, promoting a more sustainable and socially responsible supply chain [66].

Managerial implications: The research study on "Resilient Supply Chain" has several managerial implications. Firstly, it highlights the importance of identifying and assessing potential risks and vulnerabilities in supply chains. This allows managers to develop strategies to proactively manage and mitigate these risks, ensuring uninterrupted flow of goods and services. Secondly, the study emphasizes the need for collaboration and communication among supply chain partners. Managers should foster stronger relationships and coordination with partners to effectively address disruptions and find innovative solutions. Sharing information and coordinating efforts can lead to more efficient and effective responses, minimizing the social impact of disruptions. Thirdly, the research underscores the role of technology and digital tools in supply chain operations. Managers should consider implementing real-time tracking systems and automation technologies to improve efficiency, reduce waste, and contribute to sustainable practices. This not only results in cost savings but also promotes a more socially responsible supply chain [67].

5. Limitations and future research

The study on the "Resilient Supply Chain" has limitations that should be considered. Firstly, it focuses on a specific industry, limiting the generalizability of the findings to other sectors. Future research should explore the applicability of these findings across different industries. Secondly, the study may have relied on subjective measures, introducing bias or inaccuracies. Future research could use more objective and standardized measures for greater validity. Additionally, the study may not have considered all factors that impact supply chain resilience, such as political instability or natural disasters. Future studies could explore these variables for a more comprehensive understanding. Furthermore, the study did not examine the long-term effects or sustainability of the suggested strategies. Future research should evaluate the long-term impact on performance, profitability, and environmental sustainability. Finally, the study could have explored the role of human resources and organizational culture in building resilient supply chains. Future research should investigate how employee competencies and corporate culture contribute to supply chain resilience.

6. The contribution and originality

6.1 Value of the research

The main contribution of this study is the development of the Multi-level Integrated Process theory for the conceptual model. It focuses on understanding and improving the resilience of supply chains, providing valuable insights into strategies, practices, and factors that enhance resilience. The research examines specific industries, offering recommendations to practitioners in those sectors and identifying key factors for building resilient supply chains. It emphasizes the consideration of external factors like political instability and natural disasters, providing a comprehensive understanding of the complexities involved. The study also highlights the need for objective measures and rigorous research methods to enhance the validity of findings, guiding future research in the field.

7. Conclusion

In conclusion, the Multi-level Integrated Process theory offers a comprehensive framework for understanding the drivers of Resilient Supply Chain and its practical usefulness. This study has made significant contributions to the field by providing valuable insights into strategies, practices, and factors that can enhance the resilience of supply chains. By focusing on specific industries or contexts, the research has provided relevant and practical recommendations for practitioners in those sectors. The study's emphasis on considering external factors, such as political instability and natural disasters, further enhances its value in understanding and enhancing supply chain resilience. Additionally, the study highlights the importance of objective and standardized measures to improve the validity of research findings. Overall, this study has significantly advanced the existing literature on resilient supply chains, offering valuable insights, recommendations, and a comprehensive understanding of the complexities involved. It serves as a foundational work for future research and provides practical guidance for practitioners seeking to enhance the resilience of their supply chains.

DOI: http://dx.doi.org/10.5772/intechopen.113128

Author details

Shankar Subramanian Iyer[1]* and Ameeta Rawool[2]

1 S.P. Jain School of Global Management and Westford University College, UK

2 Self-Employed, Sharjah, UAE

*Address all correspondence to: shankar.subramanien@gmail.com

References

[1] Shashi, Centobelli P, Cerchione R, Ertz M. Managing supply chain resilience to pursue business and environmental strategies. Business Strategy and the Environment. 2020; **29**(3):1215-1246. DOI: 10.1002/bse.2428

[2] Butt AS. Strategies to mitigate the impact of COVID-19 on supply chain disruptions: A multiple case analysis of buyers and distributors. The International Journal of Logistics Management. 2021. DOI: 10.1108/IJLM-11-2020-0455 [Ahead-of-print]

[3] Siagian H, Tarigan ZJH, Jie F. Supply chain integration enables resilience, flexibility, and innovation to improve business performance in COVID-19 era. Sustainability. 2021;**13**(9):4669. DOI: 10.3390/su13094669

[4] Er Kara M, Ghadge A, Bititci US. Modelling the impact of climate change risk on supply chain performance. International Journal of Production Research. 2021;**59**(24):7317-7335. DOI: 10.1080/00207543.2020.1849844

[5] Soyer A, Bozdag E, Kadaifci C, Asan U, Serdarasan S. A hesitant approach to sustainable supply chain risk assessment. Journal of Cleaner Production. 2023;**418**:138103. DOI: 10.1016/j.jclepro.2023.138103

[6] Mukhwana C, Levasseur RE. Embodying authentic leadership in nascent entrepreneurship for sustainable success. Open Journal of Business and Management. 2023;**11**(4):1417-1439. DOI: 10.4236/ojbm.2023.114078

[7] Song M, Ma X, Zhao X, Zhang L. How to enhance supply chain resilience: A logistics approach. The International Journal of Logistics Management. 2022; **33**(4):1408-1436. DOI: 10.1108/IJLM-04-2021-0211

[8] Beuren IM, Santos VD, Bernd DC. Effects of the management control system on empowerment and organizational resilience. BBR. Brazilian Business Review. 2020;**17**:211-232. Available from: https://www.scielo.br/j/bbr/a/9gD6R3BqPNtcXM7frbvJKSB/

[9] Ghomi V, Nooraei SVR, Shekarian N, Shokoohyar S, Parast M. Improving supply chain resilience through investment in flexibility and innovation. International Journal of Systems Science: Operations & Logistics. 2023;**10**(1): 2221068. DOI: 10.1080/23302674.2023.2221068

[10] Martínez-Peláez R, Ochoa-Brust A, Rivera S, Félix VG, Ostos R, Brito H, et al. Role of digital transformation for achieving sustainability: Mediated role of stakeholders, key capabilities, and technology. Sustainability. 2023;**15**(14): 11221. DOI: 10.3390/su151411221

[11] Grewal D, Hulland J, Kopalle PK, Karahanna E. The future of technology and marketing: A multidisciplinary perspective. Journal of the Academy of Marketing Science. 2020;**48**:1-8. DOI: 10.1007/s11747-019-00711-4

[12] Kiradoo G. Exploring the opportunities and challenges for entrepreneurs in industry 4.0. Current Topics on Business, Economics and Finance. 2023;**2**:180-196. Available from: https://papers.ssrn.com/sol3/papers.cfm?abstract_id=4388004

[13] Silva ME, Pereira MM, Hendry LC. Embracing change in tandem: Resilience and sustainability together transforming supply chains. International Journal of Operations & Production Management.

2023;**43**(1):166-196. DOI: 10.1108/IJOPM-09-2022-0625

[14] Karmaker CL, Al Aziz R, Palit T, Bari AM. Analyzing supply chain risk factors in the small and medium enterprises under fuzzy environment: Implications towards sustainability for emerging economies. Sustainable Technology and Entrepreneurship. 2023a; **2**(1):100032. DOI: 10.1016/j.stae.2022.100032

[15] Karmaker CL, Bari AM, Anam MZ, Ahmed T, Ali SM, de Jesus Pacheco DA, et al. Industry 5.0 challenges for post-pandemic supply chain sustainability in an emerging economy. International Journal of Production Economics. 2023b; **258**:108806. DOI: 10.1016/j.ijpe.2023.108806

[16] Irfan I, Sumbal MSUK, Khurshid F, Chan FT. Toward a resilient supply chain model: Critical role of knowledge management and dynamic capabilities. Industrial Management & Data Systems. 2022;**122**(5):1153-1182. DOI: 10.1108/IMDS-06-2021-0356

[17] Hervani AA, Nandi S, Helms MM, Sarkis J. A performance measurement framework for socially sustainable and resilient supply chains using environmental goods valuation methods. Sustainable Production and Consumption. 2022;**30**:31-52. DOI: 10.1016/j.spc.2021.11.026

[18] Pretorius OR, Drewes JE, Engelbrecht WH, Malan GC. Developing resilient supply chains in the southern African development community: Lessons from the impact of COVID-19. Journal of Transport and Supply Chain Management. 2022;**16**:737. DOI: 10.4102/jtscm.v16i0.737

[19] Chang SE, Brown C, Handmer J, Helgeson J, Kajitani Y, Keating A, et al. Business recovery from disasters: Lessons from natural hazards and the COVID-19 pandemic. International Journal of Disaster Risk Reduction. 2022; **80**:103191. DOI: 10.1016/j.ijdrr.2022.103191

[20] Sirisomboonsuk P, Burns J. Sustainability in supply chains through rapid capacity increases and minimized disruptions. Sustainability. 2023;**15**(7):5629. DOI: 10.3390/su15075629

[21] LaBelle J, Santacreu AM. Global supply chain disruptions and inflation during the COVID-19 pandemic. 2022. Available at SSRN 4029211. https://papers.ssrn.com/sol3/papers.cfm?abstract_id=4029211

[22] Panwar R, Pinkse J, De Marchi V. The future of global supply chains in a post-COVID-19 world. California Management Review. 2022;**64**(2):5-23. DOI: 10.1177/0008125621107

[23] Shetty SK, Bhat KS. Green supply chain management practices implementation and sustainability–a review. Materials Today: Proceedings. 2022;**52**:735-740. DOI: 10.1016/j.matpr.2021.10.135

[24] Schoenherr T, Mena C, Vakil B, Choi TY. Creating resilient supply chains through a culture of measuring. Journal of Purchasing and Supply Management. 2023;**29**(4):100824. DOI: 10.1016/j.pursup.2023.100824

[25] Xing Y. China and global value chain restructuring. China Economic Journal. 2022;**15**(3):310-329. DOI: 10.1080/17538963.2022.2117198

[26] Azmat M, Ahmed S, Mubarik MS. Supply chain resilience in the fourth industrial revolution. In: Supply Chain Resilience: Insights from Theory and Practice. Cham: Springer International

Publishing; 2022. pp. 149-163. DOI: 10.1007/978-3-030-95401-7_13

[27] Riglietti FG. Business continuity management as a key enabler of supply chain resilience: A conceptual paper. IFAC-PapersOnLine. 2022;**55**(10): 2197-2202. DOI: 10.1016/j.ifacol.2022.10.034

[28] Dubey R, Bryde DJ, Dwivedi YK, Graham G, Foropon C, Papadopoulos T. Dynamic digital capabilities and supply chain resilience: The role of government effectiveness. International Journal of Production Economics. 2023;**258**: 108790. DOI: 10.1016/j.ijpe.2023.108790

[29] Yuan R, Luo J, Liu MJ, Yu J. Understanding organizational resilience in a platform-based sharing business: The role of absorptive capacity. Journal of Business Research. 2022;**141**:85-99. DOI: 10.1016/j.jbusres.2021.11.012

[30] Hendren K, Newcomer K, Pandey SK, Smith M, Sumner N. How qualitative research methods can be leveraged to strengthen mixed methods research in public policy and public administration? Public Administration Review. 2023;**83**(3):468-485. DOI: 10.1111/puar.13528

[31] Mehralian MM. Identifying and explaining the effective factors of digital marketing strategies in consumers' emotional states and sales rates: A mixed methods research. In: 20th International Conference of the Business and Strategic Management. 2022. Available from: https://papers.ssrn.com/sol3/papers.cfm?abstract_id=4195988

[32] Iyer SS, Seetharaman A, Maddulety K. Education transformation using block chain technology—A student centric model. In: Sharma SK, Dwivedi YK, Metri B, Rana NP, editors. Re-Imagining Diffusion and Adoption of Information Technology and Systems: A Continuing Conversation. TDIT 2020. IFIP Advances in Information and Communication Technology. Vol. 617. Cham: Springer; 2020. DOI: 10.1007/978-3-030-64849-7_19

[33] Chenger D, Pettigrew RN. Leveraging data-driven decisions: A framework for building intracompany capability for supply chain optimization and resilience. Supply Chain Management: An International Journal. 2023. DOI: 10.1108/SCM-12-2022-0464 [Ahead-of-print]

[34] Silva ME, Ruel S. Inclusive purchasing and supply chain resilience capabilities: Lessons for social sustainability. Journal of Purchasing and Supply Management. 2022;**28**(5):100767. DOI: 10.1016/j.pursup.2022.100767

[35] Singh J, Hamid ABA, Garza-Reyes JA. Supply chain resilience strategies and their impact on sustainability: An investigation from the automobile sector. Supply Chain Management: An International Journal. 2023;**28**(4): 787-802. DOI: 10.1108/SCM-06-2022-0225

[36] Gupta H, Yadav AK, Kusi-Sarpong S, Khan SA, Sharma SC. Strategies to overcome barriers to innovative digitalisation technologies for supply chain logistics resilience during pandemic. Technology in Society. 2022; **69**:101970. DOI: 10.1016/j.techsoc.2022.101970

[37] Cui L, Wu H, Wu L, Kumar A, Tan KH. Investigating the relationship between digital technologies, supply chain integration and firm resilience in the context of COVID-19. Annals of Operations Research. 2023;**327**(2):825-853

[38] Münch C, Hartmann E. Transforming resilience in the context of

a pandemic: Results from a cross-industry case study exploring supply chain viability. International Journal of Production Research. 2023;**61**(8): 2544-2562. DOI: 10.1080/00207543.2022.2029610

[39] Zighan S, Ruel S. SMEs' resilience from continuous improvement lenses. Journal of Entrepreneurship in Emerging Economies. 2023;**15**(2):233-253. DOI: 10.1108/JEEE-06-2021-0235

[40] Aslam H, Syed TA, Blome C, Ramish A, Ayaz K. The multifaceted role of social capital for achieving organizational ambidexterity and supply chain resilience. IEEE Transactions on Engineering Management. 2022;**1**:1-14. DOI: 10.1109/TEM.2022.3174069

[41] Dolgui A, Ivanov D. 5G in digital supply chain and operations management: Fostering flexibility, end-to-end connectivity and real-time visibility through internet-of-everything. International Journal of Production Research. 2022;**60**(2): 442-451. DOI: 10.1080/00207543.2021.2002969

[42] Khan SAR, Piprani AZ, Yu Z. Supply chain analytics and post-pandemic performance: Mediating role of triple-a supply chain strategies. International Journal of Emerging Markets. 2023; **18**(6):1330-1354. DOI: 10.1108/IJOEM-11-2021-1744

[43] Kano L, Narula R, Surdu I. Global value chain resilience: Understanding the impact of managerial governance adaptations. California Management Review. 2022;**64**(2):24-45. DOI: 10.1177/0008125621106

[44] Obrenovic B, Du J, Godinic D, Tsoy D, Khan MAS, Jakhongirov I. Sustaining enterprise operations and productivity during the COVID-19 pandemic: "Enterprise effectiveness and sustainability model". Sustainability. 2020;**12**(15):5981. DOI: 10.3390/su12155981

[45] Anderson B, Poeschel F, Ruhs M. Rethinking labour migration: Covid-19, essential work, and systemic resilience. Comparative Migration Studies. 2021;**9**: 1-19. DOI: 10.1186/s40878-021-00252-2

[46] Alamoush AS, Ballini F, Dalaklis D. Port sustainable supply chain management framework: Contributing to the United Nations' sustainable development goals. Maritime Technology and Research. 2021;**3**(2): 137-161. DOI: 10.33175/mtr.2021.247076

[47] Lund S, Manyika J, Woetzel J, Barriball E, Krishnan M. Risk, Resilience, and Rebalancing in Global Value Chains. Boston: McKinsey Global Institute; 2020, 2020. Available from: https://www.mckinsey.com/business-functions/operations/our-insights/risk-resilience-and-rebalancing-in-global-value-chains

[48] Yun C, Shun M, Jackson K, Newiduom L, Browndi I. Integrating life cycle assessment and green supply chain Management for Sustainable Business Practices. International Journal of Engineering and Applied Sciences. 2023; **12**(01):198-202. Available from: https://papers.ssrn.com/sol3/papers.cfm?abstract_id=4464723

[49] Modgil S, Singh RK, Hannibal C. Artificial intelligence for supply chain resilience: Learning from Covid-19. The International Journal of Logistics Management. 2022;**33**(4):1246-1268. DOI: 10.1108/IJLM-02-2021-0094

[50] Ambrogio G, Filice L, Longo F, Padovano A. Workforce and supply chain disruption as a digital and technological innovation opportunity for resilient manufacturing systems in the

COVID-19 pandemic. Computers & Industrial Engineering. 2022;**169**:108158. DOI: 10.1016/j.cie.2022.108158

[51] Annamalah S, Paraman P, Ahmed S, Pertheban TR, Marimuthu A, Venkatachalam KR. Exploitation, exploration and ambidextrous strategies of SMES in accelerating organisational effectiveness. Journal of Global Operations and Strategic Sourcing. 2023. DOI: 10.1108/JGOSS-08-2022-0090 [Ahead-of-print]

[52] Butt AS, Alghababsheh M, Arshi TA, Shah SHH. Strategies to streamline supplier relationship management during crises: Lessons learned from COVID-19 and future pathways. Benchmarking: An International Journal. 2022. DOI: 10.1108/BIJ-04-2022-0226 [Ahead-of-print]

[53] Ferreira C, Cardoso C, Travassos M, Paiva M, Pestana M, Lopes JM, et al. Disorders, vulnerabilities and resilience in the supply chain in pandemic times. Logistics. 2021;**5**(3):48. DOI: 10.3390/logistics5030048

[54] Chari A, Niedenzu D, Despeisse M, Machado CG, Azevedo JD, Boavida-Dias R, et al. Dynamic capabilities for circular manufacturing supply chains—Exploring the role of industry 4.0 and resilience. Business Strategy and the Environment. 2022;**31**(5):2500-2517. DOI: 10.1002/bse.3040

[55] Magableh GM. Supply chains and the COVID-19 pandemic: A comprehensive framework. European Management Review. 2021;**18**(3):363-382. DOI: 10.1111/emre.12449

[56] Baloch N, Rashid A. Supply chain networks, complexity, and optimization in developing economies: A systematic literature review and meta-analysis: Supply chain networks and complexity: A meta-analysis. South Asian Journal of Operations and Logistics. 2022;**1**(1): 14-19. DOI: 10.57044/SAJOL.2022.1.1.2202

[57] Aldhaheri RT, Ahmad SZ. Factors affecting organisations' supply chain agility and competitive capability. Business Process Management Journal. 2023;**29**(2):505-527. DOI: 10.1108/BPMJ-11-2022-0579

[58] Waeraas A. Thematic analysis: Making values emerge from texts. In: Espedal G, Jelstad Løvaas B, Sirris S, Waeraas A, editors. Researching Values. Cham: Palgrave Macmillan; 2022. DOI: 10.1007/978-3-030-90769-3_9

[59] Banerjee T, Trivedi A, Sharma GM, Gharib M, Hameed SS. Analyzing organizational barriers towards building postpandemic supply chain resilience in Indian MSMEs: A grey-DEMATEL approach. Benchmarking: An International Journal. 2022. DOI: 10.1108/BIJ-11-2021-0677 [Ahead-of-print]

[60] Sarstedt M, Hair JF, Pick M, Liengaard BD, Radomir L, Ringle CM. Progress in partial least squares structural equation modeling use in marketing research in the last decade. Psychology & Marketing. 2022;**39**(5): 1035-1064. DOI: 10.1002/mar.21640

[61] Hair J, Alamer A. Partial least squares structural equation modeling (PLS-SEM) in second language and education research: Guidelines using an applied example. Research Methods in Applied Linguistics. 2022;**1**(3): 100027. DOI: 10.1016/j.rmal.2022.100027

[62] Aburumman OJ, Omar K, Al Shbail M, Aldoghan M. How to Deal with the results of PLS-SEM? In: International Conference on Business and Technology.

Cham: Springer International Publishing; 2022. pp. 1196-1206. DOI: 10.1007/978-3-031-08954-1_101

[63] Goldschmidt G, Matthews B. Formulating design research questions: A framework. Design Studies. 2022;**78**: 101062. DOI: 10.1016/j.destud. 2021.101062

[64] Prataviera LB, Tappia E, Perotti S, Perego A. Estimating the national logistics outsourcing market size: A multi-method approach and an application to the Italian context. International Journal of Physical Distribution & Logistics Management. 2021;**51**(7):764-784. DOI: 10.1108/ IJPDLM-07-2020-0243

[65] Patil SM, Baramati P, Dhone NC, Chourasiya RH. Industry 4.0 technologies in the context of supply chain management 4.0. The Online Journal of Distance Education and e-Learning. 2023;**11**(2):2048-2058. Available from: https://www.tojned.net/journals/tojdel/articles/v11i02b/v11i02b-76.pdf

[66] Rosca E, Tate WL, Bals L, Huang F, Ciulli F. Coordinating multi-level collective action: How intermediaries and digital governance can help supply chains tackle grand challenges. International Journal of Operations & Production Management. 2022;**42**(12): 1937-1968. DOI: 10.1108/IJOPM-07-2022-0432

[67] Lerman LV, Benitez GB, Müller JM, de Sousa PR, Frank AG. Smart green supply chain management: A configurational approach to enhance green performance through digital transformation. Supply Chain Management: An International Journal. 2022;**27**(7):147-176. DOI: 10.1108/SCM-02-2022-0059